Principles of Database
Development and Management

Principles of Database Development and Management

Natalia Crosby

CLANRYE
INTERNATIONAL
www.clanryeinternational.com

Clanrye International,
750 Third Avenue, 9th Floor,
New York, NY 10017, USA

ISBN: 978-1-64726-092-7

Cataloging-in-Publication Data

Principles of database development and management / Natalia Crosby.
    p. cm.
Includes bibliographical references and index.
ISBN 978-1-64726-092-7
1. Database management. 2. Electronic data processing. 3. Database design. I. Crosby, Natalia.
QA76.9.D3 P75 2022
005.756 5--dc23

For information on all Clanrye International publications
visit our website at www.clanryeinternational.com

Contents

Preface

An organized collection of data which is usually stored and accessed electronically using a computer system is known as a database. Complex databases are generally developed through formal design and modeling techniques. The software which interacts with the database, end users and applications is called database management system or DBMS. The main purpose of DBMS is to capture and analyze data. A few different types of databases are in-memory database, cloud database, distributed database and embedded database. A database management system allows the user to view the database on three different levels- external level, conceptual level and internal level. This book discusses the fundamentals related to the development and management of databases. Some of the diverse topics covered herein address the varied branches that fall under this category. This book will prove to be immensely beneficial to students and researchers in this field.

A detailed account of the significant topics covered in this book is provided below:

Chapter 1- A platform which is an organized collection of data which can be stored and accessed in numerous ways is referred to as a database. Some of its aspects are database management system, database development process, elements of a database system, database languages, etc. This is an introductory chapter which will briefly introduce all the significant aspects of database systems.

Chapter 2- There are different types of database such as graph database, object oriented database, object relational database, centralized database, etc. It also comprises of specific models such as entity-attribute-value model, object model, document model, associative model, multidimensional model, etc. This chapter has been carefully written to provide an easy understanding of various database models and types.

Chapter 3- Organization of data according to the database model is termed as database design. In order to completely understand database design it is necessary to understand the concepts such as data structure, database schema, database instance, entity relationship model, etc. The following chapter elucidates the diverse concepts associated with this area of study.

Chapter 4- Database application development is used for inserting and retrieving data from a computerized database. Rule wizard framework, user interface design and format, and form creation are some aspects that fall under its domain. This chapter discusses in detail these concepts related to database application development.

Chapter 5- Data analysis services are integral part of database management. It performs services such as cleaning, inspecting, and modeling of data and sound decision making. Data warehouse, data transformation, online analytical processing are some of the area covered in this subject. This chapter closely examines these areas of data analysis services to provide an extensive understanding of the subject.

I would like to make a special mention of my publisher who considered me worthy of this opportunity and also supported me throughout the process. I would also like to thank the editing team at the back-end who extended their help whenever required.

Natalia Crosby

An Introduction to Database System

A platform which is an organized collection of data which can be stored and accessed in numerous ways is referred to as a database. Some of its aspects are database management system, database development process, elements of a database system, database languages, etc. This is an introductory chapter which will briefly introduce all the significant aspects of database systems.

Database

A database is a collection of information that is organized so that it can be easily accessed, managed and updated. Computer databases typically contain aggregations of data records or files, containing information about sales transactions or interactions with specific customers.

In a relational database, digital information about a specific customer is organized into rows, columns and tables which are indexed to make it easier to find relevant information through SQL or NoSQL queries. In contrast, a graph database uses nodes and edges to define relationships between data entries and queries require a special semantic search syntax. As of this writing, SPARQL is the only semantic query language that is approved by the World Wide Web Consortium (W3C).

Typically, the database manager provides users with the ability to control read/write access, specify report generation and analyze usage. Some databases offer ACID (atomicity, consistency, isolation and durability) compliance to guarantee that data is consistent and that transactions are complete.

Types of Databases

Databases have evolved since their inception in the 1960s, beginning with hierarchical and network databases, through the 1980s with object-oriented databases, and today with SQL and NoSQL databases and cloud databases.

In one view, databases can be classified according to content type: bibliographic, full text, numeric and images. In computing, databases are sometimes classified according to their organizational approach. There are many different kinds of databases, ranging from the most prevalent approach, the relational database, to a distributed database, cloud database, graph database or NoSQL database.

Database Management System

A database management system stores data in such a way that it becomes easier to retrieve, manipulate, and produce information.

Characteristics

Traditionally, data was organized in file formats. DBMS was a new concept then, and all the research was done to make it overcome the deficiencies in traditional style of data management. A modern DBMS has the following characteristics:

- Real-world entity: A modern DBMS is more realistic and uses real-world entities to design its architecture. It uses the behavior and attributes too. For example, a school database may use students as an entity and their age as an attribute.

- Relation-based tables: DBMS allows entities and relations among them to form tables. A user can understand the architecture of a database just by looking at the table names.

- Isolation of data and application: A database system is entirely different than its data. A database is an active entity, whereas data is said to be passive, on which the database works and organizes. DBMS also stores metadata, which is data about data, to ease its own process.

- Less redundancy: DBMS follows the rules of normalization, which splits a relation when any of its attributes is having redundancy in values. Normalization is a mathematically rich and scientific process that reduces data redundancy.

- Consistency: Consistency is a state where every relation in a database remains consistent. There exist methods and techniques, which can detect attempt of leaving database in inconsistent state. A DBMS can provide greater consistency as compared to earlier forms of data storing applications like file-processing systems.

- Query Language: DBMS is equipped with query language, which makes it more efficient to retrieve and manipulate data. A user can apply as many and as different filtering options as required to retrieve a set of data. Traditionally it was not possible where file-processing system was used.

- ACID Properties: DBMS follows the concepts of Atomicity, Consistency, Isolation, and Durability (normally shortened as ACID). These concepts are applied on transactions, which manipulate data in a database. ACID properties help the database stay healthy in multi-transactional environments and in case of failure.

- Multiuser and Concurrent Access: DBMS supports multi-user environment and allows them to access and manipulate data in parallel. Though there are restrictions on transactions when users attempt to handle the same data item, but users are always unaware of them.

- Multiple views: DBMS offers multiple views for different users. A user who is in the Sales department will have a different view of database than a person working in the Production department. This feature enables the users to have a concentrate view of the database according to their requirements.

- Security: Features like multiple views offer security to some extent where users are unable to access data of other users and departments. DBMS offers methods to impose constraints while entering data into the database and retrieving the same at a later stage. DBMS offers many different levels of security features, which enables multiple users to have different views with different features. For example, a user in the Sales department cannot see the data that belongs to the Purchase department. Additionally, it can also be managed how much data of the Sales department should be displayed to the user. Since a DBMS is not saved on the disk as traditional file systems, it is very hard for miscreants to break the code.

Users

A typical DBMS has users with different rights and permissions who use it for different purposes. Some users retrieve data and some back it up. The users of a DBMS can be broadly categorized as follows:

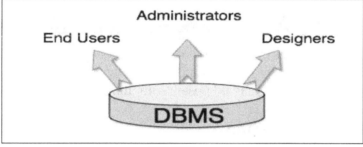

DBMS Users.

- Administrators: Administrators maintain the DBMS and are responsible for administrating the database. They are responsible to look after its usage and by whom it should be used. They create access profiles for users and apply limitations to maintain isolation and force security. Administrators also look after DBMS resources like system license, required tools, and other software and hardware related maintenance.

- Designers: Designers are the group of people who actually work on the designing part of the database. They keep a close watch on what data should be kept and in what format. They identify and design the whole set of entities, relations, constraints, and views.

- End Users: End users are those who actually reap the benefits of having a DBMS. End users can range from simple viewers who pay attention to the logs or market rates to sophisticated users such as business analysts.

Function and Purpose of Database Management System

DBMS – Purpose

It is a collection of programs that enables the user to create and maintain a database. In other words, it is general-purpose software that provides the users with the processes of defining, constructing and manipulating the database for various applications.

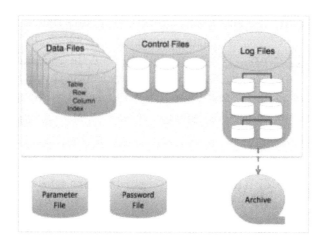

Database systems are designed to manage large bodies of information. Management of data involves both defining structures for storage of information and providing mechanisms for the manipulation of information. In addition, the database system must ensure the safety of the information stored, despite system crashes or attempts at unauthorized access. If data are to be shared among several users, the system must avoid possible anomalous results.

Disadvantages in File Processing

A database management system (DBMS) is a collection of interrelated data and a set of programs to access those data. This is a collection of related data with an implicit meaning and hence is a database. The collection of data, usually referred to as the database, contains information relevant to an enterprise. The primary goal of a DBMS is to provide a way to store and retrieve database information that is both convenient and efficient. By data, we mean known facts that can be recorded and that have implicit meaning.

For example, consider the names, telephone numbers, and addresses of the people you know. You may have recorded this data in an indexed address book, or you may have stored it on a diskette, using a personal computer and software such as DBASE IV or V, Microsoft ACCESS, or EXCEL.

The following are the main disadvantages of DBMS in File Processing:

- Data redundancy and inconsistency,

- Difficult in accessing data,

- Data isolation,

- Data integrity,

- Concurrent access is not possible,

- Security Problems.

Advantages of DBMS

Because information is so important in most organizations, computer scientists have developed a large body of concepts and techniques for managing data. These concepts and technique form the focus of this book.

- Data Independence,

- Efficient Data Access,

- Data Integrity and security,

- Data administration,

- Concurrent access and Crash recovery,

- Reduced Application Development Time.

Application or Function of DBMS

Following fields are where the main Database Applications lie:

- Banking: All transactions.

- Airlines: Reservations, schedules.

- Universities: Registration, grades.

- Sales: Customers, products, purchases.

- Online retailers: Order tracking, customized recommendations.

- Manufacturing: Production, inventory, orders, supply chain.

- Human resources: Employee records, salaries, tax deductions.

Data Processing vs. Data Management Systems

Although Data Processing and Data Management Systems both refer to functions that take raw data and transform it into usable information, the usage of the terms is very different. Data Processing is the term generally used to describe what was done by large mainframe computers from the late 1940's until the early 1980's (and which continues to be done in most large organizations to a greater or lesser extent even today): large volumes of raw transaction data fed into programs that update a master file, with fixed format reports written to paper.

The term Data Management Systems refers to an expansion of this concept, where the raw data, previously copied manually from paper to punched cards, and later into data entry terminals, is now fed into the system from a variety of sources, including ATMs, EFT, and direct customer entry through the Internet.

The master file concept has been largely displaced by database management systems, and static reporting replaced or augmented by ad-hoc reporting and direct inquiry, including downloading of data by customers. The ubiquity of the Internet and the Personal Computer have been the driving force in the transformation of Data Processing to the more global concept of Data Management Systems.

Key Terms

- A database management system (DBMS) is a collection of interrelated data and a set of programs to access those data. This is a collection of related data with an implicit meaning and hence is a database.

- A datum – a unit of data – is a symbol or a set of symbols which is used to represent something. This relationship between symbols and what they represent is the essence of what we mean by information.

- Knowledge refers to the practical use of information. The collection of information stored in the database at a particular moment is called an instance of the database.

- The overall design of the database is called the database schema. The physical schema describes the database design at the physical level, while the logical schema describes the database design at the logical level.

- A database may also have several schemas at the view level, sometimes called subschemas that describe different views of the database.

- Application programs are said to exhibit physical data independence if they do not depend on the physical schema, and thus need not be rewritten if the physical schema changes.

- Underlying the structure of a database is the data model: a collection of conceptual tools for describing data, data relationships, data semantics, and consistency constraints.

- A database system provides a data definition language to specify the database schema and a data manipulation language to express database queries and updates.

One of the main reasons for using DBMSs is to have central control of both the data and the programs that access those data. A person who has such central control over the system is called a database administrator (DBA).

Components of Database Management System

DBMS have several components, each performing very significant tasks in the database management system environment. Below is a list of components within the database and its environment:

- Software: This is the set of programs used to control and manage the overall database. This includes the DBMS software itself, the Operating System, the network software being used to share the data among users, and the application programs used to access data in the DBMS.

- Hardware: Consists of a set of physical electronic devices such as computers, I/O devices, storage devices, etc., this provides the interface between computers and the real world systems.

- Data: DBMS exists to collect, store, process and access data, the most important component. The database contains both the actual or operational data and the metadata.

- Users: The users are the people who manage the databases and perform different operations on the databases in the database system. There are three kinds of people who play different roles in database system:

  ○ Application Programmers: The people who write application programs in programming languages (such as Visual Basic, Java, or C++) to interact with databases are called Application Programmer.

  ○ Database Administrators: A person who is responsible for managing the overall database management system is called database administrator or simply DBA. DBA is a person or group of persons who is responsible for management of the database in the database management system. DBA is a highly skilled person with strong technical background to monitor various operations such as creating, modifying, and maintaining which help in handling three levels of the database. DBA has most of the powers such as defining schemas, storage structures and access method strategies, physical organization, authorization and integrity constraints etc. DBA even grants permission to the users of the database and the stores the profiles of the users in the database. The user profile describes the activities a user can perform on the database that is whether a user can perform a given operation or not. So the DBA has all the power that system can give on all the database objects. DBA is top level authority among all persons connected to the database.

  ○ End-Users: The end-users are the people who interact with database management system to perform different operations on database such as retrieving, updating, inserting, deleting data etc.

- Procedures: These are the instructions and rules that assist on how to use the DBMS, and in designing and running the database, using documented procedures, to guide the users that operate and manage it.

- Database Access Language: This is used to access the data to and from the database, to enter new data, update existing data, or retrieve required data from databases. The user writes a set of appropriate commands in a database access language, submits these to the DBMS, which then processes the data and generates and displays a set of results into a user readable form.

- Query Processor: This transforms the user queries into a series of low level instructions. This reads the online user's query and translates it into an efficient series of operations in a form capable of being sent to the run time data manager for execution.

- Run Time Database Manager: Sometimes referred to as the database control system, this is the central software component of the DBMS that interfaces with user submitted application programs and queries, and handles database access at run time. Its function is to convert operations in user's queries. It provides control to maintain the consistency, integrity and security of the data.

- Data Manager: Also called the cache manger, this is responsible for handling of data in the database, providing a recovery to the system that allows it to recover the data after a failure.

- Database Engine: The core service for storing, processing, and securing data, this provides controlled access and rapid transaction processing to address the requirements of the most demanding data consuming applications. It is often used to create relational databases for online transaction processing or online analytical processing data.

- Data Dictionary: This is a reserved space within a database used to store information about the database itself. A data dictionary is a set of read-only table and views, containing the different information about the data used in the enterprise to ensure that database representation of the data follow one standard as defined in the dictionary.

- Report Writer: Also referred to as the report generator, it is a program that extracts information from one or more files and presents the information in a specified format. Most report writers allow the user to select records that meet certain conditions and to display selected fields in rows and columns, or also format the data into different charts.

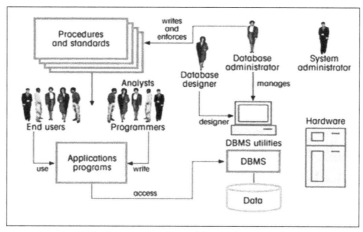

DBMS components and its environment.

Database Development Process

A core aspect of Database Management is the subdivision of the development process into a series of phases, or steps, each of which focuses on one aspect of the development. The collection of these steps is sometimes referred to as the Database Development Process. Ideally, each phase in the life cycle can be checked for correctness before moving on to the next phase. The Waterfall Model was the first Process Model to be introduced. It is very simple to understand and use.

We can use the waterfall cycle as the basis for a model of database development that incorporates three assumptions:

- We can separate the development of a database – that is, specification and creation of a schema to define data in a database – from the user processes that make use of the database.

- We can use the three-schema architecture as a basis for distinguishing the activities associated with a schema.

- We can represent the constraints to enforce the semantics of the data once within a database, rather than within every user process that uses the data.

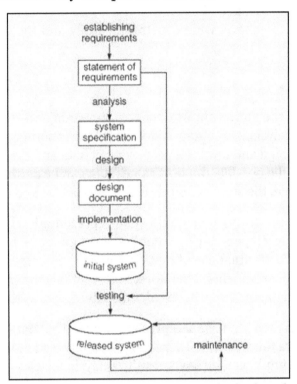

A waterfall model of the activities and their outputs for database development.

Using these assumptions and figure, we can see that this diagram represents a model of the activities and their outputs for database development. It is applicable to any class of DBMS, not just a relational approach.

Database application development is the process of obtaining real-world requirements, analyzing requirements, designing the data and functions of the system, and then implementing the operations in the system.

Requirements Gathering

The first step is *requirements gathering*. During this step, the database designers have to interview the customers (database users) to understand the proposed system and obtain and document the data and functional requirements. The result of this step is a document that includes the detailed requirements provided by the users.

Establishing requirements involves consultation with, and agreement among, all the users as to what persistent data they want to store along with an agreement as to the meaning and interpretation of the data elements. The data administrator plays a key role in this process as they overview the business, legal and ethical issues within the organization that impact on the data requirements.

The *data requirements document* is used to confirm the understanding of requirements with users. To make sure that it is easily understood, it should not be overly formal or highly encoded. The document should give a concise summary of all users' requirements – not just a collection of individuals' requirements – as the intention is to develop a single shared database.

The requirements should not describe how the data is to be processed, but rather what the data items are, what attributes they have, what constraints apply and the relationships that hold between the data items.

Analysis

Data analysis begins with the statement of data requirements and then produces a conceptual data model. The aim of analysis is to obtain a detailed description of the data that will suit user requirements so that both high and low level properties of data and their use are dealt with. These include properties such as the possible range of values that can be permitted for attributes (e.g., in the school database example, the student course code, course title and credit points).

The conceptual data model provides a shared, formal representation of what is being communicated between clients and developers during database development – it is focused on the data in a database, irrespective of the eventual use of that data in user processes or implementation of the data in specific computer environments. Therefore, a conceptual data model is concerned with the meaning and structure of data, but not with the details affecting how they are implemented.

The conceptual data model then is a formal representation of what data a database should contain and the constraints the data must satisfy. This should be expressed in terms that are independent of how the model may be implemented. As a result, analysis focuses on the questions, "What is required?" not "How is it achieved?"

Logical Design

Database design starts with a conceptual data model and produces a specification of a logical schema; this will determine the specific type of database system (network, relational, object-oriented) that is required. The relational representation is still independent of any specific DBMS; it is another conceptual data model.

We can use a relational representation of the conceptual data model as input to the logical design process. The output of this stage is a detailed relational specification, the logical schema, of all the tables and constraints needed to satisfy the description of the data in the conceptual data model. It is during this design activity that choices are made as to which tables are most appropriate for representing the data in a database. These choices must take into account various design criteria including, for example, flexibility for change, control of duplication and how best to represent the constraints. It is the tables defined by the logical schema that determine what data are stored and how they may be manipulated in the database.

Database designers familiar with relational databases and SQL might be tempted to go directly to implementation after they have produced a conceptual data model. However, such a direct transformation of the relational representation to SQL tables does not necessarily result in a database that has all the desirable properties: completeness, integrity, flexibility, efficiency and usability.

A good conceptual data model is an essential first step towards a database with these properties, but that does not mean that the direct transformation to SQL tables automatically produces a good database. This first step will accurately represent the tables and constraints needed to satisfy the conceptual data model description, and so will satisfy the completeness and integrity requirements, but it may be inflexible or offer poor usability. The first design is then flexed to improve the quality of the database design. *Flexing* is a term that is intended to capture the simultaneous ideas of bending something for a different purpose and weakening aspects of it as it is bent.

Figure summarizes the iterative (repeated) steps involved in database design, based on the overview given. Its main purpose is to distinguish the general issue of what tables should be used from the detailed definition of the constituent parts of each table – these tables are considered one at a time, although they are not independent of each other. Each iteration that involves a revision of the tables would lead to a new design; collectively they are usually referred to as *second-cut designs*, even if the process iterates for more than a single loop.

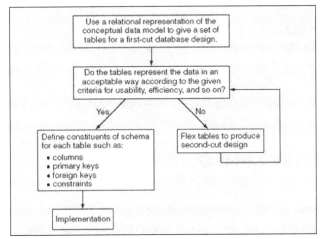

A summary of the iterative steps involved in database design.

First, for a given conceptual data model, it is not necessary that all the user requirements it represents be satisfied by a single database. There can be various reasons for the development of more than one database, such as the need for independent operation in different locations or departmental control over "their" data. However, if the collection of databases contains duplicated data and users need to access data in more than one database, then there are possible reasons that one database can satisfy multiple requirements, or issues related to data replication and distribution need to be examined.

Second, one of the assumptions about database development is that we can separate the development of a database from the development of user processes that make use of it. This is based on the expectation that, once a database has been implemented, all data required by currently identified user processes have been defined and can be accessed; but we also require flexibility to allow us to meet future requirements changes. In developing a database for some applications, it may be possible to predict the common requests that will be presented to the database and so we can optimize our design for the most common requests.

Third, at a detailed level, many aspects of database design and implementation depend on the particular DBMS being used. If the choice of DBMS is fixed or made prior to the design task, that choice can be used to determine design criteria rather than waiting until implementation. That is, it is possible to incorporate design decisions for a specific DBMS rather than produce a generic design and then tailor it to the DBMS during implementation.

It is not uncommon to find that a single design cannot simultaneously satisfy all the properties of a good database. So it is important that the designer has prioritized these properties (usually using information from the requirements specification); for example, to decide if integrity is more important than efficiency and whether usability is more important than flexibility in a given development.

At the end of our design stage, the logical schema will be specified by SQL data definition language (DDL) statements, which describe the database that needs to be implemented to meet the user requirements.

Implementation

Implementation involves the construction of a database according to the specification of a logical schema. This will include the specification of an appropriate storage schema, security enforcement, and external schema and so on. Implementation is heavily influenced by the choice of available DBMSs, database tools and operating environment. There are additional tasks beyond simply creating a database schema and implementing the constraints – data must be entered into the tables, issues relating to the users and user processes need to be addressed, and the management activities associated with wider aspects of corporate data management need to be supported. In keeping with the DBMS approach, we want as many of these concerns as possible to be addressed within the DBMS.

In practice, implementation of the logical schema in a given DBMS requires a very detailed knowledge of the specific features and facilities that the DBMS has to offer. In an ideal world, and in keeping with good software engineering practice, the first stage of implementation would involve matching the design requirements with the best available implementing tools and then using those tools for the implementation. In database terms, this might involve choosing vendor products with DBMS and SQL variants most suited to the database we need to implement. However, we don't live in an ideal world and more often than not, hardware choice and decisions regarding the DBMS will have been made well in advance of consideration of the database design. Consequently, implementation can involve additional flexing of the design to overcome any software or hardware limitations.

Realizing the Design

After the logical design has been created, we need our database to be created according to the definitions we have produced. For an implementation with a relational DBMS, this will probably involve the use of SQL to create tables and constraints that satisfy the logical schema description and the choice of appropriate storage schema (if the DBMS permits that level of control).

One way to achieve this is to write the appropriate SQL DDL statements into a file that can be executed by a DBMS so that there is an independent record, a text file, of the SQL statements defining the database. Another method is to work interactively using a database tool like SQL Server

Management Studio or Microsoft Access. Whatever mechanism is used to implement the logical schema, the result is that a database, with tables and constraints, is defined but will contain no data for the user processes.

Populating the Database

After a database has been created, there are two ways of populating the tables – either from existing data or through the use of the user applications developed for the database.

For some tables, there may be existing data from another database or data files. For example, in establishing a database for a hospital, you would expect that there are already some records of all the staff that have to be included in the database. Data might also be brought in from an outside agency (address lists are frequently brought in from external companies) or produced during a large data entry task (converting hard-copy manual records into computer files can be done by a data entry agency). In such situations, the simplest approach to populate the database is to use the import and export facilities found in the DBMS.

Facilities to import and export data in various standard formats are usually available (these functions are also known in some systems as loading and unloading data). Importing enables a file of data to be copied directly into a table. When data are held in a file format that is not appropriate for using the import function, then it is necessary to prepare an application program that reads in the old data, transforms them as necessary and then inserts them into the database using SQL code specifically produced for that purpose. The transfer of large quantities of existing data into a database is referred to as a *bulk load*. Bulk loading of data may involve very large quantities of data being loaded, one table at a time so you may find that there are DBMS facilities to postpone constraint checking until the end of the bulk loading.

Elements of a Database System

Data Model

The power of model-based engineering is the ability to visualize, analyze and design all aspects of a system. Being able to view and manage information and data alongside other models of a system provides great clarity and reduces the chance of error.

Enterprise Architect has extensive support for the data modeling discipline, ranging from the representation of information in a conceptual model right down to the generation of database objects. Whether you are generating database objects from the UML model or reverse engineering legacy DBMS into a model for analysis, the tool features will save time and valuable project resources.

Information Modelers, Data Modelers and Architects are responsible for creating models of an organization's information that span multiple levels of abstraction, from conceptual through to logical and physical. The conceptual models are technology independent and can be used for discussions with business people and domain experts, allowing the basic concepts in the domain to be represented, discussed and agreed upon. The logical model elaborates the conceptual model, adding more detail and precision but is still typically technology neutral, allowing Information Analysts to discuss and agree on logical structures. The physical model applies technology specific data to the models and allows engineers to discuss and agree on technology decisions in preparation for generation to a target environment, such as a database management system.

Enterprise Architect provides a number of features to assist in this process, including the ability to develop conceptual, logical and physical models and to be able to trace the underlying concepts between the models. The physical models can be developed for a wide range of database systems and forward and reverse engineering allows these models to be synchronized with live databases.

Type	Description
Conceptual Data Models	Conceptual data models, also called Domain models, establish the basic concepts and semantics of a given domain and help to communicate these to a wide audience of stakeholders.
	Conceptual models also serve as a common vocabulary during the analysis stages of a project; they can be created in Enterprise Architect using Entity-Relationship or UML Class models.
Logical Data Models	Logical data models add further detail to conceptual model elements and refine the structure of the domain; they can be defined using Entity-Relationship or UML Class models.
	One benefit of a Logical data model is that it provides a foundation on which to base the Physical model and subsequent database implementation.
	Entity-relationship modeling is an abstract and conceptual database modeling method, used to produce a schema or semantic data model of, for example, a relational database and its requirements, visualized in Entity-Relationship Diagrams (ERDs).
	ERDs assist you in building conceptual data models through to generating Data Definition Language (DDL) for the target DBMS.
	A Logical model can be transformed to a Physical data model using a DDL Transformation.
Physical Data Models	Physical data models in Enterprise Architect help you visualize your database structure and automatically derive the corresponding database schema; you use Enterprise Architect's UML Profile for Data Modeling specifically for this purpose.
	The profile provides useful extensions of the UML standard that map database concepts of Tables and relationships onto the UML concepts of Classes and Associations; you can also model database columns, keys, constraints, indexes, triggers, referential integrity and other relational database features.
	Because Enterprise Architect helps you visualize each type of data model in the same repository, you can easily manage dependencies between each level of abstraction to maximize traceability and verify completeness of system implementation.

Conceptual Data Model

A Conceptual data model is the most abstract form of data model. It is helpful for communicating ideas to a wide range of stakeholders because of its simplicity. Therefore platform-specific information, such as data types, indexes and keys, are omitted from a Conceptual data model. Other implementation details, such as procedures and interface definitions, are also excluded.

This is an example of a Conceptual data model, rendered using two of the notations supported by Enterprise Architect.

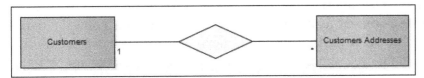

Using Entity-Relationship (ER) notation, we represent the data concepts 'Customers' and 'Customers Addresses' as Entities with a 1-to-many relationship between them. We can represent the exactly the same semantic information using UML Classes and Associations.

Whether you use UML or ER notation to represent data concepts in your project depends on the experience and preferences of the stakeholders involved. The detailed structure of the data concepts illustrated in a Conceptual data model is defined by the Logical data model.

Logical Data Model

Logical data models help to define the detailed structure of the data elements in a system and the relationships between data elements. They refine the data elements introduced by a Conceptual data model and form the basis of the Physical data model. In Enterprise Architect, a Logical data model is typically represented using the UML Class notation.

Example:

This is a simple example of a Logical data model:

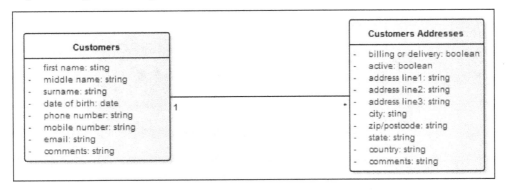

The data elements 'Customers' and 'Customers Addresses' contain UML attributes; the names and generic data types to remain platform-independent. Platform-specific data types and other meta-data that relate to a specific DBMS implementation are defined by the Physical data model.

Three-tier Architecture

A 3-tier architecture is a type of software architecture which is composed of three "tiers" or "layers" of logical computing. They are often used in applications as a specific type of client-server system. 3-tier architectures provide many benefits for production and development environments by modularizing the user interface, business logic, and data storage layers. Doing so gives greater flexibility to development teams by allowing them to update a specific part of an application independently of the other parts. This added flexibility can improve overall time-to-market and decrease development cycle times by giving development teams the ability to replace or upgrade independent tiers without affecting the other parts of the system.

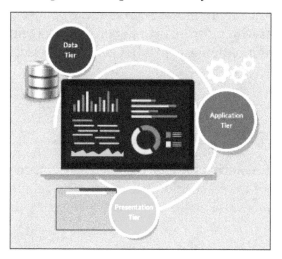

For example, the user interface of a web application could be redeveloped or modernized without affecting the underlying functional business and data access logic underneath. This architectural system is often ideal for embedding and integrating 3rd party software into an existing application. This integration flexibility also makes it ideal for embedding analytics software into pre-existing applications and is often used by embedded analytics vendors for this reason. 3-tier architectures are often used in cloud or on-premises based applications as well as in software-as-a-service (SaaS) applications.

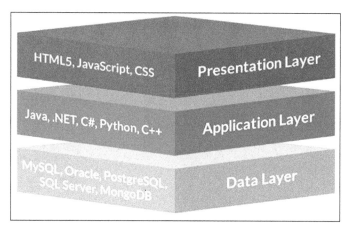

- Presentation Tier: The presentation tier is the front end layer in the 3-tier system and consists of the user interface. This user interface is often a graphical one accessible through a web browser or web-based application and which displays content and information useful to an end user. This tier is often built on web technologies such as HTML5, JavaScript, CSS, or through other popular web development frameworks, and communicates with others layers through API calls.

- Application Tier: The application tier contains the functional business logic which drives an application's core capabilities. It's often written in Java, .NET, C#, Python, C++, etc.

- Data Tier: The data tier comprises of the database/data storage system and data access layer. Examples of such systems are MySQL, Oracle, PostgreSQL, Microsoft SQL Server, MongoDB, etc. Data is accessed by the application layer via API calls.

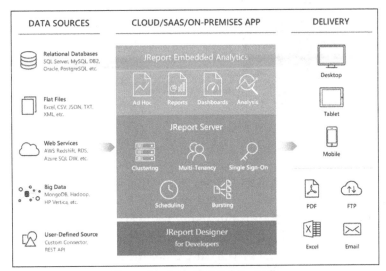

Example of a 3-tier architecture.

The typical structure for a 3-tier architecture deployment would have the presentation tier deployed to a desktop, laptop, tablet or mobile device either via a web browser or a web-based application utilizing a web server. The underlying application tier is usually hosted on one or more application servers, but can also be hosted in the cloud, or on a dedicated workstation depending on the complexity and processing power needed by the application. And the data layer would normally comprise of one or more relational databases, big data sources, or other types of database systems hosted either on-premises or in the cloud.

A simple example of a 3-tier architecture in action would be logging into a media account such as Netflix and watching a video. You start by logging in either via the web or via a mobile application. Once you've logged in you might access a specific video through the Netflix interface which is the presentation tier used by you as an end user. Once you've selected a video that information is passed on to the application tier which will query the data tier to call the information or in this case a video back up to the presentation tier. This happens every time you access a video from most media sites.

Benefits of using 3-Layer Architecture

There are many benefits to using a 3-layer architecture including speed of development, scalability, performance, and availability. Modularizing different tiers of an application gives development teams the ability to develop and enhance a product with greater speed than developing a singular code base because a specific layer can be upgraded with minimal impact on the other layers. It can also help improve development efficiency by allowing teams to focus on their core competencies. Many development teams have separate developers who specialize in front- end, server back-end, and data back-end development, by modularizing these parts of an application you no longer have to rely on full stack developers and can better utilize the specialties of each team.

Scalability is another great advantage of a 3-layer architecture. By separating out the different layers you can scale each independently depending on the need at any given time. For example, if you are receiving many web requests but not many requests which affect your application layer, you can scale your web servers without touching your application servers. Similarly, if you are receiving many large application requests from only a handful of web users, you can scale out your application and data layers to meet those requests without touch your web servers. This allows you to load balance each layer independently, improving overall performance with minimal resources. Additionally, the independence created from modularizing the different tiers gives you many deployment options. For example, you may choose to have your web servers hosted in a public or private cloud while you're application and data layers may be hosted onsite. Or you may have your application and data layers hosted in the cloud while your web servers may be locally hosted, or any combination thereof.

By having disparate layers you can also increase reliability and availability by hosting different parts of your application on different servers and utilizing cached results. With a full stack system you have to worry about a server going down and greatly affecting performance throughout your entire system, but with a 3-layer application, the increased independence created when physically separating different parts of an application minimizes performance issues when a server goes down.

Database Users and Administrators

Database users are the one who really use and take the benefits of database. There will be different types of users depending on their need and way of accessing the database:

- Application Programmers: They are the developers who interact with the database by means of DML queries. These DML queries are written in the application programs like C,

C++, JAVA, Pascal etc. These queries are converted into object code to communicate with the database. For example, writing a C program to generate the report of employees who are working in particular department will involve a query to fetch the data from database. It will include an embedded SQL query in the C Program.

- Sophisticated Users: They are database developers, who write SQL queries to select/insert/ delete/update data. They do not use any application or programs to request the database. They directly interact with the database by means of query language like SQL. These users will be scientists, engineers, analysts who thoroughly study SQL and DBMS to apply the concepts in their requirement. In short, we can say this category includes designers and developers of DBMS and SQL.

- Specialized Users: These are also sophisticated users, but they write special database application programs. They are the developers who develop the complex programs to the requirement.

- Stand-alone Users: These users will have stand –alone database for their personal use. These kinds of database will have readymade database packages which will have menus and graphical interfaces.

- Native Users: These are the users who use the existing application to interact with the database. For example, online library system, ticket booking systems, ATMs etc which has existing application and users use them to interact with the database to fulfill their requests.

Database Administrators

The life cycle of database starts from designing, implementing to administration of it. A database for any kind of requirement needs to be designed perfectly so that it should work without any issues. Once all the design is complete, it needs to be installed. Once this step is complete, users start using the database. The database grows as the data grows in the database. When the database becomes huge, its performance comes down. Also accessing the data from the database becomes challenge. There will be unused memory in database, making the memory inevitably huge. These administration and maintenance of database is taken care by database Administrator – DBA. A DBA has many responsibilities. A good performing database is in the hands of DBA.

- Installing and upgrading the DBMS Servers: DBA is responsible for installing a new DBMS server for the new projects. He is also responsible for upgrading these servers as there are new versions comes in the market or requirement. If there is any failure in up gradation of the existing servers, he should be able revert the new changes back to the older version, thus maintaining the DBMS working. He is also responsible for updating the service packs/ hot fixes/ patches to the DBMS servers.

- Design and implementation: Designing the database and implementing is also DBA's responsibility. He should be able to decide proper memory management, file organizations, error handling, log maintenance etc. for the database.

- Performance tuning: Since database is huge and it will have lots of tables, data, constraints and indices, there will be variations in the performance from time to time. Also, because of some designing issues or data growth, the database will not work as expected. It is responsibility of the DBA to tune the database performance. He is responsible to make sure all the queries and programs works in fraction of seconds.

- Migrate database servers: Sometimes, users using oracle would like to shift to SQL server or Netezza. It is the responsibility of DBA to make sure that migration happens without any failure, and there is no data loss.

- Backup and Recovery: Proper backup and recovery programs needs to be developed by DBA and has to be maintained him. This is one of the main responsibilities of DBA. Data/objects should be backed up regularly so that if there is any crash, it should be recovered without much effort and data loss.

- Security: DBA is responsible for creating various database users and roles, and giving them different levels of access rights.

- Documentation: DBA should be properly documenting all his activities so that if he quits or any new DBA comes in, he should be able to understand the database without any effort. He should basically maintain all his installation, backup, recovery, security methods. He should keep various reports about database performance.

In order to perform his entire task, he should have very good command over DBMS.

Types of DBA

There are different kinds of DBA depending on the responsibility that he owns:

- Administrative DBA: This DBA is mainly concerned with installing, and maintaining DBMS servers. His prime tasks are installing, backups, recovery, security, replications, memory management, configurations and tuning. He is mainly responsible for all administrative tasks of a database.

- Development DBA: He is responsible for creating queries and procedure for the requirement. Basically his task is similar to any database developer.

- Database Architect: Database architect is responsible for creating and maintaining the users, roles, access rights, tables, views, constraints and indexes. He is mainly responsible for designing the structure of the database depending on the requirement. These structures will be used by developers and development DBA to code.

- Data Warehouse DBA: DBA should be able to maintain the data and procedures from various sources in the data warehouse. These sources can be files, COBOL, or any other programs. Here data and programs will be from different sources. A good DBA should be able to keep the performance and function levels from these sources at same pace to make the data warehouse to work.

- Application DBA: He acts like a bridge between the application program and the database. He makes sure all the application program is optimized to interact with the database. He ensures all the activities from installing, upgrading, and patching, maintaining, backup, recovery to executing the records works without any issues.

- OLAP DBA: He is responsible for installing and maintaining the database in OLAP systems. He maintains only OLAP databases.

Database Languages

Structured Query Language (SQL)

SQL is Structured Query Language, which is a computer language for storing, manipulating and retrieving data stored in a relational database.

SQL is the standard language for Relational Database System. All the Relational Database Management Systems (RDMS) like MySQL, MS Access, Oracle, Sybase, Informix, Postgres and SQL Server use SQL as their standard database language.

Also, they are using different dialects, such as:

- MS SQL Server using T-SQL,

- Oracle using PL/SQL,

- MS Access version of SQL is called JET SQL (native format) etc.

SQL is widely popular because it offers the following advantages:

- Allows users to access data in the relational database management systems.

- Allows users to describe the data.

- Allows users to define the data in a database and manipulate that data.

- Allows embedding within other languages using SQL modules, libraries & pre-compilers.

- Allows users to create and drop databases and tables.

- Allows users to create view, stored procedure, functions in a database.

- Allows users to set permissions on tables, procedures and views.

SQL Process

When you are executing an SQL command for any RDBMS, the system determines the best way to carry out your request and SQL engine figures out how to interpret the task. There are various components included in this process.

These components are:

- Query Dispatcher,

- Optimization Engines,

- Classic Query Engine,

- SQL Query Engine, etc.

A classic query engine handles all the non-SQL queries, but a SQL query engine won't handle logical files.

Following is a simple diagram showing the SQL Architecture:

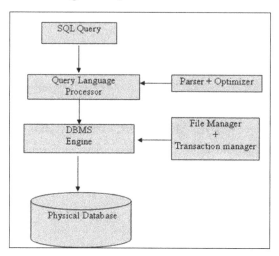

SQL Commands

The standard SQL commands to interact with relational databases are CREATE, SELECT, INSERT, UPDATE, DELETE and DROP. These commands can be classified into the following groups based on their nature:

DDL - Data Definition Language

Command	Description
CREATE	Creates a new table, a view of a table, or other object in the database.
ALTER	Modifies an existing database object, such as a table.
DROP	Deletes an entire table, a view of a table or other objects in the database.

DML - Data Manipulation Language

Command	Description
SELECT	Retrieves certain records from one or more tables.
INSERT	Creates a record.
UPDATE	Modifies records.
DELETE	Deletes records.

DCL - Data Control Language

Command	Description
GRANT	Gives a privilege to user.
REVOKE	Takes back privileges granted from user.

RDBMS stands for Relational Database Management System. RDBMS is the basis for SQL, and for all modern database systems like MS SQL Server, IBM DB2, Oracle, MySQL, and Microsoft Access.

A Relational database management system (RDBMS) is a database management system (DBMS) that is based on the relational model as introduced by E. F. Codd.

Table in RDBMS

The data in an RDBMS is stored in database objects which are called as tables. This table is basically a collection of related data entries and it consists of numerous columns and rows.

Remember, a table is the most common and simplest form of data storage in a relational database. The following program is an example of a CUSTOMERS table:

ID	NAME	AGE	ADDRESS	SALARY
1	Ramesh	32	Ahmedabad	2000.00
2	Khilan	25	Delhi	1500.00
3	kaushik	23	Kota	2000.00
4	Chaitali	25	Mumbai	6500.00
5	Hardik	27	Bhopal	8500.00
6	Komal	22	MP	4500.00
7	Muffy	24	Indore	10000.00

Fields in RDBMS

Every table is broken up into smaller entities called fields. The fields in the CUSTOMERS table consist of ID, NAME, AGE, ADDRESS and SALARY.

A field is a column in a table that is designed to maintain specific information about every record in the table.

Record or Row in RDBMS

A record is also called as a row of data is each individual entry that exists in a table. For example, there are 7 records in the above CUSTOMERS table. Following is a single row of data or record in the CUSTOMERS table:

1	Ramesh	32	Ahmedabad	2000.00

A record is a horizontal entity in a table.

Column in RDBMS

A column is a vertical entity in a table that contains all information associated with a specific field in a table.

For example, a column in the CUSTOMERS table is ADDRESS, which represents location description and would be as shown below:

ADDRESS
Ahmedabad
Delhi
Kota
Mumbai
Bhopal
MP
Indore

NULL Value

A NULL value in a table is a value in a field that appears to be blank, which means a field with a NULL value is a field with no value.

It is very important to understand that a NULL value is different than a zero value or a field that contains spaces. A field with a NULL value is the one that has been left blank during a record creation.

SQL Constraints

Constraints are the rules enforced on data columns on a table. These are used to limit the type of data that can go into a table. This ensures the accuracy and reliability of the data in the database.

Constraints can either be column level or table level. Column level constraints are applied only to one column whereas; table level constraints are applied to the entire table.

Following are some of the most commonly used constraints available in SQL:

- NOT NULL Constraint: Ensures that a column cannot have a NULL value.

- DEFAULT Constraint: Provides a default value for a column when none is specified.

- UNIQUE Constraint: Ensures that all the values in a column are different.

- PRIMARY Key: Uniquely identifies each row/record in a database table.

- FOREIGN Key: Uniquely identifies a row/record in any another database table.

- CHECK Constraint: The CHECK constraint ensures that all values in a column satisfy certain conditions.

- INDEX: Used to create and retrieve data from the database very quickly.

Data control language (DCL)

A Data Control Language (DCL) can be defined as a computer language that is used for controlling privilege in the database. The privileges are required for performing all the database operations, such as creating sequences, views or tables. It is a part of the Structured Query Language.

Types of Privileges

There are two main types of privileges in the database:

- System Privileges: System privileges are used for performing a particular type of action on objects, such as cache groups, synonyms, materialized views, tables, views, sequences, indexes, replication schemes, and PL/SQL procedures & functions. This type of privileges can only be granted or revoked by the instance administrator or a user.

- Object Privileges: Object privileges can be defined as the right for performing a special type of action on objects like materialized views, sequences, replication schemes, cache groups, synonyms, tables, views, etc. This type of privilege cannot be revoked and the owner of the object can grant object privileges.

Data Control Languages (DCL) Commands

There are two types of commands in the data control languages:

Grant Command

Grant Command is used for offering access or privileges to the users on the objects of the database. Through this command, the users get access to the privileges in the database.

The General Syntax for the Grant Command is mentioned below:

```
GRANT privilege_name

ON object_name

TO {user_name I PUBLIC I role_name}

[WITH GRANT OPTION];
```

For Example

```
GRANT ALL ON workers

TO MNO;

[WITH GRANT OPTION]
```

In the given example, the permission to view and modify the details in the 'workers table' has been given to the user MNO.

Revoke Command

The main purpose of the revoke command is canceling the previously denied or granted permissions. Through the revoke command, the access to the given privileges can be withdrawn. In simple words, the permission can be taken back from the user with this command.

The general syntax for the revoke command is mentioned below:

```
REVOKE<privilege list>

ON <relation name or view name>

From <user name>
```

For Example:

```
REVOKE UPDATE

ON worker

FROM MNO;
```

Differences between the Grant and Revoke Command:

Grant Command	Revoke Command
A user is allowed to perform some particular activities on the database by using Grant Command.	A user is disallowed to performing some particular activities by using the revoke command.
The access to privileges for database objects is granted to the other users.	The access to privileges for database objects that is granted previously to the users can be revoked.

Data Definition Language (DDL)

DDL is a standard subset of SQL that is used to define tables (database structure), and other metadata related things. The few basic commands include: CREATE DATABASE, CREATE TABLE, DROP TABLE, and ALTER TABLE.

There are many other statements, but those are the ones most commonly used.

CREATE DATABASE

Many database servers allow for the presence of many databases. In order to create a database, a relatively standard command 'CREATE DATABASE' is used.

The general format of the command is:

```
CREATE DATABASE <database-name>;
```

The name can be pretty much anything; usually it shouldn't have spaces (or those spaces have to be properly escaped). Some databases allow hyphens, and/or underscores in the name. The name is usually limited in size (some databases limit the name to 8 characters, others to 32—in other words, it depends on what database you use).

DROP DATABASE

Just like there is a 'create database' there is also a 'drop database', which simply removes the database. Note that it doesn't ask you for confirmation, and once you remove a database, it is *gone forever*.

```
DROP DATABASE <database-name>;
```

CREATE TABLE

Probably the most common DDL statement is 'CREATE TABLE'. Intuitively enough, it is used to create tables. The general format is something along the lines of:

```
CREATE TABLE <table-name>    (

) ;      ...
```

The ... is where column definitions go. The general format for a column definition is the column name followed by column type. For example:

```
PERSONID INT
```

Which defines a column name PERSONID, of type INT. Column names have to be comma separated, ie:

```
CREATE TABLE PERSON (

    PERSONID INT,

    LNAME VARCHAR(20),

    FNAME VARCHAR(20) NOT NULL,

    DOB DATE,

    PRIMARY KEY(PERSONID)

) ;
```

The above creates a table named person, with person id, last name, first name, and date of birth. There is also the 'primary key' definition. A primary key is a column value that uniquely identifies a database record. So for example, we can have two 'person' records with the same last name and first name, but with different ids.

Besides for primary key, there are many other flags we can specify for table columns. For example, in the above example, FNAME is marked as NOT NULL, which means it is not allowed to have NULL values.

Many databases implement various extensions to the basics, and you should read the documentation to determine what features are present/absent, and how to use them.

DROP TABLE

Just like there is a 'create table' there is also a 'drop table', which simply removes the table. Note that it doesn't ask you for confirmation, and once you remove a table, it is *gone forever*.

```
DROP TABLE <table-name> ;
```

ALTER TABLE

There is a command to 'alter' tables after you create them. This is usually only useful if the table already has data, and you don't want to drop it and recreate it (which is generally much simpler). Also, most databases have varying restrictions on what 'alter table' is allowed to do. For example, Oracle allows you do add a column, but not remove a column.

The general syntax to add a field is:

```
ALTER TABLE  <table-name> ;

ADD <field-name> <data-type>
```

The field declaration is pretty much exactly what it is in the 'create table' statement. The general syntax to drop a field is:

```
ALTER TABLE <table-name>

DROP <field-name>
```

Note that very few databases let you drop a field. The drop command is mostly present to allow for dropping of constraints (such as indexes, etc.) on the table.

The general syntax to modify a field (change its type, etc.) is:

```
ALTER TABLE <table-name>

MODIFY <field-name> <new-field-declaration>
```

Note that you can only do this to a certain extent on most databases. Just as with 'drop', this is mostly useful for working with table constraints (changing 'not null' to 'null', etc).

Data Manipulation Language (DML)

Data Manipulation Language is a standard subset of SQL that is used for data manipulation. In-tuitively, we need to first inset data into the database. Once it's there, we can retrieve it, modify it, and delete it. These directly correspond to: INSERT, SELECT, UPDATE, and DELETE statements.

INSERT Statement

To get data into a database, we need to use the 'insert' statement. The general syntax is:

```
INSERT INTO <table-name>(<column1>, <column2>, <column3>,…)

    VALUES (<column-value1> ,<column-value2>, <column-value3>);
```

The column names (i.e.: column1, etc.) must correspond to column values (i.e.: column-value1, etc.). There is a short-hand for the statement:

```
INSERT INTO <table-name>

    VALUES (column-value1> , <column-value2> , <column-value3>);
```

In which the column values must correspond exactly to the order columns appear in the 'create table' declaration. It must be noted, that this sort of statement should (or rather, must) be avoided! If someone changes the table, moves columns around in the table declaration, the code using the shorthand insert statement will fail.

A typical example, of inserting the 'person' record we've created earlier would be:

```
INSERT INTO PERSON(PERSONID,LNAME,FNAME,DOB)

        VALUES (1,'DOE','JOHN','1956-11-23');
```

SELECT Statement

Probably the most used statement in all of SQL is the SELECT statement. The select statement has the general format of:

```
SELECT <column-list>

FROM <table-list>

WHERE <search-condition>
```

The column-list indicates what columns you're interested in (the ones which you want to appear in the result), the table-list is the list of tables to be used in the query, and search-condition specifies what criteria you're looking for.

An example of a short-hand version to retrieve all 'person' records we've been using:

```
SELECT * FROM PERSON;
```

The WHERE Clause

The WHERE clause is used in UPDATE, DELETE, and SELECT statements, and has the same format in all these cases. It has to be evaluated to either true or false. Table 1 lists some of the common operators.

Table: SQL Operators.

=	equals to
>	greater than
<	less than
>=	greater than or equal to
<=	less than or equal to
<>	not equal to

There is also IS, which can be used to check for NULL values, for example:

```
column-name IS NULL
```

We can also use AND, OR and parenthesis to group expressions.

Besides for these operators, we can also call built-in functions (as well as stored procedures we define ourselves—that is, if the database supports stored procedures).

An example of the operators in use would be: something < 5 OR something is NULL AND some-date = TO DATE('01/03/93','MM/DD/YY').

UPDATE Statement

The update statement is used for changing records. The general syntax is:

```
UPDATE <table-name>
SET <column1> = <value1>, <column2> = <value2>, …
WHERE <criteria>
```

The criteria are what select the records for update. The 'set' portion indicates which columns should be updated and to what values. An example of the use would be:

```
UPDATE PERSON
SET FNAME='Clark', LNAME='Kent'
WHERE FNAME='Superman';
```

DELETE Statement

The 'delete' is used to remove elements from the database. The syntax is very similar to update and select statements:

```
DELETE FROM <table-name>
WHERE <criteria>
```

Basically we select which records we want to delete using the where clause. An example use would be:

```
DELETE FROM PERSON
WHERE PERSONID=12345;
```

Data Query Language (DQL)

The commands of SQL that are used to create database objects, alter the structure of the database objects and delete database objects from database are collectively called as DDL. Examples include Create, Alter, Drop, Truncate, Rename and Comment Commands.

Create

Create command is used to create database and its Objects like tables, index, stored procedure, views, triggers, functions and etc.

Example:

To create Employee table:

```
create table tblEmployee(
```

```
    Id int primary key identity(1,1) not null,

    Name nvarchar(50) ,

    Gender nvarchar(50) ,

    Salary int ,

    DepartmentId int ,

)
```

Alter: Alter command is used to create database and its Objects.

Drop: Drop command is used to delete objects from database.

Truncate: Trunctae table command is used to remove all records from a table, including all spaces allocated for records are removed.

Rename: It is used to rename the objects.

Comment: // -> Single line Comments, /* --Multi Line Comments-- */ used to comment the sql statements.

References

- Database: searchsqlserver.techtarget.com, Retrieved 05 January, 2019

- Function-purpose-dbms, computer-aptitude-and-knowledge-dbms: toppr.com, Retrieved 29 march, 2019

- Database-development-process, dbdesign01: opentextbc.ca, Retrieved 22 August 2019

- 3-tier-architecture-complete-overview, bi-defined: jinfonet.com, Retrieved 18 July, 2019

- Sql-tutorial: tutorialspoint.com, Retrieved 02 August, 2019

- Explain-data-control-language-dcl-with-examples-in-dbms: whatisdbms.com, Retrieved 05 June, 2019

Database Models and Types

There are different types of database such as graph database, object oriented database, object relational database, centralized database, etc. It also comprises of specific models such as entity-attribute-value model, object model, document model, associative model, multidimensional model, etc. This chapter has been carefully written to provide an easy understanding of various database models and types.

Entity–attribute–value Model

In an EAV model, the HTML <form> fields represent a one-to-many relationship between a primary Entity table and a Value table. Each row in the Value table corresponds to a "field", which is defined as a row in a third Attribute table. In effect, the Value table creates a many-to-many link between the Entity table and the Attribute table. Django does not provide much support for EAV out of the box, though there are a number of plugins that do so.

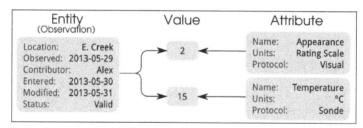

In wq, the EAV approach typically means defining classes as subclasses of the base Entity type you want to use. For example, to define a model that uses the EAV-style annotate structure, you would create it as a subclass of AnnotatedModel. Any relational fields can then be defined on your model as usual. Our general rule of thumb is that if a field is critical to the interpretation of a record, is a foreign key, or is going too referenced by name anywhere in the code, it should be defined as a traditional relational field. All other fields can be defined as rows in the Attribute table, and new attributes can be added on the fly via a web interface if needed.

The key weakness of the EAV approach is not performance - this can be optimized with appropriate database indices. Instead, the key weakness of EAV is the level of abstraction that obfuscates the application code. For example, the <form> in your edit template will need to contain a "loop" over an indeterminate number of Attribute definitions. If you want to support different field types (e.g. number, text) in a relational model, you can do so by changing the HTML <input type> for just that field. With an EAV model, you will instead need to create branching logic that can adapt to each field type on the fly. There will not be a single reference to a specific Attribute name anywhere in your code - which makes reasoning about changes more difficult. That said, if you are comfortable with this abstraction, it can be a very powerful tool for building adaptable applications that don't need any further developer intervention when project definitions change.

Network Model

A network database consists of a collection of records connected to one another through links. A record is in many respects similar to an entity in the E-R model. Each record is a collection of fields (attributes), each of which contains only one data value. A link is an association between precisely two records. Thus, a link can be viewed as a restricted (binary) form of relationship in the sense of the E-R model.

As an illustration, consider a database representing a customer-account relationship in a banking system. There are two record types, customer and account. As we saw earlier, we can define the customer record type, using Pascal-like notation:

```
type customer = record
        customer_name: string;
        customer_street: string;
        customer_city: string;
    end
```

The account record type can be defined as,

```
type account = record
        account_number: string;
        balance: integer;
    end
```

The sample database in figure shows that Hayes has account A-102, Johnson has accounts A-101 and A-201, and Turner has account A-305.

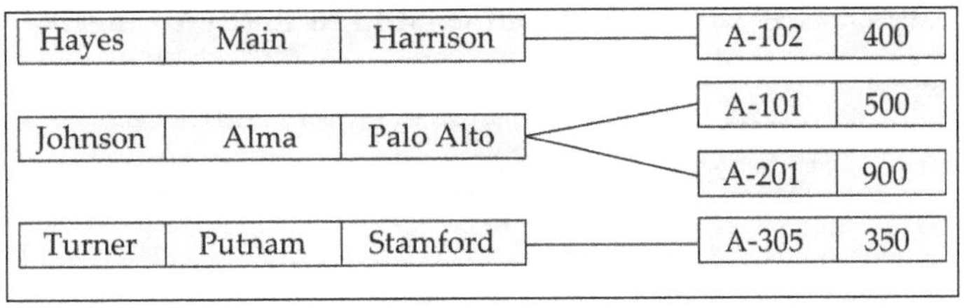

Hayes	Main	Harrison		A-102	400
				A-101	500
Johnson	Alma	Palo Alto			
				A-201	900
Turner	Putnam	Stamford		A-305	350

Sample database.

Data-Structure Diagrams

A data-structure diagram is a schema representing the design of a network database. Such a diagram consists of two basic components:

- Boxes, which correspond to record types.

- Lines, which correspond to links.

A data-structure diagram serves the same purpose as an E-R diagram; namely, it specifies the overall logical structure of the database. So that you will understand how such diagrams are structured, we shall show how to transform E-R diagrams into their corresponding data-structure diagrams.

Binary Relationship

Consider the E-R diagram of figure, consisting of two entity sets, customer and account, related through a binary, many-to-many relationship depositor, with no descriptive attributes. This diagram specifies that a customer may have several accounts, and that an account may belong to several different customers.

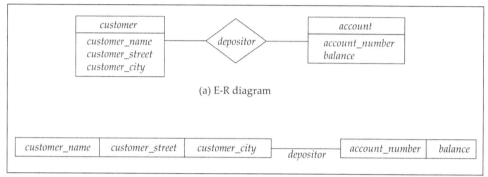

E-R diagram and its corresponding data-structure diagram.

The corresponding data-structure diagram appears in figure. The record type customer corresponds to the entity set customer. It includes three fields—*customer-name, customer_street*, and *customer_city*. Similarly, account is the record type corresponding to the entity set account. It includes the two fields *account_number* and *balance*. Finally, the relationship depositor has been replaced with the link *depositor*.

The relationship depositor is many to many. If the relationship *depositor* were one to many from customer to account, then the link *depositor* would have an arrow pointing to *customer* record type. Similarly, if the relationship depositor were one to one, then the link *depositor* would have two arrows: one pointing to account record type and one pointing to customer record type. Since, in the E-R diagram of figure, the depositor relationship is many to many, we draw no arrows on the link *depositor* in figure.

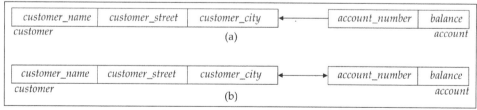

Two data-structure diagrams.

A database corresponding to the described schema may thus contain a number of *customer* records linked to a number of account records. A sample database corresponding to the data-structure diagram of figure appears in figure. Since the relationship is many to many, we show that Johnson has accounts A-101 and A-201 and that account A-201 is owned by both Johnson and Smith. A sample database corresponding to the data-structure diagram of figure is depicted in figure. Since the relationship is one to many from customer to account, a customer may have more than one account, as Johnson does—she owns both A-101 and A-201. An *account*, however, cannot belong to more than one customer, and the database observes this restriction. Finally, a sample database corresponding to the data-structure diagram of figure is shown in figure. Since the relationship is one to one, an account can be owned by precisely one customer, and a customer can have only one account; the sample database follows those rules.

Hayes	Main	Harrison		A-102	400
				A-101	500
Johnson	Alma	Palo Alto		A-201	900
Turner	Putnam	Stamford		A-305	350

Hayes	Main	Harrison		A-102	400
Lindsay	Park	Pittsfield		A-222	700
Turner	Putnam	Stamford		A-305	350

Sample database corresponding to diagram.

If a relationship includes descriptive attributes, the transformation from an E-R diagram to a data-structure diagram is more complicated. A link cannot contain any data value, so a new record type needs to be created and links need to be established.

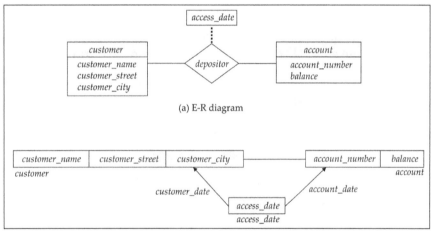

E-R diagram and its corresponding network diagram.

Consider the E-R diagram of figure. Suppose that we add the attribute access date to the relationship depositor, to denote the most recent time that a customer accessed the account. This newly derived E-R diagram appears in figure. To transform this diagram to a data-structure diagram, we must.

- Replace entities `customer` and `account` with record type's `customer` and `account`, respectively.

- Create a new record type `access date` with a single field to represent the date.

- Create the following many-to-one links:

  - `customer_date` from the `access date` record type to the `customer` record type.

  - `account_date` from the `access date` record type to the `account` record type.

The resulting data-structure diagram appears in figure.

An instance of a database corresponding to the described schema appears in figure. It shows that:

- Account A-201 is held by Johnson alone, and was last accessed by her on 17 June.

- Account A-305 is held by Turner alone, and was last accessed by him on 28 May.

- Account A-102 is held by both Hayes and Johnson. Hayes accessed it last on 10 June, and Johnson accessed it last on 24 May.

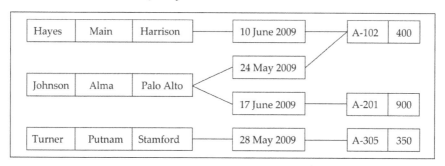

General Relationships

Consider the E-R diagram of figure, which consists of three entity sets— account, customer, and branch—related through the general relationship CAB with no descriptive attribute.

Since a link can connect precisely two different record types, we need to connect these three record types through a new record type that is linked to each of them directly.

To transform the E-R diagram of figure to a network data-structure diagram, we need to do the following:

- Replace entity sets account, customer, and branch with record types account, customer, and branch, respectively.

- Create a new record type Rlink that may either have no fields or have a single field containing a unique identifier. The system supplies this identifier, and the application program does not use it directly. This new type of record is sometimes referred to as a dummy (or link or junction) record type.

- Create the following many-to-one links:

  ◦ CustRlnk from Rlink record type to customer record type.

  ◦ AcctRlnk from Rlink record type to account record type.

  ◦ BrncRlnk from Rlink record type to branch record type.

The resulting data-structure diagram appears in figure.

A sample database corresponding to the described schema appears in figure. It shows that Hayes has account A-102 in the Perryridge branch, Johnson has accounts A-101 and A-201 in the Downtown and Perryridge branches, respectively, and Turner has account A-305 in the Round Hill branch. We can extend this technique in a straightforward manner to deal with relationships that span more than three entity sets. We create a many-to-one link from the *Rlink* record to the record types corresponding to each entity set involved in the relationship. We can also extend the technique to deal with a general relationship that has descriptive attributes. We need to add one field to the dummy record type for each descriptive attribute.

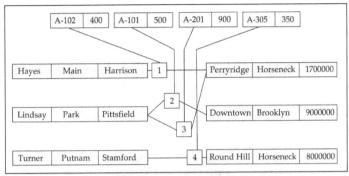

Sample database corresponding to diagram.

The DBTG CODASYL Model

The first database-standard specification, called the CODASYL DBTG 1971 report, was written in the late 1960s by the Database Task Group. Since then, a number of changes have been proposed many of which are reflected in our discussion concerning the DBTG model.

Link Restriction

In the DBTG model, only many-to-one links can be used. Many-to-many links are disallowed to simplify the implementation. We represent one-to-one links using a many-to-one link. These restrictions imply that the various algorithms for transforming an E-R diagram to a data-structure diagram must be revised. Consider a binary relationship that is either one to many or one to one. In this case, the transformation algorithm can be applied directly. Thus, for our customer-account database, if the depositor relationship is one to many with no descriptive attributes, then the appropriate data-structure diagram is as shown in figure. If the relationship has a descriptive attribute (for example, access-date), then the appropriate data-structure diagram is as shown in figure.

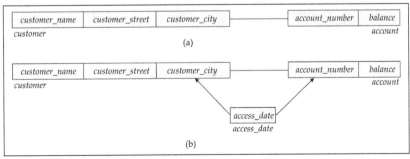

Two data-structure diagrams.

If the depositor relationship, however, is many to many, then our transformation algorithm must be refined; if the relationship has no descriptive attributes, then this algorithm must be employed:

- Replace the entity sets `customer` and account with record type's `customer` and `account`, respectively.

- Create a new dummy record type, `Rlink`, that may either have no fields or have a single field containing an externally defined unique identifier.

- Create the following two many-to-one links:

  ○ `CustRlnk` from `Rlink` record type to `customer` record type.

  ○ `AcctRlnk` from `Rlink` record type to `account` record type.

The corresponding data-structure diagram is as shown in figure. An instance of a database corresponding to the described schema appears in figure. We encourage you to compare this sample database with the one described in figure.

If the relationship depositor is many to many with a descriptive attribute (for example, `access date`), then the transformation algorithm is similar to the one described. The only difference is that the new record type `Rlink` now contains the field `access_date`.

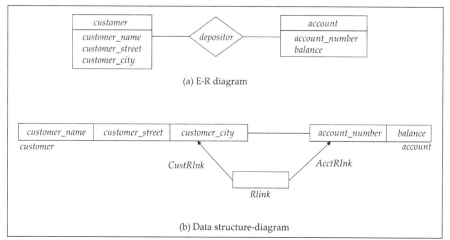

E-R diagram and its corresponding data-structure diagram.

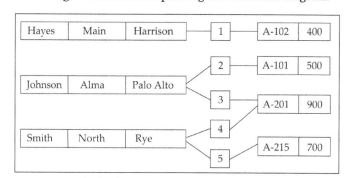

Sample database corresponding to the diagram.

In the case of general (that is, nonbinary) relationships, the transformation algorithm is the same. Thus, the E-R diagram of figure is transformed into the data-structure diagram of figure.

DBTG Sets

Given that only many-to-one links can be used in the DBTGmodel, a data-structure diagram consisting of two record types that are linked together has the general form of figure. This structure is referred to in the DBTG model as a DBTG set. The name of the set is usually chosen to be the same as the name of the link connecting the two record types.

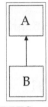

DBTG set.

In each such DBTG set, the record type A is designated as the *owner* (or *parent*) of the set, and the record type B is designated as the *member* (or *child*) of the set. Each DBTG set can have any number of *set occurrences*— that is, actual instances of linked records. For example, in figure, we have three set occurrences corresponding to the DBTG set of figure. Since many-to-many links are disallowed, each set occurrence has precisely one owner, and has zero or more member records. In addition, no member record of a set can participate in more than one occurrence of the set at any point.

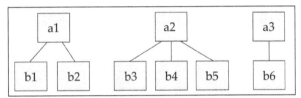

Three set occurrences.

A member record, however, can participate simultaneously in several set occurrences of different DBTG sets.

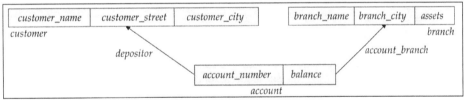

Data-structure diagram.

As an illustration, consider the data-structure diagram of figure. There are two DBTG sets:

- depositor, which has customer as the owner of the DBTG set, and account as the member of the DBTG set.

- account_branch, which has branch as the owner of the DBTG set, and account as the member of the DBTG set.

The set depositor can be defined as follows:

set name is depositor

owner is customer

member is account

The set account branch can be defined similarly:

set name is `account_branch`

owner is `branch`

member is `account`

An instance of the database appears in figure. There are six set occurrences listed next: three of set `depositor` (sets 1, 2, and 3), and three of set `account_branch` (sets 4, 5, and 6).

- Owner is `customer` record Hayes, with a single member `account` record A-102.

- Owner is `customer` record Johnson, with two member `account` records A-101 and A-201.

- Owner is `customer` record Turner, with three member `account` records A-305, A-402, and A-408.

- Owner is `branch` record Perryridge, with three member `account` records A-102, A-201, and A-402.

- Owner is `branch` record Downtown, with one member `account` record A-101.

- Owner is `branch` record Round Hill, with two member `account` records A-305 and A-408.

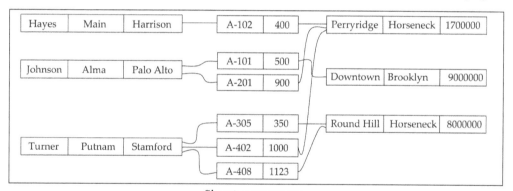

Six set occurrences.

An `account` record (which is, in this case, a member of both DBTG sets) cannot appear in more than one set occurrence of one individual set type. This restriction exists because an account can belong to exactly one customer, and can be associated with only one bank branch. An account, however, can appear in two set occurrences of different set types. For example, account A-102 is a member of set occurrence 1 of type `depositor`, and is also a member of set occurrence 4 of type `account branch`.

The member records of a set occurrence can be ordered in a variety of ways. The DBTG model allows more complicated set structures, in which one single owner type and several different member types exist. For example, suppose that we have two types of bank accounts: checking and saving. Then, the datastructure diagram for the customer-account schema is as depicted in figure. Such a schema is similar in nature to the E-R diagram of figure. The DBTG model also provides for the definition of a special kind of set, referred to as a `singular set` (or `system set`). In such a set, the owner is a systemdefined, unique record type, called `system`, with no fields. Such a set has a `single` set occurrence.

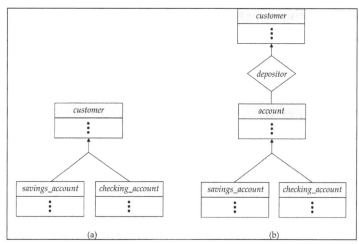

Data-structure and E-R diagram.

Repeating Groups

The DBTG model provides a mechanism for a field (or collection of fields) to have a set of values, rather than one single value. For example, suppose that a customer has several addresses. In this case, the customer record type will have the (street, city) pair of fields defined as a repeating group. Thus, the customer record for Turner may be as in figure.

Turner	Putnam	Stamford
	Field	Horseneck

A customer record.

The repeating-groups construct provides another way to represent the notion of weak entities in the E-R model. As an illustration, let us partition the entity set customer into two sets:

- Customer, with descriptive attribute customer name.

- Customer_address, with descriptive attributes customer street and customer city.

The customer_address entity set is a weak entity set, since it depends on the strong entity set customer.

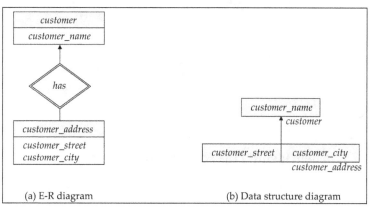

E-R and data-structure diagram.

The E-R diagram describing this schema appears in figure. If we do not use the repeating-group construct in the schema, then the corresponding data structure diagram is the one in Figure. If, on the other hand, we do use the repeating-group construct, then the data-structure diagram consists of simply one single record type `customer`.

DBTG Data-Retrieval Facility

The data-manipulation language of the DBTG proposal consists of commands that are embedded in a host language.

Program Work Area

Each application program executing in the system consists of a sequence of statements; some are Pascal statements, whereas others are DBTG command statements. Each such program is called a `run unit`. These statements access and manipulate database items, as well as locally declared variables. For each such application program, the system maintains a `program work area` (referred to in the DBTG model as a `user work area`), which is a buffer storage area that contains the following variables:

- Record templates: A record (in the Pascal sense) for each record type accessed by the application program.

- Currency pointers: A set of pointers to various database records most recently accessed by the application program; currency pointers are of the following types:

  - Current of record type: One currency pointer for each record type T referenced by the application program; each pointer contains the `address` (location on disk) of the most recently accessed record of type T.

  - Current of set type: One currency pointer for each set type S referenced by the application program; each pointer contains the address of the most recently accessed record of that set type; note that this pointer may point to a record of either the owner or member type, depending on whether an owner or a member was most recently accessed.

  - Current of run unit: One single currency pointer, containing the `address` of the record (regardless of type) most recently accessed by the application program.

- Status flags: A set of variables used by the system to communicate to the application program the outcome of the last operation applied to the database; the most frequently used one is DB-status, set to 0 if the most recent operation succeeded and otherwise set to an error code.

The additional status variables (DB-set-name, DB-record-name, and DB-data-name) are set when the final operation fails, to help identify the source of the difficulty.

We emphasize that a particular program work area is associated with precisely one application program.

For our customer-account-branch database example, a particular program work area contains the following:

- Templates: three record types:

  ○ `customer` **record**

  ○ `account` **record**

  ○ `branch` **record**

- Currency pointers: six pointers:

  ○ Three currency pointers for record types: one to the most recently accessed `customer` record, one to the most recently accessed `account` record, and one to the most recently accessed `branch` record.

  ○ Two currency pointers for set types: one to the most recently accessed record in an occurrence of the set `depositor`, and one to the most recently accessed record in an occurrence of the set `account branch`.

  ○ One current of run-unit pointer.

- Status flags: the four status variables that we defined previously.

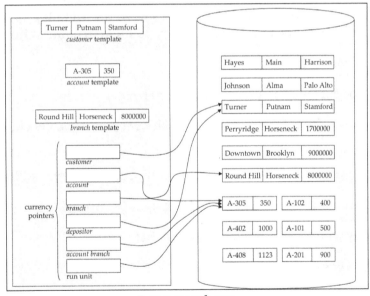

Program work area.

The Find and Get Commands

The two most frequently used DBTG commands are:

- Find, which locates a record in the database and sets the appropriate currency pointers.

- Get, which copies the record to which the current of run unit points from the database to the appropriate program work area template.

Let us illustrate the general effect that the find and get statements have on the program work area. Consider the sample database of figure. Suppose that the current state of the program work area of a particular application program is as shown in figure. Further suppose that a find command is issued to locate the customer record belonging to Johnson. This command causes the following changes to occur in the state of the program work area:

- The current of record type `customer` now points to the record of Johnson.

- The current of set type `depositor` now points to the record of Johnson.

- The current of run unit now points to `customer` record Johnson.

If the get command is executed, the result is that the information pertaining to Johnson is loaded into the customer record template.

Access of Individual Records

The find command has a number of forms. We shall present only a few of these commands in this appendix. There are two different find commands for locating individual records in the database. The simplest command has the form:

```
find any <record type> using <record-field>
```

This command locates a record of type <record type> whose <record-field> value is the same as the value of <record-field> in the <record type> template in the program work area. Once the system finds such a record, it sets the following currency pointers to point to that record:

- The current of run-unit pointer.

- The record-type currency pointer for `<record type>`.

- The set currency pointer for every set in which `<record type>` is either the owner type or member type.

As an illustration, let us construct the DBTG query that prints the street address of Hayes:

> `customer.customer_name` := "Hayes";
>
> find any `customer` using `customer_name`;
>
> get `customer`;
>
> print (`customer.customer_street`);

There may be several records with the specified value. The find command locates the first of these in some prespecified ordering. To locate other database records that match the <record-field>, we use the command:

```
find duplicate <record type> using <record-field>
```

which locates (according to a system-dependent ordering) the next record that matches the <record-field>. The currency pointers noted previously are affected.

As an example, let us construct the DBTG query that prints the names of all the customers who live in Harrison:

```
customer.customer_city := "Harrison";

find any customer using customer_city;

while DB-status = 0 do

        begin

                get customer;

                print (customer.customer_name);

                find duplicate customer using customer_city;

end;
```

We have enclosed part of the query in a while loop, because we do not know in advance how many such customers exist. We exit from the loop when DB-status ≠ 0. This action indicates that the most recent find duplicate operation failed, implying that we have exhausted all customers residing in Harrison.

Access of Records within a Set

The previous find commands located `any` database <record type>. The set in question is the one that is pointed to by the currency pointer. There are three different types of commands. The basic find command is:

```
find next <record type> within <set-type>
```

which locates the first member record of type `<record type>` belonging to the current occurrence of `<set-type>`.

To step through the other members of type `<record type>` belonging to the set occurrence, we repeatedly execute the following command:

```
find next <record type> within <set-type>
```

The find first and find next commands need to specify the record type since a DBTG set can have members of different record types. As an illustration of how these commands execute, let us construct the DBTG query that prints the total balance of all accounts belonging to Hayes.

```
sum := 0;

customer.customer_name := "Hayes";

find any customer using customer_name;

find first account within depositor;

while DB-status = 0 do
```

             begin

                   get `account;`

                   `sum := sum + account.balance;`

                   find next `account` within `depositor;`

         end

      print `(sum);`

Note that we exit from the while loop and print out the value of `sum` only when the DB-status is set to a value not equal to zero. Such a nonzero value results after the find next operation fails, indicating that we have exhausted all the members of a set occurrence of type `depositor`, whose owner is the record of customer Hayes.

The previous find commands locate member records within a particular DBTG set occurrence. There are many circumstances, however, under which it may be necessary to locate the owner of a particular DBTG set occurrence. We can do so through the following command:

      find owner within `<set-type>`

The set in question is `<set-type>`. Note that, for each set occurrence, there exists precisely one single owner.

As an illustration, consider the DBTG query that prints all the customers of the Perryridge branch:

         `branch.branch_name := "Perryridge";`

         find any `branch` using `branch_name;`

         find first `account` within `account_branch;`

         while `DB-status = 0` do

            begin

               find owner within `depositor;`

               get `customer;`

               print `(customer.customer_name);`

               find next `account` within `account_branch;`

         end

Note that, if a customer has several accounts in the Perryridge branch, then his name will be printed several times.

As a final example, consider the DBTG query that prints the names of all the customers of the bank. Such a query cannot be formed easily with the mechanism that we have described thus far, since no one single set has all the customer records as its members. The remedy is to define a singular set consisting of members of type `customer`. This set is defined as follows:

> set name is `AllCust`
>
> owner is `system`
>
> member is `customer`

Once such a set has been defined, we can form our query as follows:

> find first `customer` within `AllCust`;
>
> while `DB-status` = 0 do
>
> > begin
> >
> > > get `customer`;
> > >
> > > print (`customer.customer_name`);
> > >
> > > find next `customer` within `AllCust`;
> >
> > end

Predicates

The find statements that we have described allow the value of a field in one of the record templates to be matched with the corresponding field in the appropriate database records. Although, with this technique, we can formulate a variety of DBTG queries in a convenient and concise way, there are many queries in which a field value must be matched with a specified range of values, rather than to only one. To accomplish this match, we need to get the appropriate records into memory, to examine each one separately for a match, and thus to determine whether each is the target of our find statement.

As an illustration, consider the DBTG query to print the total number of accounts in the Perryridge branch with a balance greater than $10,000:

> count := 0;
>
> branch.branch_name := "Perryridge";
>
> find any `branch` using `branch_name`;
>
> find first `account` within `account_branch`;
>
> while `DB-status` = 0 do
>
> > begin
> >
> > > get `account`;
> > >
> > > if `account.balance` > 10000 then count := count + 1;
> > >
> > > find next `account` within `account_branch`;
> >
> > end
>
> print (count);

DBTG Update Facility

Creation of New Records

To create a new record of type `<record type>`, we insert the appropriate values in the corresponding `<record type>` template. We then add this new record to the database by executing.

```
store <record type>
```

This technique allows us to create and add new records only one at a time.

As an illustration, consider the DBTG program for adding a new customer, Jackson, to the database:

```
customer.customer_name := "Jackson";

customer.customer_street := "Old Road";

customer.customer_city := "Richardson";

store customer;
```

If a new record is created that must belong to a particular DBTG set occurrence (for example, a new account), then, in addition to the store operation, we need a mechanism for inserting records into set occurrences.

Modification of an Existing Record

To modify an existing record of type `<record type>`, we must find that record in the database, get that record into memory, and then change the desired fields in the template of `<record type>`. Then, we reflect the changes to the record to which the currency pointer of `<record type>` points by executing:

```
modify <record type>
```

The DBTG model requires that the find command executed prior to modification of a record must have the additional clause for update, so that the system is aware that a record is to be modified. We are not required to update a record that we "find for update." However, we cannot update a record unless it is found for update.

As an example, consider the DBTG program to change the street address of Turner to North Loop:

```
customer.customer_name := "Turner";

find for update any customer using customer_name;

get customer;

customer.customer_street := "North Loop";

modify customer;
```

Deletion of a Record

To delete an existing record of type `<record type>`, we must make the currency pointer of that type point to the record in the database to be deleted. Then, we can delete that record by executing:

```
erase <record type>
```

Note that, as in the case of record modification, the find command must have the attribute for update attached to it.

As an illustration, consider the DBTG program to delete account A-402 belonging to Turner:

```
finish := false;

customer.customer_name := "Turner";

find any customer using customer_name;

find for update first account within depositor;

while DB-status = 0 and not finish do
    begin
        get account;
        if account.account_number = "A-402" then
        begin
            erase account;
            finish := true;
        end
        else find for update next account within depositor;
    end
```

We can delete an entire set occurrence by finding the owner of the set—say, a record of type `<record type>`—and executing:

```
erase all <record type>
```

This command will delete the owner of the set, as well as all the set's members. If a member of the set is an owner of another set, the members of that second set also will be deleted. Thus, the erase all operation is recursive.

Consider the DBTG program to delete customer "Johnson" and all her accounts:

```
customer.customer_name := "Johnson";

find for update any customer using customer_name;

erase all customer;
```

A natural question is what happens when we wish to delete a record that is an owner of a set, but we do not specify all in the erase statement. In this case, several possibilities exist:

- Delete only that record.

- Delete the record and all its members.

- Do not delete any records.

It turns out that each of these options can be specified in the DBTG model.

DBTG Set-processing Facility

The store and erase statements are closely tied to the set-processing facility. In particular, a mechanism must be provided for inserting records into and removing records from a particular set occurrence. In the case of deletion, we have a number of different options to consider if the record to be deleted is the owner of a set.

The connect Statement

To insert a new record of type `<record type>` into a particular occurrence of `<settype>`, we must first insert the record into the database (if it is not already there). Then, we need to set the currency pointers of `<record type>` and `<set-type>` to point to the appropriate record and set occurrence. Then, we can insert the new record into the set by executing.

```
connect <record type> to <set-type>
```

A new record can be inserted as follows:

- Create a new record of type `<record type>`. This action sets the appropriate `<record type>` currency pointer.

- Find the appropriate owner of the set `<set-type>`. This automatically sets the appropriate currency pointer of `<set-type>`.

- Insert the new record into the set oocurrence by executing the connect statement.

As an illustration, consider the DBTG query for creating new account A-267, which belongs to Jackson:

```
account.account_number := "A-267";

account.balance := 0;

store account;

customer.customer_name := "Jackson";

find any customer using customer name;

connect account to depositor;
```

The Disconnect Statement

To remove a record of type `<record type>` from a set occurrence of type `<settype>`, we need to set the currency pointer of `<record type>` and `<set-type>` to point to the appropriate record and set occurrence. Then, we can remove the record from the set by executing

```
disconnect <record type> from <set-type>
```

Assume that we wish to close account A-201. To do so, we need to delete the relationship between account A-201 and its customer. However, we need to keep the record of account A-201 in the database for the bank's internal archives. The following program shows how to perform these two actions within the DBTG model. This program will remove account A-201 from the set occurrence of type `depositor`. The account will still be accessible in the database for record-keeping purposes.

> account.account_number := "A-201";
>
> find for update any account using account number;
>
> find owner within depositor;
>
> disconnect account from depositor;

The Reconnect Statement

To move a record of type `<record type>` from one set occurrence to another set occurrence of type `<set-type>`, we need to find the appropriate record and the owner of the set occurrences to which that record is to be moved. Then, we can move the record by executing:

```
reconnect <record type> to <set-type>
```

Consider the DBTG program to move all accounts of Hayes that are currently at the Perryridge branch to the Downtown branch:

> customer.customer_name := "Hayes";
>
> find any customer using customer_name;
>
> find first account within depositor;
>
> while DB-status = 0 do
>
> > begin
> >
> > > find owner within account branch;
> > >
> > > get branch;
> > >
> > > if branch.branch_name = "Perryridge" then
> > >
> > > > begin
> > > >
> > > > > branch.branch_name := "Downtown";

> find any `branch` using `branch_name`;
>
> reconnect `account` to `account branch`;

    end

    find next `account` within `depositor`;

end

Insertion and Retention of Records

When a new set is defined, we must specify how member records are to be inserted. In addition, we must specify the conditions under which a record must be retained in the set occurrence in which it was initially inserted.

Set Insertion

A newly created member record of type <record type> of a set type <set-type> can be added to a set occurrence either explicitly (manually) or implicitly (automatically). This distinction is specified at set-definition time via:

```
insertion is <insert mode>
```

where <insert mode> can take one of two forms:

- Manual: We can insert the new record into the set manually (explicitly) by executing:

```
connect <record type> to <set-type>
```

- Automatic. The new record is inserted into the set automatically (implicitly) when it is created— that is, when we execute:

```
store <record type>
```

In either case, just prior to insertion, the <set-type> currency pointer must point to the set occurrence into which the insertion is to be made.

As an illustration, consider the creation of account A-535 that belongs to Hayes and is at the Downtown branch. Suppose that set insertion is manual for set type depositor and is automatic for set type account branch. The appropriate DBTG program is:

> `branch.branch_name` := "Downtown";
>
> find any `branch` using `branch_name`;
>
> `account.account_number` := "A-535";
>
> `account.balance` := 0;
>
> store `account`;
>
> `customer.customer_name` := "Hayes";

> find any `customer` using `customer_name`;
>
> connect `account` to `depositor`;

Set Retention

There are various restrictions on how and when a member record can be removed from a set occurrence into which it has been inserted previously. These restrictions are specified at set-definition time via:

```
retention is <retention-mode>
```

where `<retention-mode>` can take one of the three forms:

- Fixed: Once a member record has been inserted into a particular set occurrence, it cannot be removed from that set. If retention is fixed, then, to reconnect a record to another set, we must erase that record, re-create it, and then insert it into the new set occurrence.

- Mandatory: Once a member record has been inserted into a particular set occurrence, it can be reconnected to another set occurrence of only type `<set-type>`. It can neither be disconnected nor be reconnected to a set of another type.

- Optional: No restrictions are placed on how and when a member record can be removed from a set occurrence. A member record can be reconnected, disconnected, and connected at will.

The decision of which option to choose depends on the application. For example, in our banking database, the optional retention mode is appropriate for the depositor set because we may have defunct accounts not owned by anybody. On the other hand, the mandatory retention mode is appropriate for the account branch set, since an account has to belong to some branch.

Deletion

When a record is deleted (erased) and that record is the owner of set occurrence of type `<set-type>`, the best way of handling this deletion depends on the specification of the set retention of `<set-type>`.

Network Model

- If the retention status is optional, then the record will be deleted and every member of the set that it owns will be disconnected. These records, however, will remain in the database.

- If the retention status is fixed, then the record and all its owned members will be deleted. This action occurs because the fixed status means that a member record cannot be removed from the set occurrence without being deleted.

- If the retention status is mandatory, then the record cannot be erased, because the mandatory status indicates that a member record must belong to a set occurrence. The record cannot be disconnected from that set.

Set Ordering

The members of a set occurrence of type `<set-type>` can be ordered in a variety of ways. These orders are specified by a programmer when the set is defined via:

```
order is <order-mode>
```

where `<order-mode>` can be any of the following:

- First: When a new record is added to a set, it is inserted in the first position. Thus, the set is in reverse chronological order.

- Last: When a new record is added to a set, it is inserted in the final position. Thus, the set is in chronological order.

- Next: Suppose that the currency pointer of `<set-type>` points to record X. If X is a member type, then, when a new record is added to the set, that record is inserted in the next position following X. If X is an owner type, then, when a new record is added, that record is inserted in the first position.

- Prior: Suppose that the currency pointer of `<set-type>` points to record X. If X is a member type, then, when a new record is added to the set, that record is inserted in the position just prior to X. If X is an owner type, then, when a new record is added, that record is inserted in the last position.

- System default: When a new record is added to a set, it is inserted in an arbitrary position determined by the system.

- Sorted: When a new record is added to a set, it is inserted in a position that ensures that the set will remain sorted. The sorting order is specified by a particular key value when a programmer defines the set. The programmer must specify whether members are ordered in ascending or descending order relative to that key.

Consider again figure, where the set occurrence of type `depositor` with the owner-record customer Turner and member-record accounts A-305, A-402, and A-408 are ordered as indicated. Suppose that we add a new account A-125 to that set. For each `<order-mode>` option, the new set ordering is as follows:

- First: {A-125, A-305, A-402, A-408}

- Last: {A-305, A-402, A-408, A-125}

- Next: Suppose that the currency pointer points to record "Turner"; then the new set order is {A-125, A-305, A-402, A-408}

- Prior: Suppose that the currency pointer points to record A-402; then the new set order is {A-305, A-125, A-402, A-408}

- System default: Any arbitrary order is acceptable; thus, {A-305, A-402, A-125, A-408} is a valid set ordering.

- Sorted: The set must be ordered in ascending order with account number being the key; thus, the ordering must be {A-125, A-305, A-402, A-408}

Mapping of Networks to Files

A network database consists of records and links. We implement links by adding pointer fields to records that are associated via a link. Each record must have one pointer field for each link with which it is associated. As an illustration, return to the data-structure diagram of figure and to the sample database corresponding to it in figure shows the sample instance with pointer fields to represent the links. Each line in figure is replaced in figure by two pointers.

Since the depositor link is many to many, each record can be associated with an arbitrary number of records. Thus, it is not possible to limit the number of pointer fields in a record. Therefore, even if a record itself is of fixed length, the actual record used in the physical implementation is a variable-length record.

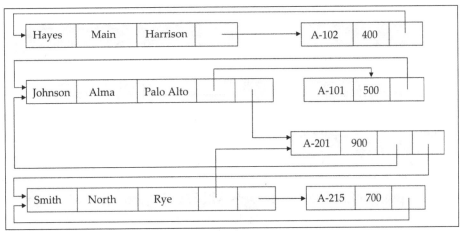

Implementation of instance of figure.

These complications led the architects of the DBTG model to restrict links to be either one to one or one to many. We shall see that, under this restriction, the number of pointers needed is reduced, and it is possible to retain fixed-length records. To illustrate the implementation of the DBTG model, we assume that the depositor link is one to many and is represented by the DBTG set depositor as defined here:

> set name is depositor
>
> owner is customer
>
> member is account

A sample database corresponding to this schema is in figure.

An account record can be associated with only one customer record. Thus, we need only one pointer in the account record to represent the depositor relationship. However, a customer record can be associated with many account records. Instead of using multiple pointers in the customer record, we can use a ring structure to represent the entire occurrence of the DBTG set depositor. In a ring structure, the records of both the owner and member types for a set occurrence are organized into a circular list. There is one circular list for each set occurrence (that is, for each record of the owner type).

Figure shows the ring structure for the example of figure. Let us examine the DBTG-set occurrence owned by the "Johnson" record. There are two member-type (`account`) records. Instead of containing one pointer to each member record, the owner (Johnson) record contains a pointer to only the first member record (account A-101). This member record contains a pointer to the next member record (account A-201). Since the record for account A-201 is the final member record, it contains a pointer to the owner record.

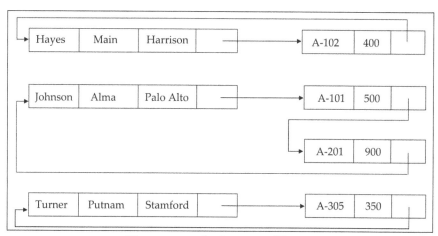

Ring structure for instance of figure.

If we represent DBTG sets by using the ring structure, a record contains exactly one pointer for each DBTG set in which it is involved, regardless of whether it is of the owner type or member type. Thus, we can represent fixed-length records within a ring structure without resorting to variable-length records. This structural simplicity is offset by added complexity in accessing records within a set. To find a particular member record of a set occurrence, we must traverse the pointer chain to navigate from the owner record to the desired member record. The ring-structure implementation strategy for the DBTG model provided the basis for the DBTG data retrieval facility. Recall these statements:

- find first <record type> within <set type>

- find next <record type> within <set type>

The terms first and next in these statements refer to the ordering of records given by the ring-structure pointers. Thus, once the owner has been found, it is easy to do a find first, since all the system must do is to follow a pointer. Similarly, all the system must do in response to a find next is to follow the ring-structure pointer. The find owner statement of the DBTG query language can be supported efficiently by a modified form of the ring structure in which every member type record contains a second pointer, which points to the owner record. This structure appears in figure. Under this implementation strategy, a record has one pointer for each DBTG set for which it is of the owner type, and two pointers (a `next-member` pointer and an `owner` pointer) for each DBTG set for which it is of the member type. This strategy allows efficient execution of a find owner statement. Under our earlier strategy, it is necessary to traverse the ring structure until we find the owner.

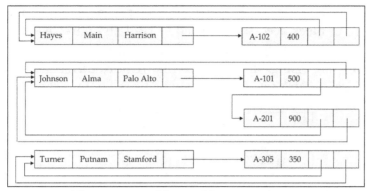

Ring structure of figure with owner pointers.

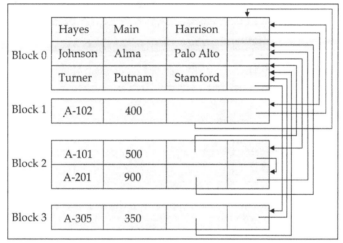

Clustered record placement for instance of figure.

The physical placement of records is important for an efficient implementation of a network database, as it is for a relational database. The statements find first, find next, and find owner are designed for processing a sequence of records within a particular DBTG-set occurrence. Since these statements are the ones most frequently used in a DBTG query, it is desirable to store records of a DBTG-set occurrence physically close to one another on disk. To specify the strategy that the system is to use to store a DBTG set, we add a placement clause to the definition of the member record type. Consider the DBTG set depositor and the example shown in figure. If we add the clause to the definition of record type account (the member-record type of the depositor DBTG set), the system will store members of each set occurrence close to one another physically on disk. To the extent possible, members of a set occurrence will be stored in the same block. Figure illustrates this storage strategy for the instance of figure:

placement clustered via `depositor`

The clustered placement strategy does not require the owner record of a DBTG set to be stored near the set's members. Thus, each record type can be stored in a distinct file. If we are willing to store more than one record type in a file, we can specify that owner and member records are to be stored close to one another physically on disk. We do so by adding the clause near owner to the placement clause. For our example of the depositor set, we add the clause to the definition of the record type account.

placement clustered via `depositor` near owner

Figure illustrates this storage strategy. By storing member records in the same block as the owner, we reduce the number of block accesses required to read an entire set occurrence. This form of storage is analogous to the clustering file structure that we proposed earlier for the relational model. This similarity is not surprising, since queries that require traversal of DBTG-set occurrences under the network model require natural joins under the relational model.

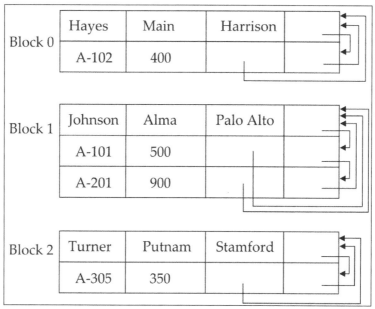

Record placement using clustering with the near owner option.

Semi-structured Model

The semi-structured data model is a data model where the information that would normal be connected to a schema is instead contained within the data, this is often referred to as self-describing model.

With this type of database there is no clear separation between the data and the schema, also the level to which it is structured relies on the application being used.

Certain forms of semi-structured data have no separate schema, while in others there is a separate schema but only in areas of little restriction on the data.

Modeling semi-structured data in graphs which have labels that give semantics to its fundamental structure is a natural process. Databases of this type include the modeling power of other extensions of flat relational databases, to sheathed databases which enable the encapsulation of entities, as well as to the object databases, which also enable recurring references between objects.

Data that is semi-structured has just recently come into view as an important area of study for various reasons. One reason is that there are data sources like the World Wide Web, which we often treat as a database but it cannot be controlled by a schema.

Another reason is it might be advantageous to have a very flexible format for data exchange between contrasting databases. Finally there is also the reason that when dealing with structured data it sometimes may still be helpful to view it as semi-structured data for the tasks of browsing.

Semi-Structured Data

We are familiar with structured data, which is the data that has been clearly formed, formatted, modeled, and organized into customs that are easy for us to work and manage. We are also familiar with unstructured data.

Unstructured data combines the bulk of information that does not fit into a set of databases. The most easily recognized form of unstructured data is the text in a document.

What you may not have known is that there is a middle ground for data; this is the data we refer to as semi-structured. This would be data sets that some implied structure is usually followed, but still not a standard enough structured to meet the criteria needed for the types of management and mechanization that is normally applied to structured data.

We deal with semi-structured data every day; this applies in both technical and non-technical environments. Web pages track definite distinctive forms, and the content entrenched within HTML usually have a certain extent of metadata within the tags.

Details about the data are implied instantly when using this information. This is why semi-structured data is so intriguing, though there is no set formatting rule, and there is still adequate reliability in which some interesting information can be taken from.

Advantages of the Semi-structured Data Model

Some advantages to the semi-structured data model include:

- Representation of the information about data sources that normally cannot be constrained by schema.
- The model provides a flexible format used for the data switch over amongst dissimilar kinds of databases.
- Semi-structured data models are supportive in screening structured data as semi-structured data.
- The schema is effortlessly altered with the model
- The data transportation configuration can be convenient.

The most important exchange being made in using a semi-structured database model is quite possibly that the queries will not be made as resourcefully as in the more inhibited structures, like the relational model.

Normally the records in a semi-structured database are stored with only one of a kind IDs that are referenced with indicators to their specific locality on a disk. Due to this the course-plotting or path based queries are very well-organized, yet for the purpose of doing searches over scores of records it is not as practical for the reason that it is forced to seek in the various regions of the disk by following the indicators.

We can clearly see that there are some disadvantages with semi-structured data model, as there are with all other models, lets take a moment to outline a few of these disadvantages.

Issues with Semi-Structured Data

Semi-structured data need to be characterized, turned over, stored, manipulated or analyzed with adeptness. Even so there are challenges in semi-structured data use. Some of these challenges include:

- Data Diversity: The issues of data diversity in federated systems is a complex issue, it also involves areas such as unit and semantic incompatibilities, grouping incompatibilities, and non-consistent overlapping of sets.

- Extensibility: It is vital to realize that extensibility as used to data is in indication to data presentation and not data processing. Data processing should be able to happen without the aid of database updates.

- Storage: Transfer formats like XML are universally in text or in Unicode; they are also prime candidates for transference, yet not so much for storage. The presentations are instead stored by deep seated and accessible systems that support such standards.

In short, many academic, open source, or other direct attention to these particular issues have been at an on-the-surface level of resolving representation or definitions, or even units.

The formation of sufficient processing engines for well-organized and scalable storage recovery has been wholly deficient in the complete driving force for a semi-structured data model.

Hierarchical Database Model

A hierarchical database consists of a collection of records that are connected to each other through `links`. A record is similar to a record in the network model. Each record is a collection of fields (attributes), each of which contains only one data value. A link is an association between precisely two records. Thus, a link here is similar to a link in the network model.

Consider a database that represents a `customer-account` relationship in a banking system. There are two record types: `customer` and `account`. The `customer` record type can be defined in the same manner as in Appendix A. It consists of three fields: `customer name`, `customer street`, and `customer city`. Similarly, the account record consists of two fields: `account number` and `balance`.

A sample database appears in figure. It shows that customer Hayes has account A-102, customer Johnson has accounts A-101 and A-201, and customer Turner has account A-305.

Note that the set of all customer and account records is organized in the form of a rooted tree, where the root of the tree is a dummy node. As we shall see, a hierarchical database is a collection of such rooted trees, and hence forms a forest. We shall refer to each such rooted tree as a `database tree`.

The content of a particular record may have to be replicated in several different locations. For example, in our customer-account banking system, an account may belong to several customers. The information pertaining to that account, or the information pertaining to the various customers to which that account may belong, will have to be replicated.

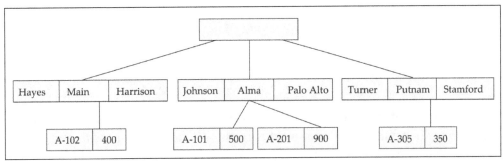

Sample database.

This replication may occur either in the same database tree or in several different trees. Record replication has two major drawbacks:

- Data inconsistency may result when updating takes place.

- Waste of space is unavoidable.

Tree-Structure Diagrams

A tree-structure diagram is the schema for a hierarchical database. Such a diagram consists of two basic components:

- Boxes, which correspond to record types.

- Lines, which correspond to links.

A tree-structure diagram serves the same purpose as an entity–relationship (E-R) diagram; namely, it specifies the overall logical structure of the database. A tree structure diagram is similar to a data-structure diagram in the network model. The main difference is that, in the latter, record types are organized in the form of an arbitrary graph, whereas in the former, record types are organized in the form of a rooted tree.

We have to be more precise about what a rooted tree is. First, there can be no cycles in the underlying graph. Second, there is a record type that is designated as the root of the tree. The relationships formed in the tree-structure diagram must be such that only one-to-many or one-to-one relationships exist between a parent and a child. The general form of a tree-structure diagram appears in figure. Note that the arrows are pointing from children to parents. A parent may have an arrow pointing to a child, but a child must have an arrow pointing to its parent.

The database schema is represented as a collection of tree-structure diagrams. For each such diagram, there exists one single instance of a database tree. The root of this tree is a dummy node. The children of the dummy node are instances of the root record type in the tree-structure diagram. Each record instance may, in turn, have several children, which are instances of various record types, as specified in the corresponding tree-structure diagram.

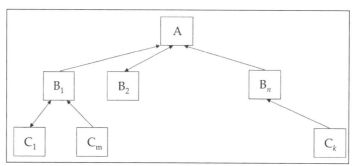

General structure of a tree-structure diagram.

To understand how tree-structure diagrams are formed, we shall show how to transform E-R diagrams to their corresponding tree-structure diagrams. We first show how to apply such transformations to single relationships. We then explain how to ensure that the resulting diagrams are in the form of rooted trees.

Single Relationships

Consider the E-R diagram of figure; it consists of the two entity sets `customer` and `account` related through a binary, one-to-many relationship `depositor`, with no descriptive attributes. This diagram specifies that a customer can have several accounts, but an account can belong to only one customer. The corresponding treestructure diagram appears in figure. The record type `customer` corresponds to the entity set `customer`. It includes three fields: `customer name`, `customer_street`, and `customer city`. Similarly, `account` is the record type corresponding to the entity set account. It includes two fields: `account number` and `balance`. Finally, the relationship `depositor` has been replaced with the link `depositor`, with an arrow pointing to `customer` record type.

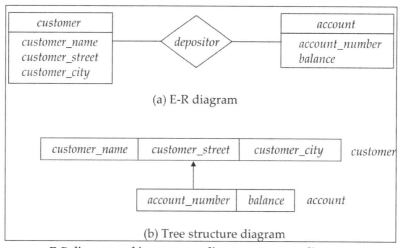

E-R diagram and its corresponding tree-structure diagram.

An instance of a database corresponding to the described schema may thus contain a number of `customer` records linked to a number of `account` records. Since the relationship is one to many from `customer` to `account`, a customer can have more than one account, as does Johnson, who has both accounts A-101 and A-201. An account, however, cannot belong to more than one customer; none do in the sample database.

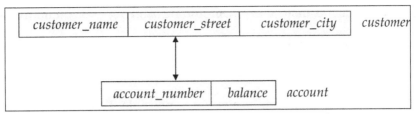

Tree-structure diagram with one-to-one relationship.

If the relationship `depositor` is one to one, then the link `depositor` has two arrows: one pointing to `account` record type, and one pointing to `customer` record type). A sample database corresponding to this schema appears in figure. Since the relationship is one to one, an account can be owned by precisely one customer, and a customer can have only one account, as is indeed the case in the sample database.

If the relationship depositor is one to one, then the link depositor has two arrows: one pointing to account record type, and one pointing to customer record type. A sample database corresponding to this schema appears in figure. Since the relationship is one to one, an account can be owned by precisely one customer, and a customer can have only one account, as is indeed the case in the sample database.

If the relationship `depositor` is many to many, then the transformation from an E-R diagram to a tree-structure diagram is more complicated. Only one-to-many and one-to-one relationships can be directly represented in the hierarchical model.

There are many different ways to transform this E-R diagram to a tree-structure diagram. All these diagrams, however, share the property that the underlying database tree (or trees) will have replicated records.

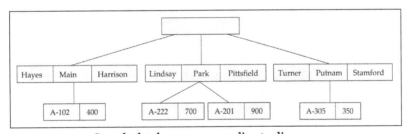

Sample database corresponding to diagram.

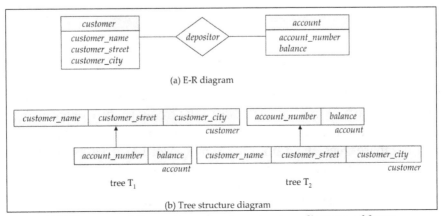

E-R diagram and its corresponding tree-structure diagrams of figure.

The decision regarding which transformation should be used depends on many factors, including:

- The type of queries expected on the database.

- The degree to which the overall database schema being modeled fits the given E-R diagram.

We shall present a transformation that is as general as possible. That is, all other possible transformations are a special case of this one transformation.

To transform the E-R diagram of figure into a tree-structure diagram, we take these steps:

- Create two separate tree-structure diagrams, T_1 and T_2, each of which has the `customer` and `account` record types. In tree T_1, `customer` is the root; in tree T_2, `account` is the root.

- Create the following two links:

    ○ `Depositor`, a many-to-one link from `account` record type to `customer` record type, in T_1

    ○ `Account_customer`, a many-to-one link from `customer` record type to `account` record type, in T_2.

The resulting tree-structure diagrams appear in figure. The presence of two diagrams (1) permits customers who do not participate in the `depositor` relationship as well as accounts that do not participate in the `depositor` relationship, and (2) permits efficient access to account information for a given customer as well as customer information for a given account.

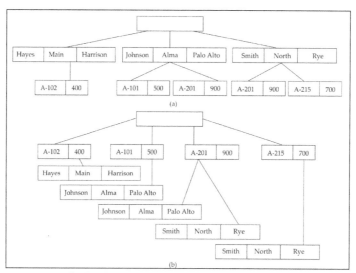

Sample database corresponding to diagram of figure.

A sample database corresponding to the tree-structure diagram of figure appears in figure. There are two database trees. The first tree corresponds to the tree-structure diagram T_1; the second tree corresponds to the tree-structure diagram T_2. As we can see, all `customer` and `account` records are replicated in both database trees. In addition, `account` record A-201 appears twice in the first tree, whereas `customer` records Johnson and Smith appear twice in the second tree.

If a relationship also includes a descriptive attribute, the transformation from an E-R diagram to a tree-structure diagram is more complicated. A link cannot contain any data value. In this case, a new record type needs to be created, and the appropriate links need to be established. The manner in which links are formed depends on the way the relationship depositor is defined.

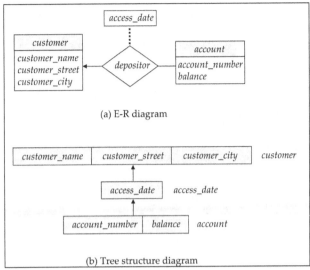

(a) E-R diagram

(b) Tree structure diagram

E-R diagram and its corresponding tree-structure diagram.

Consider the E-R diagram of figure. Suppose that we add the attribute access_date to the relationship depositor, to denote the most recent date on which a customer accessed the account. This newly derived E-R diagram appears in figure. To transform this diagram into a tree-structure diagram, we must:

- Create a new record type access_date with a single field.

- Create the following two links:

  ○ Customer_date, a many-to-one link from access_date record type to customer record type.

- Date_account, a many-to-one link from account record type to access_date record type.

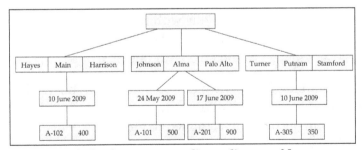

Sample database corresponding to diagram of figure.

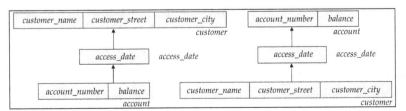

Tree-structure diagram with many-to-many relationships.

The resulting tree-structure diagram is illustrated in figure. An instance corresponding to the described schema appears in figure. It shows that:

- Hayes has account A-102, which was last accessed on 10 June 2009.

- Johnson has two accounts: A-101, which was last accessed on 24 May 2009, and A-201, which was last accessed on 17 June 2009.

- Turner has account A-305, which was last accessed on 10 June 2009.

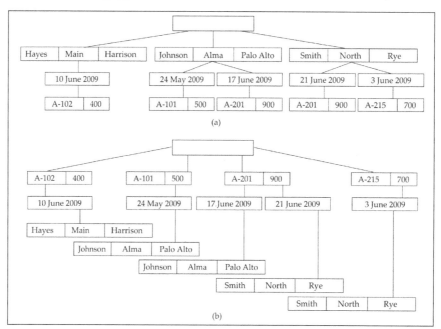

Sample database corresponding to diagram of figure.

Two different accounts can be accessed on the same date, as were accounts A-102 and A-305. These accounts belong to two different customers, so the `access_date` record must be replicated to preserve the hierarchy.

If the relationship `depositors` were one to one with the attribute `date`, then the transformation algorithm would be similar to the one described. The only difference would be that the two links `customer_date` and `date_account` would be one-to-one links.

Assume that the relationship `depositor` is many to many with the attribute `access_date`; here again, we can choose among a number of alternative transformations. We shall use the most general transformation; it is similar to the one applied to the case where the relationship `depositor` has no descriptive attribute.

The record type's `customer, account,` and `access_date` need to be replicated, and two separate tree-structure diagrams must be created, as in figure. A sample database corresponding to this schema is in figure.

Until now, we have considered only binary relationships. We shift our attention here to general relationships. The transformation of E-R diagrams corresponding to general relationships into tree-structure diagrams is complicated.

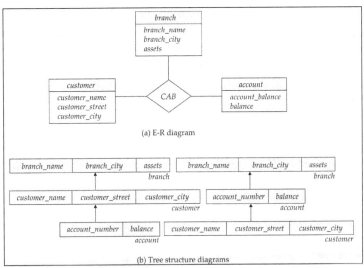

(a) E-R diagram

(b) Tree structure diagrams

E-R diagram and its corresponding tree-structure diagrams.

Rather than present a general transformation algorithm, we present a single example to illustrate the overall strategy that you can apply to deal with such a transformation.

Consider the E-R diagram of figure, which consists of the three entity sets `customer`, `account`, and `branch`, related through the general relationship set CAB with no descriptive attribute.

There are many different ways to transform this E-R diagram into a treestructure diagram. Again, all share the property that the underlying database tree (or trees) will have replicated records. The most straightforward transformation is to create two tree-structure diagrams.

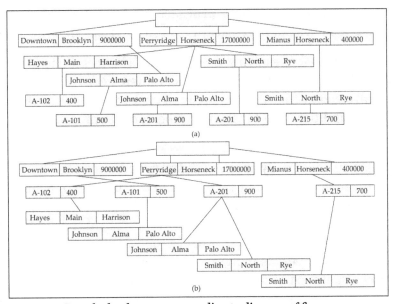

Sample database corresponding to diagram of figure.

An instance of the database corresponding to this schema is illustrated in figure. It shows that Hayes has account A-102 in the Perryridge branch; Johnson has accounts A-101 and A-201 in the Downtown and Perryridge branches, respectively; and Smith has accounts A-201 and A-215 in the Perryridge and Mianus branches, respectively.

We can extend the preceding transformation algorithm in a straightforward manner to deal with relationships that span more than three entity sets. We simply replicate the various record types, and generate as many tree-structure diagrams as necessary. We can extend this approach, in turn, to deal with a general relationship that has descriptive attributes. We need only to create a new record type with one field for each descriptive attribute, and then to insert that record type in the appropriate location in the tree-structure diagram.

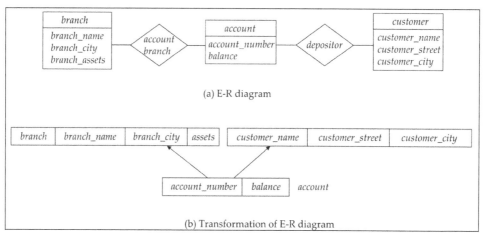

E-R diagram and its transformation.

Several Relationships

The scheme that we have described to transform an E-R diagram to a tree-structure diagram ensures that, for each single relationship, the transformation will result in diagrams that are of the form of rooted trees. Unfortunately, application of such a transformation individually to each relationship in an E-R diagram does not necessarily result in diagrams that are rooted trees.

Next, we shall discuss means for resolving the problem. The technique is to split the diagrams in question into several diagrams, each of which is a rooted tree. We present here two examples to illustrate the overall strategy that you can apply to deal with such transformations. (The large number of different possibilities would make it cumbersome to present a general transformation algorithm).

Consider the E-R diagram of figure. By applying the transformation algorithm separately to the relationships `account-branch` and `depositor`, we obtain the diagram of figure. This diagram is not a rooted tree, since the only possible root can be the record type `account`, but this record type has many-to-one relationships with both its children, and that violates our definition of a rooted tree. To transform this diagram into one that is in the form of a rooted tree, we replicate the `account` record type, and create two separate trees, as in figure. Note that each such tree is indeed a rooted tree. Thus, in general, we can split such a diagram into several diagrams, each of which is a rooted tree.

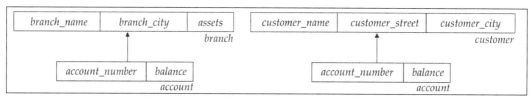

Tree-structure diagram corresponding to figure.

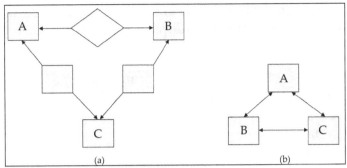

E-R diagram and its transformation.

Now consider the E-R diagram of figure. By applying the transformation algorithm we obtain the diagram in figure. This diagram is not in the form of a rooted tree, since it contains a cycle. To transform the diagram to a tree-structure diagram, we replicate all three record types, and create two separate diagrams, as in figure. Note that each such diagram is indeed a rooted tree. Thus, in general, we can split such a diagram into several diagrams, each of which is a rooted tree.

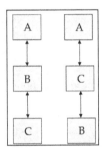

Tree-structure diagram corresponding to figure.

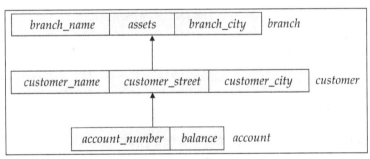

Tree-structure diagram.

Data-Retrieval Facility

Program Work Area

Each application program executing in the system consists of a sequence of statements. Some of these statements are in Pascal; others are data-manipulation language command statements. These statements access and manipulate database items, as well as locally declared variables. For each such application program, the system maintains a `program work area`, which is a buffer storage area that contains the following variables:

- Record templates: A record (in the Pascal sense) for each record type accessed by the application program.

- Currency pointers: A set of pointers, one for each database tree, containing the `address` of the record in that particular tree (regardless of type) most recently accessed by the application program.

- Status flag: A variable set by the system to indicate to the application program the outcome of the most recent database operation; we call this flag `DB-status` and use the same convention as in the DBTG model to denote failure—namely, if `DB-status` = 0, then the most recent operation succeeded.

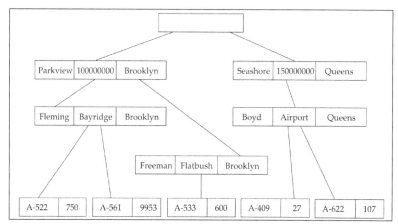

Sample database corresponding to figure.

We reemphasize that a particular program work area is associated with precisely one application program. For our `branch-customer-account` example, a particular program work area contains the following:

- Templates: One record for each of three record types:

  ◦ `Branch` record,

  ◦ `Customer` record,

  ◦ `Account` record.

- Currency pointer: A pointer to the most recently accessed record of branch, `customer`, or `account` type.

- Status: One status variable.

The Get Command

Data are retrieved through the get command. The actions taken in response to a get are as follows:

- Locate a record in the database and set the currency pointer to it.

- Copy that record from the database to the appropriate program area template.

The get command must specify which of the database trees is to be searched. For our example, we assume that the only database tree to be searched is the sample database of figure; thus, we omit this specification in our queries.

As an illustration of the general effect that the get command has on the program work area, consider the sample database of figure. Suppose that a get command is issued to locate the `customer` record belonging to Freeman. Once this command executes successfully, these changes occur in the state of the program work area:

- The currency pointer points now to the record of Freeman.

- The information pertaining to Freeman is copied into the customer record work-area template.

- `DB-status` is set to the value 0.

To scan all records in a consistent manner, we must impose an ordering on the records. The one commonly used is preorder. A preorder search starts at the root, and then searches the subtrees of the root from left to right, recursively. Thus, we start at the root, visit the leftmost child, visit its leftmost child, and so on, until we reach a leaf (childless) node. We then move back to the parent of the leaf and visit the leftmost unvisited child. We proceed in this manner until we have visited the entire tree. For example, the preordered listing of the records in the database tree of figure is:

Parkview, Fleming, A-522, A-561, Freeman, A-533,

Seashore, Boyd, A-409, A-622

Access within a Database

Tree There are two different get commands for locating records in a database tree. The simplest command has the form:

get first `<record type>`

where `<condition>`

The where clause is optional. The attached `<condition>` is a predicate that may involve any record type that is either an ancestor of `<record type>` or the `<record type>` itself.

The get command locates the first record (in preorder) of type `<record type>` in the database that satisfies the `<condition>` of the where clause. If the where clause is omitted, then the command locates the first record of type `<record type>`. Once such a record is found, the currency pointer is set to point to that record, and the content of the record is copied into the appropriate work-area template. If no such record exists in the database tree, then the search fails, and the variable DB-status is set to an appropriate error message.

As an illustration, we construct the database query that prints the address of customer Fleming:

get first `customer`

where `customer.customer_name` = "Fleming";

print (`customer.customer_address`);

As another example, consider the query that prints an account belonging to Fleming that has a balance greater than $10,000 (if one such exists).

> get first `account`
>
> > where `customer.customer_name` = "Fleming" and `account.balance` > 10000;
>
> if `DB-status` = 0 then print (`account.account_number`);

There may be several similar records in the database that we wish to retrieve. The get first command locates one of these. To locate the other database records, we can use the following command:

> > get next `<record type>`
> >
> > > where `<condition>`

This command locates the next record (in preorder) that satisfies `<condition>`. If the where clause is omitted, then the command locates the next record of type `<record type>`. Note that the system uses the currency pointer to determine where to resume the search. As before, the currency pointer, the work-area template of type `<record-type>`, and `DB-status` are affected.

As an illustration, we construct the database e query that prints the account number of all the accounts that have a balance greater than $500:

> get first `account`
>
> > where `account.balance` > 500;
>
> while `DB-status` = 0 do
>
> > begin
> >
> > print (`account.account_number`);
> >
> > get next `account`
> >
> > > where `account.balance` > 500;
>
> end

We have enclosed part of the query in a while loop, since we do not know in advance how many such accounts exist. We exit from the loop when `DB-status` ≠ 0. This value indicates that the last get next operation failed, implying that we have exhausted all account records with `account.balance > 500`.

The two previous get commands locate a database record of type `<record type>` within a particular database tree. There are, however, many circumstances in which we wish to locate such a record within a particular subtree. That is, we want to limit the search to one specific subtree, rather than search the entire database tree. The root of the subtree in question is the most recent record that was located with either a get first or get next command. This record is known as the `current` parent. There is only one current parent record per database tree. The get command to locate a record within the subtree rooted at the current parent has the form:

> get next within parent `<record type>`
>
> > where `<condition>`

It locates the next record (in preorder) of type `<record type>` that satisfies `<condition>` and is in the subtree rooted at the current parent. If the where clause is omitted, then the command locates the next record of type `<record type>` within the designated subtree. The system uses the currency pointer to determine where to resume the search. As before, the currency pointer and the work-area template of type `<record type>` are affected. In this case, however, the DB-status is set to a nonzero value if no such record exists in the designated subtree, rather than if none exists in the entire tree. Note that a get next within parent command will not modify the pointer to the current parent.

To illustrate how this get command executes, we shall construct the query that prints the total balance of all accounts belonging to Boyd:

> `sum := 0;`
>
> get first `customer`
>
> > where `customer.customer_name` = "Boyd";
>
> get next within parent `account;`
>
> while `DB-status` = 0 do
>
> > begin
> >
> > > `sum := sum + account.balance;`
> > >
> > > get next within parent `account;`
> >
> > end
> >
> > print (`sum`);

Note that we exit from the while loop and print out the value of `sum` only when the `DB-status` is set to a value not equal to 0. Such a value exists after the get next within parent operation fails, indicating that we have exhausted all the accounts whose owner is customer Boyd.

Update Facility

The mechanisms available for updating information in the database allow insertion and deletion of records, as well as modification of the content of existing records.

Creation of New Records

To insert a record of type `<record type>` into the database, we must first set the appropriate values in the corresponding `<record type>` work-area template. Once we set them, we add the new record to the database tree by executing:

> insert `<record type>`
>
> where `<condition>`

If the where clause is included, the system searches the database tree (in preorder) for a record that satisfies the `<condition>` in the where clause. Once it finds such a record—say, X—it inserts the newly created record into the tree as the leftmost child of X. If the where clause is omitted, the system inserts the record in the first position (in preorder) in the database tree where a record type `<record type>` can be inserted in accordance with the schema specified by the corresponding tree-structure diagram.

Consider the program for adding a new customer, Jackson, to the Seashore branch:

> `customer.customer_name` := "Jackson";
>
> `customer.customer_street` := "Old Road";
>
> `customer.customer_city` := "Queens";
>
> insert `customer`
>
> where `branch.branch_name` = "Seashore";

The result of executing this program is the database tree of figure.

As another example, consider the program for creating a new account numbered A-655 that belongs to customer "Jackson":

> `account.account_number` := "A-655";
>
> `account.balance` := 100;
>
> insert `account`
>
> where `customer.customer_name` = "Jackson";

The result of executing this program is the database tree of figure.

Modification of an Existing Record

To modify an existing record of type `<record type>`, we must get that record into the work-area template for `<record type>`, and change the desired fields in that template. Then, we reflect the changes in the database by executing:

> `replace`

The replace command does not have `<record type>` as an argument. The record that is affected is the one to which the currency pointer points, which must be the desired record.

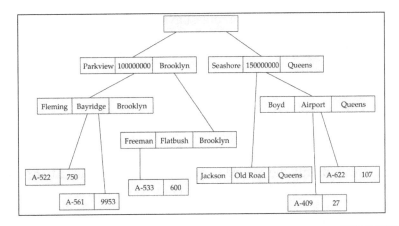

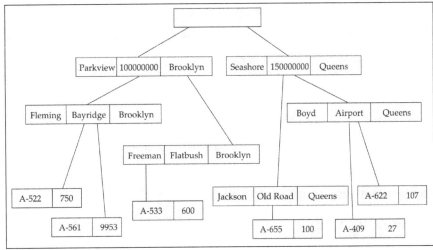

New database tree.

The DL/I language requires that, before a record can be modified, the get command must have the additional clause hold, so that the system is aware that a record is to be modified.

As an example, consider the program to change the street address of Boyd to Northview:

> get hold first `customer`
>
> > where `customer.customer_name` = "Boyd";
>
> `customer.customer_street := `"Northview";
>
> replace;

In our example, we have only one record containing the address of Boyd. If that were not the case, our program would have included a loop to search all Boyd records.

Deletion of a Record

To delete a record of type <record type>, we must set the currency pointer to point to that record. Then, we can delete that record by executing:

```
delete
```

As in record modification, the get command must have the attribute hold attached to it.

As an illustration, consider the program to delete account A-561:

> get hold first `account`
>
> > where `account.account_number` = "A-561";
>
> delete;

A delete operation deletes not only the record in question, but also the entire subtree rooted by that record. Thus, to delete customer Boyd and all his accounts, we write:

> get hold first `customer`
>
> > where `customer.customer_name` = "Boyd";
>
> delete;

Virtual Records

We have seen that, in the case of many-to-many relationships, record replication is necessary to preserve the tree-structure organization of the database. Record replication has two major drawbacks:

- Data inconsistency may result when updating takes place.

- Waste of space is unavoidable.

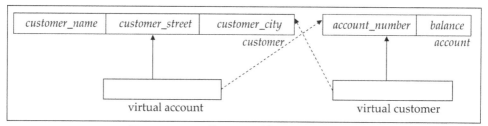

Tree-structure diagram with virtual records.

There are several ways to eliminate these drawbacks.

To eliminate record replication, we need to relax our requirement that the logical organization of data be constrained to a tree structure. We need to do that cautiously, however, since otherwise we will end up with the network model.

The solution is to introduce the concept of a `virtual record`. Such a record contains no data value; it does contain a logical pointer to a particular physical record. Instead of replication, we keep a single copy of the physical record, and everywhere else we keep virtual records containing a pointer to that physical record.

More specifically, we let R be a record type that is replicated in several tree structure diagrams—say, $T_1, T_2, \cdots, T_n$. To eliminate replication, we create a new virtual record type `virtual-R`, and replace R in each of the n−1 trees with a record of type `virtual-R`.

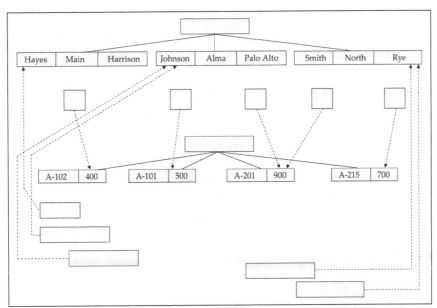

Sample database corresponding to diagram of figure.

As an example, consider the E-R diagram of figure and its corresponding tree-structure diagram, which comprises two separate trees, each consisting of both `customer` and `account` record types.

To eliminate data replication, we create two virtual record types: `virtual_customer` and `virtual_account`. We then replace record type `account` with record type `virtual_account` in the first tree, and replace record type `customer` with record type `virtual_customer` in the second tree. We also add a dashed line from `virtual_customer` record to `customer` record, and a dashed line from `virtual_account` record to `account` record, to specify the association between a virtual record and its corresponding physical record. The resulting tree-structure diagram appears in figure.

A sample database corresponding to the diagram of figure appears in figure. Note that only a single copy of the information for each customer and each account exists. Contrast this database with the same information depicted in figure, where replication is allowed.

The data-manipulation language for this new configuration remains the same as in the case where record replication is allowed. Thus, a user does not need to be aware of these changes. Only the internal implementation is affected.

Mapping of Hierarchies to Files

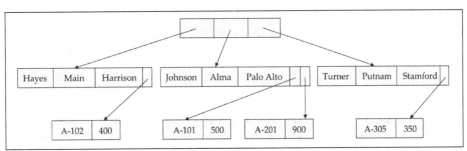

Implementation with parent-child pointers.

A straightforward technique for implementing the instance of a tree-structure diagram is to associate one pointer with a record for each child that the record has. Consider the database tree of figure. Figure shows an implementation of this database using parent-to-child pointers. Parent–child pointers, however, are not an ideal structure for the implementation of hierarchical databases, since a parent record may have an arbitrary number of children. Thus, fixed-length records become variable-length records once the parent–child pointers are added.

Instead of parent–child pointers, we can use `leftmost-child` and `next-sibling` pointers. Figure shows this structure for the database tree of figure. Under this structure, every record has exactly two pointer fields. Thus, fixed length records retain their fixed length when we add the necessary pointers. Note that the leftmost-child pointers for the account record are null, since account is a leaf of the tree.

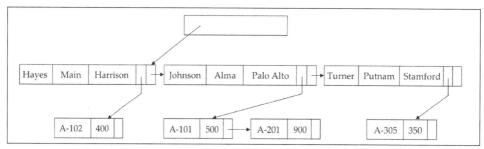

Implementation with leftmost-child and next-sibling pointers.

Observe that several pointer fields are unused in figure. In general, the final child of a parent has no next sibling; thus, its next-sibling field is set to null. Rather than place nulls in such fields, we can place pointers there to facilitate the preorder traversal required to process queries on hierarchical databases. Thus, for each record that is a rightmost sibling, we place a pointer in the next-sibling field to the next record in preorder after traversing its subtree. Figure shows this modification to the structure of figure. These pointers allow us to process a tree instance in preorder simply by following pointers. For this reason, the pointers are sometimes referred to as `preorder threads`.

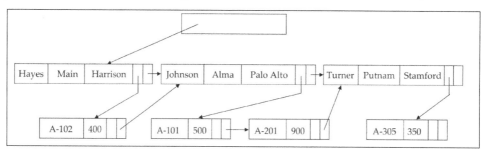

Implementation using preorder threads.

A parent pointer is often added to records in an implementation of a hierarchical database. This pointer facilitates the processing of queries that give a value for a child record and request a value from the corresponding parent record. If we include parent pointers, a total of exactly three pointer fields is added to each record.

To see how best to locate records of a hierarchical database physically on disk, we draw an analogy between the parent–child relationship within a hierarchy and the owner–member relationship within a DBTG set. In both cases, a one-to-many relationship is being represented. We want to store together the members and the owners of a set occurrence. Similarly, we want to store physically close on disk the child records and their parent. This form of storage allows a sequence of get first, get next, and get next within parent statements to be executed with a minimal number of block accesses.

The IMS Database System

The hierarchical model is significant primarily because of the importance of IBM's IMS database system.

The IBM Information Management System (IMS) is one of the oldest and most widely used database systems. Since IMS databases have historically been among the largest, the IMS developers were among the first to deal with such issues as concurrency, recovery, integrity, and efficient query processing. Through several releases, IMS acquired a large number of features and options. As a result, IMS is a highly complex system. We shall consider only a few features of IMS here.

Queries on IMS databases are issued through embedded calls in a host language. The embedded calls are part of the IMS database language DL/I. (The language used in this appendix is a simplified form of DL/I.)

Since performance is critically important in large databases, IMS allows the database designer a broad number of options in the data-definition language. The database designer defines a physical hierarchy as the database schema. She can define several subschemas (or views) by constructing a logical hierarchy from the record types constituting the schema. The various options available in the data-definition language (block sizes, special pointer fields, and so on) allow the database administrator to tune the system for improved performance.

Several record access schemes are available in IMS:

- The hierarchical sequential-access method (HSAM) is used for physically sequential files (such as tape files). Records are stored physically in preorder.

- The hierarchical indexed-sequential-access method (HISAM) is an index- sequential organization at the root level of the hierarchy. Records are stored physically in preorder.

- The hierarchical indexed-direct-access method (HIDAM) is an ordered index organization at the root level with pointers to child records.

- The hierarchical direct-access method (HDAM) is similar to HIDAM, but with hashed access at the root level.

The original version of IMS predated the development of concurrency-control theory. Early versions of IMS had a simple form of concurrency control. Only one update application program could run at a time. However, any number of read-only applications could run concurrently with an update application. This feature permitted applications to read uncommitted updates and allowed nonserializable executions. Exclusive access to the database was the only option available to applications that demanded a greater degree of isolation from the anomalies of concurrent processing.

Later versions of IMS included a more sophisticated `program-isolation` feature that allowed for both improved concurrency control and more sophisticated transaction-recovery techniques (such as logging). These features increased in importance as more IMS users began to use online transactions, as opposed to the batch transactions that were originally the norm.

The need for high-performance transaction processing led to the introduction of `IMS Fast Path`. Fast Path uses an alternative physical data organization designed to allow the most active parts of the database to reside in main memory. Instead of forcing updates to disk at the end of a transaction (as standard IMS does), Fast Path defers update until a checkpoint or synchronization point. In the event of a crash, the recovery subsystem must redo all committed transactions whose updates were not forced to disk. These tricks and others allow for extremely high rates of transaction throughput. IMS Fast Path is a forerunner of much of the work on developing main-memory database systems that has emerged as main memory has become larger and less expensive.

Object Model

Increasingly complex real-world problems demonstrated a need for a data model that more closely represented the real world.

In the object oriented data model (OODM), both data and their relationships are contained in a single structure known as an object.

In turn, the OODM is the basis for the object-oriented database management system (OODBMS).

The Components of the Object Oriented Data Model

- An object is an abstraction of a real-world entity. In general terms, an object may be considered equivalent to an ER model's entity. More precisely, an object represents only one occurrence of an entity. (The object's semantic content is defined through several of the items in this list).

- Attributes describe the properties of an object. For example, a PERSON object includes the attributes Name, Social Security Number, and Date of Birth.

- Objects that share similar characteristics are grouped in classes. A class is a collection of similar objects with shared structure (attributes) and behavior (methods). In a general sense, a class resembles the ER model's entity set. However, a class is different from an entity set in that it contains a set of procedures known as methods. A class's method represents a real-world action such as finding a selected PERSON's name, changing a PERSON's name, or printing a PERSON's address. In other words, methods are the equivalent of procedures in traditional programming languages. In OO terms, methods define an object's behavior.

- Classes are organized in a class hierarchy. The class hierarchy resembles an upside-down tree in which each class has only one parent. For example, the CUSTOMER class and the EMPLOYEE class share a parent PERSON class. (Note the similarity to the hierarchical data model in this respect).

- Inheritance is the ability of an object within the class hierarchy to inherit the attributes and methods of the classes above it. For example, two classes, CUSTOMER and EMPLOYEE, can be created as subclasses from the class PERSON. In this case, CUSTOMER and EM- PLOYEE will inherit all attributes and methods from PERSON.

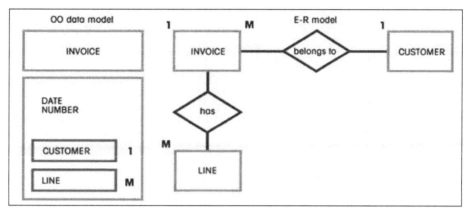

A comparison of OO data model and ER model.

Advantages of Object Oriented Data Model

- Add semantic content.
- Visual presentation includes semantic content.
- Database integrity.
- Both structural and data independence.

Disadvantages of Object Oriented Data Model

- Lack of OODM standards.
- Complex navigational data access.
- Steep learning curve.
- High system overhead slows transactions.

Document Model

A document store database (also known as a document-oriented database, aggregate database, or simply document store or document database) is a database that uses a document-oriented model to store data.

Document store databases store each record and its associated data within a single document. Each document contains semi-structured data that can be queried against using various query and analytics tools of the DBMS.

Document Examples

Here are two examples of documents that could be stored in a document database. Both examples use the same data – they are just written in different languages.

Here's the first example, written in XML.

```xml
<artist>

    <artistname>Iron Maiden</<artistname>

    <albums>

      <album>

        <albumname>The Book of Souls</albumname>

        <datereleased>2015</datereleased>

        <genre>Hard Rock</genre>

      </album>

      <album>

        <albumname>Killers</albumname>

        <datereleased>1981</datereleased>

        <genre>Hard Rock</genre>

      </album>

      <album>

        <albumname>Powerslave</albumname>

        <datereleased>1984</datereleased>

        <genre>Hard Rock</genre>

      </album>

      <album>

        <albumname>Somewhere in Time</albumname>

        <datereleased>1986</datereleased>

        <genre>Hard Rock</genre>

      </album>

    </albums>

  </artist>
```

And here's the same example, but this time written in JSON:

```
{
    '_id' : 1,
    'artistName' : { 'Iron Maiden' },
    'albums' : [
        {
            'albumname' : 'The Book of Souls',
            'datereleased' : 2015,
            'genre' : 'Hard Rock'
        }, {
            'albumname' : 'Killers',
            'datereleased' : 1981,
            'genre' : 'Hard Rock'
        }, {
            'albumname' : 'Powerslave',
            'datereleased' : 1984,
            'genre' : 'Hard Rock'
        }, {
            'albumname' : 'Somewhere in Time',
            'datereleased' : 1986,
            'genre' : 'Hard Rock'
        }
    ]
}
```

Notice that we decided to add an _id field in the second example. This may or may not be required by the DBMS, however, some DBMSs will automatically insert a unique ID field if one isn't supplied.

Document Store vs. Relational Databases

If we were to enter the above data into a relational database, the info would typically be stored across three different tables — with a relationship linking them together via their primary key and foreign key fields.

Here's how a relational database might store the above data.

Artists

Artist Id	ArtistName
1	Iron Maiden
2	Devin Townsend
3	The Wiggles
4	...

Albums

AlbumId	AlbumName	DateReleased	ArtistId	GenreId
1	The Book of Souls	2015	1	3
2	Killers	1981	1	3
3	Powerslave	1984	1	3
4	Somewhere in Time	1986	1	3
5	Ziltoid the Omniscient	2007	2	3
6	...	...	...	...

Genre

GenreId	Genre
1	Country
2	Blues
3	Hard Rock
4	...

And here's the relationship between those tables (done in MySQL):

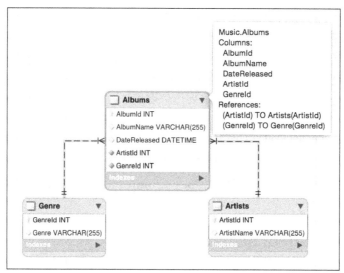

Diagram of a relationship between three tables. The primary
key and foreign key fields have been highlighted.

So this indicates that there are some significant differences between document store databases and relational databases.

Here are some of the main ones:

Tables

Relational databases store data within multiple tables, each table containing columns, and each row represents each record. Information about any given entity could be spread out among many tables. Data from different tables can only be associated by establishing a relationship between the tables.

Document databases on the other hand, don't use tables as such. They store all data on a given entity within a single document. Any associated data is stored inside that one document.

Schemas

With relational databases, you must create a schema before you load any data. With document store databases (and most other NoSQL databases), you have no such requirement. You can just go ahead and load the data without any predefined schema.

So with a document store, any two documents can contain a different structure and data type. For example, if one user chooses not to supply his date of birth, that wouldn't even be a field within the document. If another user does supply her date of birth, that would be a field in that document. If this was a relational database, date of birth would still be a field for both users – it just wouldn't contain a value.

Scalability

Document databases can scale horizontally very well. Data can be stored over many thousands of computers and the system will perform well. This is often referred to as sharding.

Relational databases are not well suited to scaling in this fashion. Relational DBs are more suited towards scaling vertically (i.e. adding more memory, storage, etc). Seeing as there's a limit to how many resources you can fit inside one machine, there could come a point where horizontal scaling becomes the only option.

Relationships

Document stores don't have foreign keys, like relational databases have. Foreign keys are used by relational databases to enforce relationships between tables. If a relationship needs to be established with a document database, it would need to be done at the application level.

However, the whole idea behind the document model is that any data associated with a record is stored within the same document. So the need to establish a relationship when using the document model should not be as prevalent as in a relational database.

NoSQL

Most relational databases use SQL as the standard query language. Document store databases tend to use other query languages (although some are built to support SQL). Many document databases can be queried using languages such as XQuery, XSLT, SPARQL, Java, JavaScript, Python, etc.

Document Store vs. Key-Value Databases

Document databases are similar to key-value databases in that, there's a key and a value. Data is stored as a value. Its associated key is the unique identifier for that value.

The difference is that, in a document database, the value contains structured or semi-structured data. This structured/semi-structured value is referred to as a document.

The structured/semi-structured data that makes up the document can be encoded using one of any number of methods, including XML, JSON, YAML, BSON, etc. It could also be encoded using binary, such as PDFs, MS Office documents, etc.

A Benefit of the Document Model over Key-Value Stores

One benefit that document store databases have over key-value databases, is that you can query the data itself. You can query against the structure of the document, as well as the elements within that structure. Therefore, you can return only those parts of the document that you require.

With a key-value database, you get the whole value – no matter how big (and seemingly structured) it might be. You can't query within the value.

Associative Model

The Associative data model is a model for databases unlike any of those we spoke of in prior topcs. Unlike the relational model, which is record based and deals with entities and attributes, this model works with entities that have a discreet independent existence, and their relationships are modeled as associations.

The Associative model was bases on a subject-verb-object syntax with bold parallels in sentences built from English and other languages. Some examples of phrases that are suitable for the Associative model could include:

- Cyan **is a** Color,

- Marc **is a** Musician,

- Musicians **play** instruments,

- Swings **are in** a park,

- A Park **is in** a City (the bold text indicates the verbs).

By studying the example above it is easy to see that the verb is actually a way of association. The association's sole purpose is to identify the relationship between the subject and the object.

The Associative database had two structures, there are a set of items and a set of links that are used to connected them together. With the item structure the entries must contain a unique indication, a type, and a name. Entries in the links structure must also have a unique indicator along with indicators for the related source, subject, object, and verb.

The Associative model structure is efficient with the storage room fore there is no need to put aside existing space for the data that is not yet available. This differs from the relational model structure. With the relational model the minimum of a single null byte is stored for missing data in any given row. Also some relational databases set aside the maximum room for a specified column in each row.

The Associative database creates storage of custom data for each user, or other needs clear cut and economical when considering maintenance or network resources. When different data needs to be stored the Associative model is able to manage the task more effectively then the relational model.

With the Associative model there are entities and associations. The entity is identified as discrete and has an independent existence, whereas the association depends on other things. Let's try to simplify this a little before moving on.

Let's say the entity is an organization, the associations would be the customer and the employees. It is possible for the entity to have many business roles at the same time, each role would be recorded as an association. When the circumstances change, one or more of the associations may no longer apply, but the entity will continue to endure.

The Associative model is designed to store metadata in the same structures where the data itself is stored. This metadata describes the structure of the database and the how different kinds of data can interconnect. Simple data structures need more to transport a database competent of storing the varying of data that a modernized business requires along with the protection and managements that is important for internet implementation.

The Associative model is built from chapters and the user's view the content of the database is controlled by their profile. The profile is a list of chapters. When some links between items in the chapters inside as well as outside of a specific profile exist, those links will not be visible to the user.

There is a combination of chapters and profiled that can simplify the making of the database to specific users or ever subject groups. The data that is related to one of the user groups would remain unseen to another, and would be replaced by a different data set.

Potential Disadvantages to the Associative Data Model

With the Associative model there is not record. When assembling all of the current information on a complex order the data storage needs to be re-visited multiple times. This could pose as a disadvantage. Some calculations seem to suggest that Associative database would need as many as four times the data reads as the relational database.

All of the changes and deletions to the Associative model are directly affected by adding links to the database. However we must not that a deleted association is not actually deleted itself. Rather it is linked to an assertion that has been deleted. Also when an entity is re-named it is not actually re-named but rather linked to its new name.

In order to reduce the complexity that is a direct result from the parameterization required by heftier software packages we can rely on the chapters, profiles and the continuation of database engines that expect data stored to be different between the individual entities or associations. To set of or hold back program functions in a database the use of "Flags" has begun to be practiced.

The packages that are based on an Associative model would use the structure of the database along with the metadata to control this process. This can ultimately lead to the generalization of what are often lengthy and costly implementation processes.

A generalization such as this would produce considerable cost reductions for users purchasing or implementing bigger software packages, this could reduce risks related with the changes of post implementation as well.

Suitability of the Associative Model

Some ask if there is still an ongoing demand for a better database. Honestly, there will always be that demand. The weaker points of the current relational model are now apparent, due to the character of the data we still need to store changing. Binary structures that are supportive to multimedia have posed real challenged for relational databases in the same way that the object-oriented programming methods did.

When we look back on the Object databases we can see that they have no conquered the market, and have their cousins the hybrid relational products with their object extensions. So will the Associative model solve some of the issues surrounding the relational model? The answer is not entirely clear, though it may resolve some issues it is not completely clear how efficiently the model will manage when set against the bigger binary blocks of data.

The security of data is crucial, as is the speed of transaction. User interfaces and database management facilities should but up to pace. When a database is designed to aid in the use of internet applications it should allow backups without needing to take the data off-line as well.

Programming interfaces need to be hearty and readily available to a range of development languages, the Associative database will need to show that it is good practice to store data using the subject-verb-object method in every case as well.

Multidimensional Model

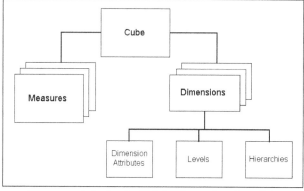

Diagram of the Logical Multidimensional Model.

The multidimensional data model is an integral part of On-Line Analytical Processing, or OLAP. Because OLAP is on-line, it must provide answers quickly; analysts pose iterative queries during interactive sessions, not in batch jobs that run overnight. And because OLAP is also analytic, the queries are complex. The multidimensional data model is designed to solve complex queries in real time.

The multidimensional data model is important because it enforces simplicity.

"The central attraction of the dimensional model of a business is its simplicity that simplicity is the fundamental key that allows users to understand databases, and allows software to navigate databases efficiently."

The multidimensional data model is composed of logical cubes, measures, dimensions, hierarchies, levels, and attributes. The simplicity of the model is inherent because it defines objects that represent real-world business entities. Analysts know which business measures they are interested in examining, which dimensions and attributes make the data meaningful, and how the dimensions of their business are organized into levels and hierarchies.

Logical Cubes

Logical cubes provide a means of organizing measures that have the same shape, that is, they have the exact same dimensions. Measures in the same cube have the same relationships to other logical objects and can easily be analyzed and displayed together.

Logical Measures

Measures populate the cells of a logical cube with the facts collected about business operations. Measures are organized by dimensions, which typically include a Time dimension.

An analytic database contains snapshots of historical data, derived from data in a legacy system, transactional database, syndicated sources, or other data sources. Three years of historical data is generally considered to be appropriate for analytic applications.

Measures are static and consistent while analysts are using them to inform their decisions. They are updated in a batch window at regular intervals: weekly, daily, or periodically throughout the day. Many applications refresh their data by adding periods to the time dimension of a measure, and may also roll off an equal number of the oldest time periods. Each update provides a fixed historical record of a particular business activity for that interval. Other applications do a full rebuild of their data rather than performing incremental updates.

A critical decision in defining a measure is the lowest level of detail (sometimes called the grain). Users may never view this base level data, but it determines the types of analysis that can be performed. For example, market analysts (unlike order entry personnel) do not need to know that Beth Miller in Ann Arbor, Michigan, placed an order for a size 10 blue polka-dot dress on July 6, 2002, at 2:34 p.m. But they might want to find out which color of dress was most popular in the summer of 2002 in the Midwestern United States.

The base level determines whether analysts can get an answer to this question. For this particular question, Time could be rolled up into months, Customer could be rolled up into regions, and

Product could be rolled up into items (such as dresses) with an attribute of color. However, this level of aggregate data could not answer the question: At what time of day are women most likely to place an order? An important decision is the extent to which the data has been pre-aggregated before being loaded into a data warehouse.

Logical Dimensions

Dimensions contain a set of unique values that identify and categorize data. They form the edges of a logical cube, and thus of the measures within the cube. Because measures are typically multi-dimensional, a single value in a measure must be qualified by a member of each dimension to be meaningful. For example, the Sales measure has four dimensions: Time, Customer, Product, and Channel. A particular Sales value (43,613.50) only has meaning when it is qualified by a specific time period (Feb-01), a customer (Warren Systems), a product (Portable PCs), and a channel (Catalog).

Logical Hierarchies and Levels

A hierarchy is a way to organize data at different levels of aggregation. In viewing data, analysts use dimension hierarchies to recognize trends at one level, drill down to lower levels to identify reasons for these trends, and roll up to higher levels to see what affect these trends have on a larger sector of the business.

Each level represents a position in the hierarchy. Each level above the base (or most detailed) level contains aggregate values for the levels below it. The members at different levels have a one-to-many parent-child relation.

Suppose a data warehouse contains snapshots of data taken three times a day, that is, every 8 hours. Analysts might normally prefer to view the data that has been aggregated into days, weeks, quarters, or years. Thus, the Time dimension needs a hierarchy with at least five levels.

Similarly, a sales manager with a particular target for the upcoming year might want to allocate that target amount among the sales representatives in his territory; the allocation requires a dimension hierarchy in which individual sales representatives are the child values of a particular territory.

Hierarchies and levels have a many-to-many relationship. A hierarchy typically contains several levels, and a single level can be included in more than one hierarchy.

Logical Attributes

An attribute provides additional information about the data. Some attributes are used for display. For example, you might have a product dimension that uses Stock Keeping Units (SKUs) for dimension members. The SKUs are an excellent way of uniquely identifying thousands of products, but are meaningless to most people if they are used to label the data in a report or graph. You would define attributes for the descriptive labels.

You might also have attributes like colors, flavors, or sizes. This type of attribute can be used for data selection and answering questions such as: Which colors were the most popular in women's dresses in the summer of 2002? How does this compare with the previous summer?

Time attributes can provide information about the Time dimension that may be useful in some types of analysis, such as identifying the last day or the number of days in each time period.

The Relational Implementation of the Model

The relational implementation of the multidimensional data model is typically a star schema or a snowflake schema. A star schema is a convention for organizing the data into dimension tables, fact tables, and materialized views. Ultimately, all of the data is stored in columns, and metadata is required to identify the columns that function as multidimensional objects.

In Oracle Database, you can define a logical multidimensional model for relational tables using the OLAP Catalog or AWXML. The metadata distinguishes level columns from attribute columns in the dimension tables and specifies the hierarchical relationships among the levels. It identifies the various measures that are stored in columns of the fact tables and aggregation methods for the measures. And it provides display names for all of these logical objects.

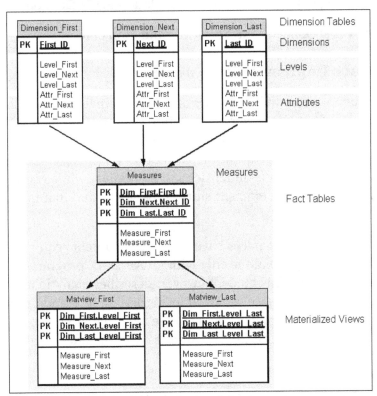

Diagram of a Star Schema.

Dimension Tables

A star schema stores all of the information about a dimension in a single table. Each level of a hierarchy is represented by a column or column set in the dimension table. A dimension object can be used to define the hierarchical relationship between two columns (or column sets) that represent two levels of a hierarchy; without a dimension object, the hierarchical relationships are defined only in metadata. Attributes are stored in columns of the dimension tables.

A snowflake schema normalizes the dimension members by storing each level in a separate table.

Fact Tables

Measures are stored in fact tables. Fact tables contain a composite primary key, which is composed of several foreign keys (one for each dimension table) and a column for each measure that uses these dimensions.

Materialized Views

Aggregate data is calculated on the basis of the hierarchical relationships defined in the dimension tables. These aggregates are stored in separate tables, called summary tables or materialized views. Oracle provides extensive support for materialized views, including automatic refresh and query rewrite.

Queries can be written either against a fact table or against a materialized view. If a query is written against the fact table that requires aggregate data for its result set, the query is either redirected by query rewrite to an existing materialized view, or the data is aggregated on the fly.

Each materialized view is specific to a particular combination of levels.

Analytic Workspace Implementation of the Model

Analytic workspaces have several different types of data containers, such as dimensions, variables, and relations. Each type of container can be used in a variety of ways to store different types of information. For example, a dimension can define an edge of a measure, or store the names of all the languages supported by the analytic workspace, or all of the acceptable values of a relation. Dimension objects are themselves one dimensional list of values, while variables and relations are designed specifically to support the efficient storage, retrieval, and manipulation of multidimensional data.

Like relational tables, analytic workspaces have no specific content requirements. You can create an empty analytic workspace, populate it only with OLAP DML programs, or define a single dimension to hold a list of values. This guide, however, describes analytic workspaces that comply with database standard form. Database standard form (or simply, standard form) is a convention for instantiating the logical multidimensional model in a particular way so that it can be managed by the current set of Oracle OLAP utilities. It defines a set of metadata that can be queried by any application.

Multidimensional Data Storage in Analytic Workspaces

In the logical multidimensional model, a cube represents all measures with the same shape, that is, the exact same dimensions. In a cube shape, each edge represents a dimension. The dimension members are aligned on the edges and divide the cube shape into cells in which data values are stored.

In an analytic workspace, the cube shape also represents the physical storage of multidimensional measures, in contrast with two-dimensional relational tables. An advantage of the cube shape is that it can be rotated: there is no one right way to manipulate or view the data. This is an important part of multidimensional data storage, calculation, and display, because different analysts need to view the data in different ways. For example, if you are the Sales Manager for the Pacific Rim, then you need to look at the data differently from a product manager or a financial analyst.

Assume that a company collects data on sales. The company maintains records that quantify how many of each product was sold in a particular sales region during a specific time period.

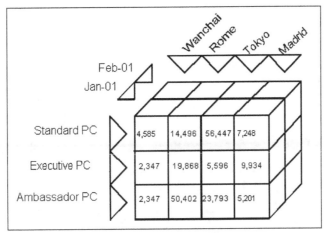

Comparison of Product Sales by City.

In figures compare the sales of various products in different cities for January 2001 (shown) and February 2001 (not shown). This view of the data might be used to identify products that are performing poorly in certain markets. Figures show sales of various products during a four-month period in Rome (shown) and Tokyo (not shown). This view of the data is the basis for trend analysis.

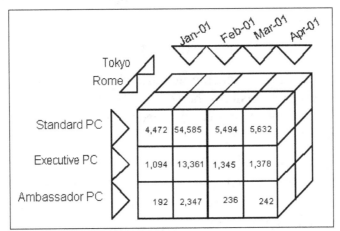

Comparison of Product Sales by Month.

A cube shape is three dimensional. Of course, measures can have many more than three dimensions, but three dimensions are the maximum number that can be represented pictorially. Additional dimensions are pictured with additional cube shapes.

Database Standard Form Analytic Workspaces

In figures shows how dimension, variable, formula, and relation objects in a standard form analytic workspace are used to implement the multidimensional model. Measures with identical dimensions compose a logical cube. All dimensions have attributes, and all hierarchical dimensions have level relations and self-relations; for clarity, these objects are shown only once in the diagram. Variables and formulas can have any number of dimensions.

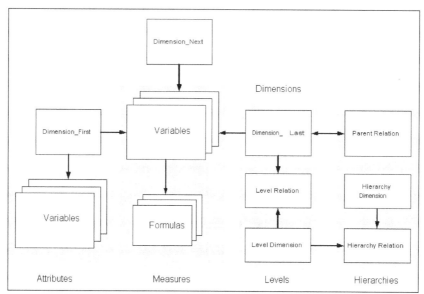

Diagram of a Standard Form Analytic Workspace.

Analytic Workspace Dimensions

A dimension in an analytic workspace is a highly optimized, one-dimensional index of values that serves as a key table. Variables, relations, formulas (which are stored equations) are among the objects that can have dimensions.

Dimensions have several intrinsic characteristics that are important for data analysis:

- Referential integrity: Each dimension member is unique and cannot be NA (that is, null). If a measure has three dimensions, then each data value of that measure must be qualified by a member of each dimension. Likewise, each combination of dimension members has a value, even if it is NA.

- Consistency: Dimensions are maintained as separate containers and are shared by measures. Measures with the same dimensionality can be manipulated together easily. For example, if the sales and expense measures are dimensioned by time and line, then you can create equations such as profit = sales - expense.

- Preserved order of members: Each dimension has a default status, which is a list of all of its members in the order they are stored. The default status list is always the same unless it is purposefully altered by adding, deleting, or moving members. Within a session, a user can change the selection and order of the status list; this is called the current status list. The current status list remains the same until the user purposefully alters it by adding, removing, or changing the order of its members.

Because the order of dimension members is consistent and known, the selection of members can be relative. For example, this function call compares the sales values of all currently selected time periods in the current status list against sales from the prior period.

```
lagdif(sales, 1, time)
```

- Highly denormalized: A dimension typically contains members at all levels of all hierarchies. This type of dimension is sometimes called an embedded total dimension.

In addition to simple dimensions, there are several special types of dimensions used in a standard form analytic workspace, such as composites and concat dimensions.

Use of Dimensions in Standard Form Analytic Workspaces

In an analytic workspace, data dimensions are structured hierarchically so that data at different levels can be manipulated for aggregation, allocation, and navigation. However, all dimension members at all levels for all hierarchies are stored in a single data dimension container. For example, months, quarters, and years are all stored in a single dimension for Time. The hierarchical relationships among dimension members are defined by a parent relation.

Not all data is hierarchical in nature, however, and you can create data dimensions that do not have levels. A line item dimension is one such dimension, and the relationships among its members require a model rather than a multilevel hierarchy. The extensive data modeling subsystem available in analytic workspaces enables you to create both simple and complex models, which can be solved alone or in conjunction with aggregation methods.

As a one-dimensional index, a dimension container has many uses in an analytic workspace in addition to dimensioning measures. A standard form analytic workspace uses dimensions to store various types of metadata, such as lists of hierarchies, levels, and the dimensions composing a logical cube.

Analytic Workspace Variables

A variable is a data value table, that is, an array with a particular data type and indexed by a specific list of dimensions. The dimensions themselves are not stored with the variable.

Each combination of dimension members defines a data cell, regardless of whether a value exists for that cell or not. Thus, the absence of data can be purposefully included or excluded from the analysis. For example, if a particular product was not available before a certain date, then the analysis may exclude null values (called NAs) in the prior periods. However, if the product was available but did not sell in some markets, then the analysis may include the NAs.

No special physical relationship exists among variables that share the same dimensions. However, a logical relationship exists because, even though they store different data that may be a different data type, they are identical containers. Variables that have identical dimensions compose a logical cube.

If you change a dimension, such as adding new time periods to the Time dimension, then all variables dimensioned by Time are automatically changed to include these new time periods, even if the other variables have no data for them. Variables that share dimensions (and thus are contained by the same logical cube) can also be manipulated together in a variety of ways, such as aggregation, allocation, modeling, and numeric calculations. This type of calculation is easy and fast in an analytic workspace, while the equivalent single-row calculation in a relational schema can be quite difficult.

Use of Variables to Store Measures

In an analytic workspace, facts are stored in variables, typically with a numeric data type. Each type of data is stored in its own variable, so that while sales data and expenses data might have the same dimensions and the same data type, they are stored in two distinct variables. The containers are identical, but the contents are unique.

An analytic workspace provides a valuable alternative to materialized views for creating, storing, and maintaining summary data. A very sophisticated aggregation system supports modeling in addition to an extensive number of aggregation methods. Moreover, finely grained aggregation rules enable you to decide precisely which data within a single measure is pre-aggregated, and which data within the same measure will be calculated at run-time.

Pre-aggregated data is stored in a compact format in the same container as the base-level data, and the performance impact of aggregating data on the fly is negligible when the aggregation rules have been defined according to known good methods. If aggregate data needed for the result set is stored in the variable, then it is simply retrieved. If the aggregate data does not exist, then it is calculated on the fly.

Use of Variables to Store Attributes

Like measures, attributes are stored in variables. However, there are significant differences between attributes and measures. While attributes are often multidimensional, only one dimension is a data dimension. A hierarchy dimension, which lists the data dimension hierarchies, and a language dimension, which provides support for multiple languages, are typical of the other dimensions.

Attributes provide supplementary information about each dimension member, regardless of its level in a dimension hierarchy. For example, a Time dimension might have three attribute variables, one for descriptive names, and another for the period end dates, and a third for period time spans. These attributes provide Time member OCT-02 with a descriptive name of October 2002, an end date of 31-OCT-02, and a time span of 31. All of the other days, months, quarters, and years in the Time dimension have similar information stored in these three attribute variables.

Analytic Workspace Formulas

A formula is a stored equation. A call to any function in the OLAP DML or to any custom program can be stored in a formula. In this way, a formula in an analytic workspace is like a relational view.

In a standard form analytic workspace, one of the uses of a formula object is to provide the interface between aggregation rules and a variable that holds the data. The name of a measure is always the name of a formula, not the underlying variable. While the variable only contains stored data (the base-level data and recalculated aggregates), the formula returns a fully solved measure containing data that is both stored and calculated on the fly. This method enables all queries against a particular measure to be written against the same column of the same relational view for the analytic workspace, regardless of whether the data is calculated or simply retrieved. That column presents data acquired from the formula.

Formulas can also be used to calculate other results like ratios, differences, moving totals, and averages on the fly.

Analytic Workspace Relations

Relations are identical to variables except in their data type. A variable has a general data type, such as DECIMAL or TEXT, while a relation has a dimension as its data type. For example, a relation with a data type of PRODUCT only accepts values that are members of the PRODUCT dimension; an attempt to store any other value causes an error. The dimension members provide a finite list of acceptable values for a relation. A relation container is like a foreign key column, except that it can be multidimensional.

In a standard form analytic workspace, two relations support the hierarchical content of the data dimensions: a parent relation and a level relation.

A parent relation is a self-relation that identifies the parent of each member of a dimension hierarchy. This relation defines the hierarchical structure of the dimension.

A level relation identifies the level of each member of a dimension hierarchy. It is used to select and sort dimension members based on level.

Flat-file Database

A flat file database is basically a giant collection of data in which the tables and records have no relation between any other tables. In fact, one could have a single table (e.g., My Small Business Data) with everything stored in it, from customers to sales to orders to invoices.

Sound too messy? Often it is. But there are uses. One doesn't necessarily have to normalize a database. By normalize, we mean break out all the repeating values in tables and save them into other, related tables. Sometimes simple is best.

In fact, if the data set is fairly simple, the flat file option makes more sense. A CD collection, a list of cell phone numbers, or results from a 10k could be stored in a flat file database. Even a web page or computer program could be written to interact with these types of databases; in fact, from a developer's perspective, it would be easy to maintain.

Flat File Database Examples

If you have ever created an Excel spreadsheet, you have created a basic flat file! A workbook with multiple tabs makes up the database of the flat-file database; there could be many values that are the same in both worksheets, but they are not linked together.

The database table shown in the table below could be used in a small web application for a running a club:

Table: Flat File Example.

Runner	Race	Age	Time
Wendy	10K	29	0:42:19
Dave	10K	31	1:01:20
Paul	5K	22	0:16:05
Jonas	10K	53	0:53:17
Tim	5K	40	0:21:15
Lacey	5K	21	0:33:18
Sandra	5K	68	0:19:22
Dave	5K	31	0:32:00
Wendy	5K	37	0:20:05
Marcus	5K	24	0:24:17
Brian	5K	38	0:32:19
Anita	5K	39	0:30:03

You will notice that some names repeat; for a small table this is not that big of a deal. However, if you wanted to change the record for Dave and add a last name, you have to find all records for him and update each one.

When starting a career in information technology, was given the task of creating a database to track all printers for a given department. He generated an overly complex relational database with over 25 tables. When presented to a colleague, the colleague replied: 'Why not just make a flat file?' This turned out to be the simplest solution; although it was a large file, it wasn't unwieldy and was user-friendly. Using Microsoft Access, a simple user form was created, and no special coding or updates to related tables were needed.

Relational databases use primary and foreign keys to index the data. A flat file database table can still use an index; however, it's specific only to that table. An index is usually an auto-generated number that identifies the record number in the table at 1.

System Design

The system based on File Input Output processing and Streams. This system also same as flatfile database the difference is we can use multiple tables. The similarity is the multiple tables querying such as Join queries are not processed currently.

Database:

The database is nothing but, It creates the folder for a database Name in application startup folder.

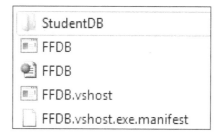

Tables:

In this system the tables are holding all the data. In this System the table structure has two parts:

    1. Header Row,

    2. Data Rows.

Header Row consists the column names. Data Rows consists the rcords related to the columns. Here some special symbols are used as delimiters.

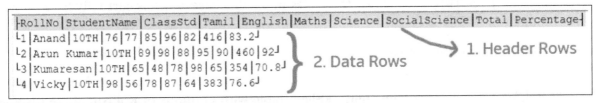

Symbols:

    ⊢ - Header Row Begining

    ⊣ - Header Row End

    L - Data Row Begining

    ⌐ - Data Row End

    | - Column Separator

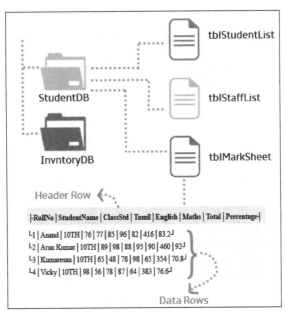

Overview of System.

Querying:

The system support 15 and more SQL Type Queries to querying the Database. The following queries are used in this system.

- CREATE DATABASE StudentDB: This is the query for creating the database named "StudendDB".

- LIST DATABASES: This query shows list of database in the system.

- DROP DATABASE StudentDB: This query deletes the Database StudentDB.

- USE StudentDB: This query holds the StudentDB database name for further database manipulation quries such as INSERT, DELETE, UPDATE, SELECT, etc.

- LIST TABLES: This query shows the tables in the database which is currenlty hold for manipulation.

- DROP TABLE tblMarkSheet: This query delete the table from the database.

- CREATE TABLE tblMarkSheet (RollNo,StudentName,ClassStd,Mark1,Mark2,Mark3,-Total,Avg):This query crates tblMarkSheet table with Columns of RollNo, StudentName, ClassStd, Mark1, Mark2, Mark3, Total and Avg. In Background It creates one file named "tblMarkSheet.fdb" in "StudentDB" Folder.

- INSERT INTO tblMarkSheet (RollNo,StudentName,ClassStd,Mark1,Mark2,Mark3,-Total,Avg) VALUES (1, ANAND,10TH,85,48,59,192,64): This query insert a record in tblMarkSheet table.

- INSERT INTO tblMarkSheet VALUES (1, ANAND,10TH,85,48,59,192,64): This query also same as previous insert query. The difference is we don't need to mention the column names.

- DELETE FROM tblMarkSheet WHERE RollNo=10: This query deletes the record which record column values is equal to 10 in tblMarkSheet table.

- DELETE FROM tblMarkSheet: This query deletes all the record from tblMarkSheet Table.

- UPDATE tblMarkSheet SET (ClassStd) VALUES (11TH) WHERE RollNo=1: This query modify the ClassStd field of the record which holds RollNo has 1.

- UPDATE tblMarkSheet SET (ClassStd) VALUES (11TH)

- UPDATE tblMarkSheet SET VALUES (1, XXX,5TH,40) WHERE RollNo=1: This query sequentiay updates the record which holds the RollNo has 1. Here we don't need to mention the updating columns, it automatically updates from the sequence and missed column values are remain in the same in previous.

- UPDATE tblMarkSheet SET VALUES (1, XXX,5TH,40): The queries 11 of 1.1 and 2.1 are executed without condition.

- SELECT * FROM tblMarkSheet

- SELECT * FROM tblMarkSheet WHERE RollNo=1

- SELECT RollNo,StudentName,Total FROM tblMarkSheet WHERE RollNo>5

- SELECT RollNo,StudentName,Avg FROM tblMarkSheet WHERE Avg>=60

This query using to view the records of the table. Here we can filter the records by using relational operators.

Bugs and Flaws in Queries

- In UPDATE and DELETE queries it supports only Equal (=) condition. It is not support for other operators like <, >, <=, etc.

- In SELECT query the data filter feature is held by use of datatable and dataview. Need to provide native support.

- There is no JOIN queries when compared to RDBMS.

Advantage

- It is our own database system. So we can modify the transaction of the database system.

- When compared to other database system is quite little and slower but security things are ours. So we feel free about data security.

- We can ensure the security by using cryptography things in this system.

- We can modify the table structure in encoded text. So that no one knows the inner structure of the database. There is no data theft.

Graph Database

A graph database, also called a graph-oriented database, is a type of NoSQL database that uses graph theory to store, map and query relationships.

A graph database is essentially a collection of nodes and edges. Each node represents an entity (such as a person or business) and each edge represents a connection or relationship between two nodes. Every node in a graph database is defined by a unique identifier, a set of outgoing edges and/or incoming edges and a set of properties expressed as key/value pairs. Each edge is defined by a unique identifier, a starting-place and/or ending-place node and a set of properties. The mantra of graph database enthusiasts is "If you can whiteboard it, you can graph it."

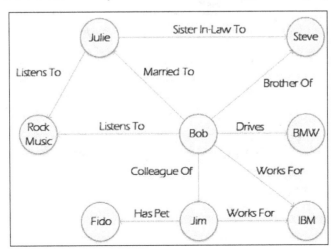

Graph databases are well-suited for analyzing interconnections, which is why there has been a lot of interest in using graph databases to mine data from social media. Graph databases are also useful for working with data in business disciplines that involve complex relationships and dynamic schema, such as supply chain management, identifying the source of an IP telephony issue and creating "customers who bought this also looked at ..." recommendations.

Object-oriented Database

Object-oriented databases (OODB) are databases that represent data in the form of objects and classes. In object-oriented terminology, an object is a real-world entity, and a class is a collection of objects. Object-oriented databases follow the fundamental principles of object-oriented programming (OOP). The combination of relational model features (concurrency, transaction, and recovery) with object-oriented principles results in an object-oriented database model.

The object-oriented database model (OODBM) is an alternative implementation to that of a relational model. An object-oriented database is similar in principle to an object-oriented programming language. An object-oriented database management system is a hybrid applications that uses a combination of object-oriented and relational database principles to process data. That said, we can use the following formula to outline the OODBM:

Object-Oriented Programming + Relational Database Features = Object-Oriented Database Model.

The figure below outlines the object-oriented database model along with its principles and features.

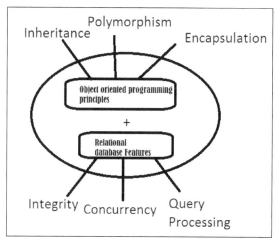

The Object-Oriented Database Model.

Fundamental Features

The object-oriented approach considers all entities as objects. An object has properties (state) and methods (behavior). Each object is identified using a unique object identifier. For example, let us consider a real-world entity called 'Student'. A student has states or properties such as a name, USN, date of birth, address, etc. Similarly, the student has behaviors or methods including attending classes, writing exams, paying fees, etc.

The figure below shows how the 'Student' object can be represented.

Representation of the Student Object.

The state and behavior cells are separate, but related. A class is a collection of similar objects. A collection of first year commerce students forms a class. In a class, the objects interact with each other using messages.

- Let's now look at the encapsulation feature.

Encapsulation is an important object-oriented feature. This hides the implementation details from the end-users and displays only the needed descriptions. For example, imagine that you are buying soap from a commercial store. You know its ingredients such as color and fragrance by looking on the box, but you aren't shown the actual method used to manufacture the soap.

- Let's now look at the inheritance feature.

Inheritance is considered important in object-oriented design because it enables re-usability. It is defined as the method of creating new classes from existing classes. The new classes not only inherit the properties of their parent class, but they also have their own unique properties. For example, when a child is born to parents, the child resembles either its mother or father, but it also has its own unique traits and personality. This figure below shows an additional example of how inheritance works.

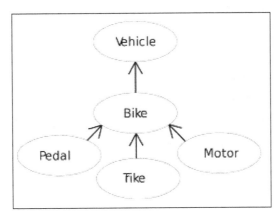

Example of Inheritance.

Association refers to links between the various entities of an application. In an object-oriented database, association is denoted as references between various objects. For example, individuals from a 'Person' class can also be associated with the 'Committee' class. The association name here can be called 'Membership' as outlined in this figure below.

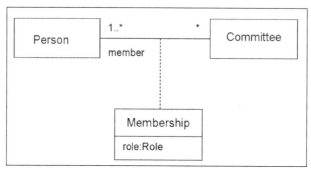

Association Example.

The concept of complex objects is derived from applying constructors to simple objects. Simple objects are mainly items such as integers, byte strings, and characters. Complex objects are items such as maps, sets, lists, tuples, or collections of many primitive objects.

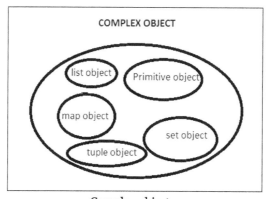

Complex objects.

The object-oriented database allows for the creation of persistent objects. A persistent object is one that lives in computer memory even after completing its execution. This is different from the lifespan of normal objects, which expire after execution, are destroyed immediately and freed from memory. Object persistent solves the database challenges of concurrency and recovery.

Object-relational Database

Relational DBMSs are currently the dominant database technology. The OODBMS has also become the favored system for financial and telecommunications applications. Although the OODBMS market is still same. The OODBMS continues to find new application areas, such as the World Wide Web. Some industry analysts expect the market for the OODBMSs to grow at over 50% per year, a rate faster than the total database market.

However, their sales are unlikely to overtake those of relational systems because of the wealth of businesses that find RDBMSs acceptable, and because businesses have invested to much money and resources in their development that change is prohibitive.

Until recently, the choice of DBMS seemed to be between the relational DBMS and the object-oriented DBMS. However, many vendors of RDBMS products are conscious of the threat and promise of the OODBMS. They agree that traditional relational DBMSs are not suited to the advanced application. The most obvious way to remedy the shortcomings of the relational model is to extend the model with these types of feature.

This is the approach that has been taken by many extended relational DBMSs, although each has implemented different combinations of features. Thus there is no single extended relational model rather, there are a variety of these models, whose characteristics depends upon the way and the degree to which extensions were made. However, all the models do share the same basic relational tables and query language, all incorporate some concept of 'object, and some have the ability to store methods (or procedures or triggers), as well as data in the database.

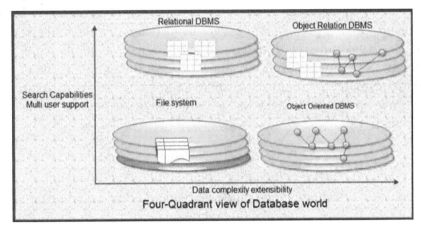

Four-Quadrant view of Database world

In a four-quadrant view of the database world, as illustrated in the figure, the lower-left quadrant are those applications that process simple data and have no requirements for querying the data.

These types of application, for example standard text processing packages such as Word.

WordPerfect, and Frame maker, can use the underlying operating system to obtain the essential DBMS functionality of persistence. In the lower-right quadrant are those applications that process complex data but again have no significant requirements for querying the data. For these types of application, for example computer-aided design packages, an OODBMS may be an appropriate choice of DBMS.

In the top-left quadrant are those applications that process simple data and also have requirements for complex querying. Many traditional business applications fall into this quadrant and an RDBMS may be the most appropriate DBMS.

Finally, in the top-right quadrant are those applications that process completed data and have complex querying requirements. This represents many of the advanced database applications and for these applications an ORDBMS may be the appropriate choice of DBMS.

Advantages and Disadvantages of ORDBMSS

ORDBMSs can provide appropriate solutions for many types of advanced database applications. However, there are also disadvantages.

Advantages of ORDBMSs

There are following advantages of ORDBMSs:

- Reuse and Sharing: The main advantages of extending the Relational data model come from reuse and sharing. Reuse comes from the ability to extend the DBMS server to perform standard functionality centrally, rather than have it coded in each application.

- Increased Productivity: ORDBMS provides increased productivity both for the developer and for the, end user.

- Use of experience in developing RDBMS: Another obvious advantage is that .the extended relational approach preserves the significant body of knowledge and experience that has gone into developing relational applications. This is a significant advantage, as many organizations would find it prohibitively expensive to change. If the new functionality is designed appropriately, this approach should allow organizations to take advantage of the new extensions in an evolutionary way without losing the benefits of current database features and functions.

Disadvantages of ORDBMSs

The ORDBMS approach has the obvious disadvantages of complexity and associated increased costs. Further, there are the proponents of the relational approach that believe the· essential simplicity' and purity of the .relational model are lost with these types of extension.

ORDBMS vendors are attempting to portray object models as extensions to the relational model with some additional complexities. This potentially misses the point of object orientation, highlighting the large semantic gap between these two technologies. Object applications are simply not as data-centric as relational-based ones.

Centralized Database

In a centralized database model, a core unit acts in a way that serves the entire company. This description is often used to describe an analytics model which has been completely centralized, though it may also refer to shared information database which is accessible to everyone.

Companies that are large and have a single-business organization have a need for information, analytics, and applications to be able to cross various boundaries. This enhances the communication within the organization, providing more effective leadership from the C-Suite as specific needs are accurately related to the specific individuals tasked with a response.

Choosing a centralized system is about funding a way for a unique business strategy to have the most potential impact. According to reporting from Deloitte, 42% of companies have established a centralized approach.

List of the Advantages of a Centralized Database:

- It allows for working on cross-functional projects

A centralized database speeds up the communication which occurs within an organization. Instead of having layers of administrative red tape in place to handle cross-functional projects between teams, the core design allows for those teams to come together whenever it is necessary. That makes it possible to absorb analytical data faster, complete specific tasks with more quality, and make more progress toward the vision, mission, or goals which have been established.

- It is easier to share ideas across analysts

Many businesses are setup in a way that creates silos for individuals and teams. By implementing a strategy which centralizes information and analytics, those silos begin to disappear. Instead of having multiple people working on the same projects or datasets independently, the organization can coordinate their work to have them collaborating more often. When everyone can share their ideas with the rest of the organization, the diversity created allows for a better growth potential.

- Analysts can be assigned to specific problems or projects centrally

There is a higher level of accountability found within a centralized database. That is because there is much more transparency about the policies and procedures being implemented. Each person can be assigned to a specific problem that the organization must address. Those with the correct authorities can monitor the progress of that person in solving the identified issue. Instead of routing through numerous sections, teams, or departments, all of the communication for each problem or project is routed centrally, which reduces confusion.

- Higher levels of security can be obtained

When there is long-term funding granted to a centralized database, then there is a higher level of data security which develops for the organization. That is because the information which is obtained by the company serves the entire company. Everyone involved with the information retention is bound by certain protocols or limits with their access, which limits the amount of data leakage which may occur. The end result is that the valuable data stays internal more often than going external.

- Higher levels of dependability are present within the system

There are fewer breakdowns of internal reporting systems when a centralized database is present. Instead of having multiple channels open, which may come to different conclusions on their own, there is one central channel which includes everyone. Each person can access the data they require, offer their opinion, and listen to the company-wide chatter as specific conclusions are created. Dependability happens because people get onto the same page faster.

- It reduces conflict

When there is a centralized database responsible for the collection and storage of data, then conflicts within the organization are reduced. That occurs because there are fewer people involved in the decision-making processes which involve the data. When there are top managers or assigned individuals responsible for this information, the lower-level managers and lower tier employees are insulated from the burdens of using the data inappropriately, which leads to a happier working environment.

- Organizations can act with greater speed

When there is a core database responsible for managing information, decisions on actions or strategies occur with greater speed because there are fewer layers of data which must be navigated. Leaders of the business are able to operate more efficiently because the communication processes are built naturally into the system. That makes it easier for everyone to evaluate the pros and cons of any decision they may face.

- It helps an organization stay close to a focused vision

The centralized database can be configured to keep tabs on an entire organization with regards to its one purpose or vision. Inconsistencies are eliminated from the workflows because the data being collected is intended for specific purposes which are clearly communicated to everyone involved.

List of the Disadvantages of a Centralized Database:

- It can become unresponsive to the needs of the business

There are heavy workload requirements which become necessary when using a centralized database. Individuals and teams find that the time constraints placed on them may be unreasonable for the expectations asked. In time, if these constraints are not addressed as they should be, a centralized database creates unresponsive teams that are focused on specific tasks instead of collaboration. The teams can essentially rebel against the system to create their own silos for self-protection.

- There are lower levels of location-based adaptability

Using a centralized database means you are trading movement efficiencies for less flexibility at the local level. If there are changes which occur locally that affect the business, this data must be sent to the centralized database. There is no option to control the data locally. That means response times to local customers or the community may not be as efficient as they could be, as there may not be any information in place to deal with a necessary response.

- It can have a negative impact on local morale

When there is a centralized database being used, the responsibilities of local managers are often reduced. That occurs because the structure of the company may forbid local managers from hiring their own employees. It may force them to use data from the centralized system which they feel has a negative impact at the local level. Instead of being able to make decisions immediately, they are forced to wait for data to come from the centralized database. For those who wish to experience higher levels of responsibility with their management role, the centralized process can be highly demoralizing

- Succession planning can be limited with a centralized database

Because the information is managed by a centralized database, there is little need to work on the development of new or upcoming managers. The only form of succession planning that is necessary with this setup involves bringing in an individual to replace a core analyst at some point. Should top-level managers experience a family issue, health event, or some other issue which interferes with their job, there may be no one with the necessary experience to take over the position, which reduces the effectiveness of the centralized database.

- It reduces the amount of legitimate feedback received

A centralized database may provide transparency. It may lead to greater levels of communication. Those are not always positive benefits. When anyone can offer an opinion or feedback on information they have received, they often feel a responsibility to send a response. Many employees may have general knowledge about certain policies or procedures, but not have access to the full picture. They waste time creating feedback which isn't needed, which wastes time for everyone who reads that feedback. Over time, this can lead to lower levels of productivity and higher levels of frustration.

- It may increase costs

When a centralized system is in place, there is a reliance on the accuracy of the data being collected. Even one small miscalculation could have a grave impact on the centralized database. That may result in higher fees for rushed deliveries, incorrect orders that are labeled as being correct, and unnecessary changes to potential inventory controlled by the organization. The costs of fixing a mistake from a decentralized system tend to be lower than fixing the mistakes generated by centralized systems.

There is a Risk of loss

When there is a centralized database, everything is stored within that database. What happens to that information if the database should be lost for some reason? Because there are no other database locations, an organization loses access immediately. That could create a long-term outage which may affect the overall viability of the company. Even with cloud backup systems in place and other protections available, there is always a risk of complete loss present when using a centralized database.

These centralized database advantages and disadvantages must be considered at the local level. For some organizations, the centralized structure makes sense because it brings people and teams together with a common bond to work toward a specific mission. For others, the system may create too many data points, bogging down overall productivity.

Cloud Database

A cloud database is a collection of informational content, either structured or unstructured, that resides on a private, public or hybrid cloud computing infrastructure platform. From a structural and design perspective, a cloud database is no different than one that operates on a business's own on-premises servers. The critical difference lies in where the database resides.

Where an on-premises database is connected to local users through a corporation's internal local area network (LAN), a cloud database resides on servers and storage furnished by a cloud or database as a service (DBaaS) provider and it is accessed solely through the internet. To a software application, for example, a SQL database residing on-premises or in the cloud should appear identical.

The behavior of the database should be the same whether accessed through direct queries, such as SQL statements, or through API calls. However, it may be possible to discern small differences in response time. An on-premises database, accessed with a LAN, is likely to provide a slightly faster response than a cloud-based database, which requires a round trip on the internet for each interaction with the database.

How Cloud Databases Work

Cloud databases, like their traditional ancestors, can be divided into two broad categories: relational and nonrelational.

A relational database, typically written in structured query language (SQL), is composed of a set of interrelated tables that are organized into rows and columns. The relationship between tables and columns (fields) is specified in a schema. SQL databases, by design, rely on data that is highly consistent in its format, such as banking transactions or a telephone directory. Popular cloud platforms and cloud providers include MySQL, Oracle, IBM DB2 and Microsoft SQL Server. Some cloud platforms such as MySQL are open sourced.

Nonrelational databases, sometimes called NoSQL, do not employ a table model. Instead, they store content, regardless of its structure, as a single document. This technology is well-suited for unstructured data, such as social media content, photos and videos.

Types of Cloud Databases

Two cloud database environment models exist: traditional and database as a service (DBaaS).

In a traditional cloud model, a database runs on an IT department's infrastructure with a virtual machine. Tasks of database oversight and management fall upon IT staffers of the organization.

The DBaaS model is a fee-based subscription service in which the database runs on the service provider's physical infrastructure. Different service levels are usually available. In a classic DBaaS arrangement, the provider maintains the physical infrastructure and database, leaving the customer to manage the database's contents and operation.

Alternatively, a customer can set up a managed hosting arrangement, in which the provider handles database maintenance and management. This latter option may be especially attractive to small businesses that have database needs but lack adequate IT expertise.

Cloud database benefits

Compared with operating a traditional database on an on-site physical server and storage architecture, a cloud database offers the following distinct advantages:

- Elimination of physical infrastructure: In a cloud database environment, the cloud computing provider of servers, storage and other infrastructure is responsible for maintenance and keeping high availability. The organization that owns and operates the database is only responsible for supporting and maintaining the database software and its contents. In a DBaaS environment, the service provider is responsible for managing and operating the database software, leaving the DBaaS users responsible only for their own data.

- Cost savings: Through the elimination of a physical infrastructure owned and operated by an IT department, significant savings can be achieved from reduced capital expenditures, less staff, decreased electrical and HVAC operating costs and a smaller amount of needed physical space.

- DBaaS benefits also include instantaneous scalability, performance guarantees, failover support, declining pricing and specialized expertise.

Migrating Legacy Databases to the Cloud

An on-premises database can migrate to a cloud implementation. Numerous reasons exist for doing this, including the following:

- Allows IT to retire on-premises physical server and storage infrastructure.

- Fills the talent gap when IT lacks adequate in-house database expertise.

- Improves processing efficiency, especially when applications and analytics that access the data also reside in the cloud.

- Achieves cost savings through several means, including:

  ○ Reduction of in-house IT staff.

  ○ Continually declining cloud service pricing.

  ○ Paying for only the resources consumed, known as pay-as-you-go pricing.

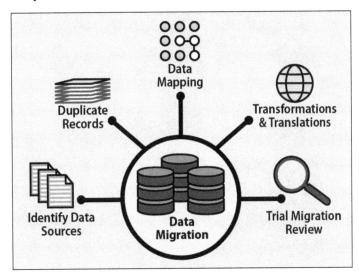

Relocating a database to the cloud can be an effective way to further enable business application performance as part of a wider software-as-a-service deployment. Doing so simplifies the processes required to make information available through internet-based connections. Storage consolidation can also be a benefit of moving a company's databases to the cloud. Databases in multiple departments of a large company, for example, can be combined in the cloud into a single hosted database management system.

References

- Eav-vs-relational: wq.io, Retrieved 17 May, 2019

- Semi-structured-model, data-modeling: learn.geekinterview.com, Retrieved 28 April, 2019

- The-object-oriented-oo-model, notes-and-studymaterial - 472: myreadingroom.co.in, Retrieved 02 April, 2019

- What-is-a-document-store-database: database.guide, Retrieved 23 August, 2019

- The-associative-model, data-modeling: learn.geekinterview.com, Retrieved 20 August, 2019

- Flat-file-database-definition-example: study.com, Retrieved 11 May, 2019

- Graph-database: whatis.techtarget.com, Retrieved 15 January, 2019

- Cloud-database: searchcloudcomputing.techtarget.com, Retrieved 23 July, 2019

Database Design and Structure

Organization of data according to the database model is termed as database design. In order to completely understand database design it is necessary to understand the concepts such as data structure, database schema, database instance, entity relationship model, etc. The following chapter elucidates the diverse concepts associated with this area of study.

Database Design Process

Conceptual Design

The purpose of the conceptual design phase is to build a conceptual model based upon the previously identified requirements, but closer to the final physical model. A commonly-used conceptual model is called an *entity-relationship* model.

Entities and Attributes

Entities are basically people, places, or things you want to keep information about. For example, a library system may have the book, *library* and *borrower* entities. Learning to identify what should be an entity, what should be a number of entities, and what should be an *attribute* of an entity takes practice, but there are some good rules of thumb. The following questions can help to identify whether something is an entity:

- Can it vary in number independently of other *entities*? For example, *person height* is probably not an entity, as it cannot vary in number independently of *person*. It is not fundamental, so it cannot be an entity in this case.

- Is it important enough to warrant the effort of maintaining. For example *customer* may not be important for a small grocery store and will not be an entity in that case, but it will be important for a video store, and will be an entity in that case.

- Is it its own thing that cannot be separated into subcategories? For example, a car-rental agency may have different criteria and storage requirements for different kinds of vehicles. *Vehicle* may not be an entity, as it can be broken up into *car* and *boat*, which are the entities.

- Does it list a type of thing, not an instance? The video game *blow-em-up 6* is not an entity, rather an instance of the *game entity*.

- Does it have many associated facts? If it only contains one attribute, it is unlikely to be an entity. For example, *city* may be an entity in some cases, but if it contains only one attribute, *city name*, it is more likely to be an attribute of another entity, such as *customer*.

The following are examples of entities involving a university with possible attributes in parentheses:

- Course (name, code, course prerequisites).

- Student (first_name, surname, address, age).

- Book (title, ISBN, price, quantity in stock).

An instance of an entity is one particular occurrence of that entity. For example, the student Rudolf Sono is one instance of the student entity. There will probably be many instances. If there is only one instance, consider whether the entity is warranted. The top level usually does not warrant an entity. For example, if the system is being developed for a particular university, *university* will not be an entity because the whole system is for that one university. However, if the system was developed to track legislation at all universities in the country, then *university* would be a valid entity.

Relationships

Entities are related in certain ways. For example, a borrower may belong to a library and can take out books. A book can be found in a particular library. Understanding what you are storing data about, and how the data relate, leads you a large part of the way to a physical implementation in the database.

There are a number of possible relationships:

Mandatory

For each instance of entity A, there must exist one or more instances of entity B. This does not necessarily mean that for each instance of entity B, there must exist one or more instances of entity A. Relationships are optional or mandatory in one direction only, so the A-to-B relationship can be optional, while the B-to-A relationship is mandatory.

Optional

For each instance of entity A, there may or may not exist instances of entity B.

One-to-one (1:1)

This is where for each instance of entity A, there exists one instance of entity B, and vice-versa. If the relationship is optional, there can exist zero or one instances, and if the relationship is mandatory, there exists one and only one instance of the associated entity.

One-to-many (1:M)

For each instance of entity A, many instances of entity B can exist, which for each instance of entity B, only one instance of entity A exists. Again, these can be optional or mandatory relationships.

Many-to-many (M:N)

For each instance of entity A, many instances of entity B can exist, and vice versa. These can be optional or mandatory relationships.

There are numerous ways of showing these relationships. The image below shows *student* and *course* entities. In this case, each student must have registered for at least one course, but a course does not necessarily have to have students registered. The student-to-course relationship is mandatory, and the course-to-student relationship is optional.

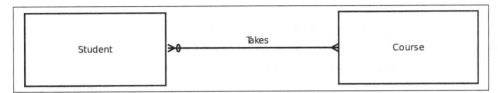

The image below shows *invoice_line* and *product* entities. Each invoice line must have at least one product (but no more than one); however each product can appear on many invoice lines, or none at all. The *invoice_line-to-product* relationship is mandatory, while the *product-to-invoice_line* relationship is optional.

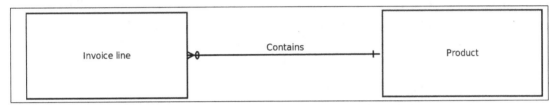

The figure below shows husband and wife entities. In this system (others are of course possible), each husband must have one and only one wife, and each wife must have one, and only one, husband. Both relationships are mandatory.

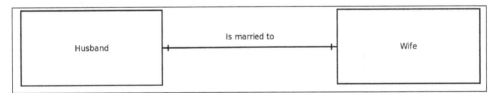

An entity can also have a relationship with itself. Such an entity is called a *recursive entity*. Take a person entity. If you're interested in storing data about which people are brothers, you wlll have an "is brother to" relationship. In this case, the relationship is a M:N relationship.

Conversely, a weak entity is an entity that cannot exist without another entity. For example, in a school, the scholar entity is related to the weak entity parent/guardian. Without the scholar, the parent or guardian cannot exist in the system. Weak entities usually derive their primary key, in part or in totality, from the associated entity. parent/guardian could take the primary key from the scholar table as part of its primary key (or the entire key if the system only stored one parent/guardian per scholar).

The term *connectivity* refers to the relationship classification.

The term cardinality refers to the specific number of instances possible for a relationship. Cardinality limits list the minimum and maximum possible occurrences of the associated entity. In the husband and wife example, the cardinality limit is, and in the case of a student who can take between one and eight courses, the cardinality limits would be represented as.

Developing an Entity-relationship Diagram

An entity-relationship diagram models how the entities relate to each other. It's made up of multiple relationships, the kind shown in the examples above. In general, these entities go on to become the database tables.

The first step in developing the diagram is to identify all the entities in the system. In the initial stage, it is not necessary to identify the attributes, but this may help to clarify matters if the designer is unsure about some of the entities. Once the entities are listed, relationships between these entities are identified and modeled according to their type: one-to-many, optional and so on. There are many software packages that can assist in drawing an entity-relationship diagram, but any graphical package should suffice.

Once the initial entity-relationship diagram has been drawn, it is often shown to the stakeholders. Entity-relationship diagrams are easy for non-technical people to understand, especially when guided through the process. This can help identify any errors that have crept in. Part of the reason for modeling is that models are much easier to understand than pages of text, and they are much more likely to be viewed by stakeholders, which reduces the chances of errors slipping through to the next stage, when they may be more difficult to fix.

It is important to remember that there is no one right or wrong answer. The more complex the situation, the more possible designs that will work. Database design is an acquired skill, though, and more experienced designers will have a good idea of what works and of possible problems at a later stage, having gone through the process before.

Once the diagram has been approved, the next stage is to replace many-to-many relationships with two one-to-many relationships. A DBMS cannot directly implement many-to-many relationships, so they are decomposed into two smaller relationships. To achieve this, you have to create an *intersection*, or *composite* entity type. Because intersection entities are less "real-world" than ordinary entities, they are sometimes difficult to name. In this case, you can name them according to the two entities being intersected. For example, you can intersect the many-to-many relationship between *student* and *course* by *a student-course* entity.

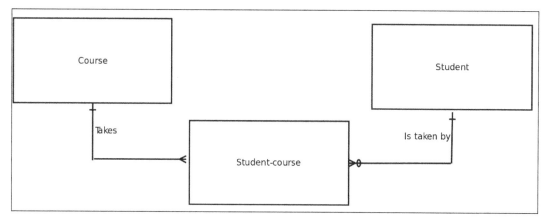

The same applies even if the entity is recursive. The person entity that has an M:N relationship "is brother to" also needs an intersection entity. You can come up with a good name for the intersection entity in this case: *brother*. This entity would contain two fields, one for each person of the brother relationship — in other words, the primary key of the first brother and the primary key of the other brother.

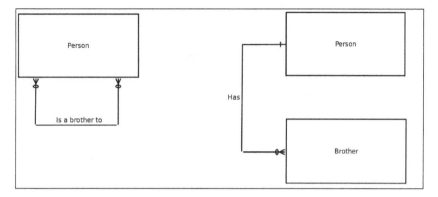

Database Design

A good database design starts with a list of the data that you want to include in your database and what you want to be able to do with the database later on. This can all be written in your own language, without any SQL. In this stage you must try not to think in tables or columns, but just think: "What do I need to know?" Don't take this too lightly, because if you find out later that you forgot something, usually you need to start all over. Adding things to your database is mostly a lot of work.

Identifying Entities

The types of information that are saved in the database are called 'entities'. These entities exist in four kinds: people, things, events, and locations. Everything you could want to put in a database fits into one of these categories. If the information you want to include doesn't fit into these categories then it is probably not an entity but a property of an entity, an attribute.

Imagine that you are creating a website for a shop, what kind of information do you have to deal with? In a shop you sell your products to customers. The "Shop" is a location; "Sale" is an event; "Products" are things; and "Customers" are people. These are all entities that need to be included in your database.

But what other things are happening when selling a product? A customer comes into the shop, approaches the vendor, asks a question and gets an answer. "Vendors" also participate, and because vendors are people, we need a vendors entity.

Entities: Types of information.

Identifying Relationships

The next step is to determine the relationships between the entities and to determine the cardinality of each relationship. The relationship is the connection between the entities, just like in the real world: what does one entity do with the other, how do they relate to each other? For example, customers buy products, products are sold to customers, a sale comprises products, a sale happens in a shop.

The cardinality shows how much of one side of the relationship belongs to how much of the other side of the relationship. First, you need to state for each relationship, how much of one side belongs to exactly 1 of the other side. For example: How many customers belong to 1 sale?; How many sales belong to 1 customer?; How many sales take place in 1 shop?

You'll get a list like this:

- Customers --> Sales; 1 customer can buy something several times.

- Sales --> Customers; 1 sale is always made by 1 customer at the time.

- Customers --> Products; 1 customer can buy multiple products.

- Products --> Customers; 1 product can be purchased by multiple customers.

- Customers --> Shops; 1 customer can purchase in multiple shops.

- Shops --> Customers, 1 shop can receive multiple customers.

- Shops --> Products; in 1 shop there are multiple products.

- Products --> Shops; 1 product (type) can be sold in multiple shops.

- Shops --> Sales; in 1 shop multiple sales can be made.

- Sales --> Shops; 1 sale can only be made in 1 shop at the time.

- Products --> Sales; 1 product (type) can be purchased in multiple sales.

- Sales --> Products; 1 sale can exist out of multiple products.

There are four entities and each entity has a relationship with every other entity, so each entity must have three relationships, and also appear on the left end of the relationship three times.

Now we'll put the data together to find the cardinality of the whole relationship. In order to do this, we'll draft the cardinalities per relationship. To make this easy to do, we'll adjust the notation a bit, by noting the 'backward'-relationship the other way around:

- Customers --> Sales; 1 customer can buy something several times.

- Sales --> Customers; 1 sale is always made by 1 customer at the time.

  The second relationship we will turn around so it has the same entity order as the first. Please notice the arrow that is now faced the other way!

- Customers <-- Sales; 1 sale is always made by 1 customer at the time.

  Cardinality exists in four types: one-to-one, one-to-many, many-to-one, and many-to-many. In a database design this is indicated as: 1:1, 1:N, M:1, and M:N. To find the right indication just leave the '1'. If there is a 'many' on the left side, this will be indicated with 'M', if there is a 'many' on the right side it is indicated with 'N'.

- Customers --> Sales; 1 customer can buy something several times; 1:N.

- Customers <-- Sales; 1 sale is always made by 1 customer at the time; 1:1.

The true cardinality can be calculated through assigning the biggest values for left and right, for which 'N' or 'M' are greater than '1'. In this example, in both cases there is a '1' on the left side. On the right side, there is a 'N' and a '1', the 'N' is the biggest value. The total cardinality is therefore '1:N'. A customer can make multiple 'sales', but each 'sale' has just one customer.

If we do this for the other relationships too, we'll get:

- Customers --> Sales; --> 1:N

- Customers --> Products; --> M:N

- Customers --> Shops; --> M:N

- Sales --> Products; --> M:N

- Shops --> Sales; --> 1:N

- Shops --> Products; --> M:N

So, we have two '1-to-many' relationships, and four 'many-to-many' relationships.

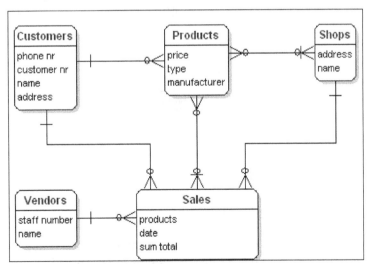

Relationships between the entities.

Between the entities there may be a mutual dependency. This means that the one item cannot exist if the other item does not exist. For example, there cannot be a sale if there are no customers, and there cannot be a sale if there are no products.

The relationships Sales --> Customers, and Sales --> Products are mandatory, but the other way around this is not the case. A customer can exist without sale, and also a product can exist without sale. This is of importance for the next step.

Recursive Relationships

Sometimes an entity refers back to itself. For example, think of a work hierarchy: an employee has a boss; and the bosschef is an employee too. The attribute 'boss' of the entity 'employees' refers back to the entity 'employees'.

In an ERD this type of relationship is a line that goes out of the entity and returns with a nice loop to the same entity.

Redundant Relationships

Sometimes in your model you will get a 'redundant relationship'. These are relationships that are already indicated by other relationships, although not directly.

In the case of our example there is a direct relationship between customers and products. But there are also relationships from customers to sales and from sales to products, so indirectly there already is a relationship between customers and products through sales. The relationship 'Customers <----> Products' is made twice, and one of them is therefore redundant. In this case, products are only purchased through a sale, so the relationships 'Customers <----> Products' can be deleted. The model will then look like this:

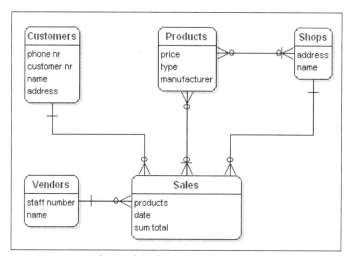

Relationships between the entities.

Solving Many-to-Many Relationships

Many-to-many relationships (M:N) are not directly possible in a database. What a M:N relationship says is that a number of records from one table belongs to a number of records from another table. Somewhere you need to save which records these are and the solution is to split the relationship up in two one-to-many relationships.

This can be done by creating a new entity that is in between the related entities. In our example, there is a many-to-many relationship between sales and products. This can be solved by creating a new entity: sales-products. This entity has a many-to-one relationship with Sales, and a many-to-one relationship with Products. In logical models this is called an associative entity and in physical database terms this is called a link table, intersection table or junction table.

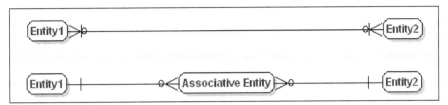

Many to many relationship implementation via associative entity.

In the example there are too many-to-many relationships that need to be solved: 'Products <---->
Sales', and 'Products <----> Shops'. For both situations there needs to be create a new entity, but
what is that entity?

For the Products <----> Sales relationship, every sale includes more products. The relationship
shows the content of the sale. In other words, it gives details about the sale. So the entity is called
'Sales details'. You could also name it 'sold products'.

The Products <----> Shops relationship shows which products are available in which the shops,
also known as 'stock'. Our model would now look like this:

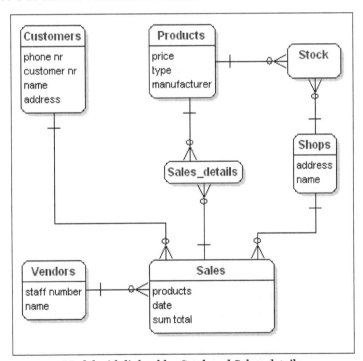

Model with link tables Stock and Sales_details.

Physical Design

Database System Architecture

Database architecture uses programming languages to design a particular type of software for
businesses or organizations. Database architecture focuses on the design, development, implementation and maintenance of computer programs that store and organize information for businesses, agencies and institutions. A database architect develops and implements software to meet
the needs of users.

The design of a DBMS depends on its architecture. It can be centralized or decentralized or hierarchical. The architecture of a DBMS can be seen as either single tier or multi-tier. The tiers are classified as follows:

- 1-tier architecture,

- 2-tier architecture,

- 3-tier architecture,

- n-tier architecture.

1-tier Architecture

One-tier architecture involves putting all of the required components for a software application or technology on a single server or platform.

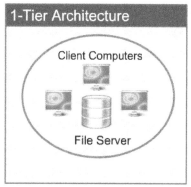

1-tier architecture.

Basically, a one-tier architecture keeps all of the elements of an application, including the interface, Middleware and back-end data, in one place. Developers see these types of systems as the simplest and most direct way.

2-tier Architecture

The two-tier is based on Client Server architecture. The two-tier architecture is like client server application. The direct communication takes place between client and server. There is no intermediate between client and server.

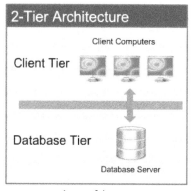

2-tier architecture.

3-tier Architecture

3-tier architecture separates its tiers from each other based on the complexity of the users and how they use the data present in the database. It is the most widely used architecture to design a DBMS.

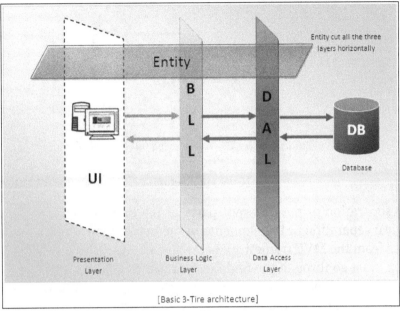

3-tier architecture.

This architecture has different usages with different applications. It can be used in web applications and distributed applications. The strength in particular is when using this architecture over distributed systems.

- Database (Data) Tier: At this tier, the database resides along with its query processing languages. We also have the relations that define the data and their constraints at this level.

- Application (Middle) Tier: At this tier reside the application server and the programs that access the database. For a user, this application tier presents an abstracted view of the database. End-users are unaware of any existence of the database beyond the application. At the other end, the database tier is not aware of any other user beyond the application tier. Hence, the application layer sits in the middle and acts as a mediator between the end-user and the database.

- User (Presentation) Tier: End-users operate on this tier and they know nothing about any existence of the database beyond this layer. At this layer, multiple views of the database can be provided by the application. All views are generated by applications that reside in the application tier.

N-tier Architecture

N-tier architecture would involve dividing an application into three different tiers. These would be the:

- Logic tier,

- The presentation tier, and

- The data tier.

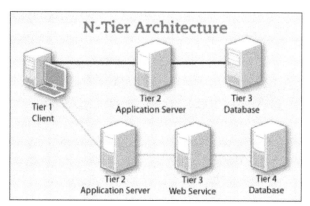

N-tier architecture.

It is the physical separation of the different parts of the application as opposed to the usually conceptual or logical separation of the elements in the model-view-controller (MVC) framework. Another difference from the MVC framework is that n-tier layers are connected linearly, meaning all communication must go through the middle layer, which is the logic tier. In MVC, there is no actual middle layer because the interaction is triangular; the control layer has access to both the view and model layers and the model also accesses the view; the controller also creates a model based on the requirements and pushes this to the view. However, they are not mutually exclusive, as the MVC framework can be used in conjunction with the n-tier architecture, with the n-tier being the overall architecture used and MVC used as the framework for the presentation tier.

Normalization of Database

Database Normalisation is a technique of organizing the data in the database. Normalization is a systematic approach of decomposing tables to eliminate data redundancy and undesirable characteristics like Insertion, Update and Deletion Anamolies. It is a multi-step process that puts data into tabular form by removing duplicated data from the relation tables.

Normalization is used for mainly two purpose:

- Eliminating reduntant(useless) data.

- Ensuring data dependencies make sense i.e data is logically stored.

Problem without Normalization

Without Normalization, it becomes difficult to handle and update the database, without facing data loss. Insertion, Updation and Deletion Anamolies are very frequent if Database is not Normalized.

Normalization Rule

Normalization rule are divided into following normal form:

- First Normal Form,

- Second Normal Form,

- Third Normal Form,

- BCNF.

First Normal Form

A database is in first normal form if it satisfies the following conditions:

- Contains only atomic values.

- There are no repeating groups.

An atomic value is a value that cannot be divided. For example, the values in the [Color] column in the first row can be divided into "red" and "green", hence [TABLE_PRODUCT] is not in 1NF.

A repeating group means that a table contains two or more columns that are closely related. For example, a table that records data on a book and its author(s) with the following columns: [Book ID], [Author 1], [Author 2], [Author 3] is not in 1NF because [Author 1], [Author 2], and [Author 3] are all repeating the same attribute.

1st Normal Form Example

How do we bring an unnormalized table into first normal form? Consider the following example:

TABLE_PRODUCT		
Product ID	Color	Price
1	red, green	15.99
2	yellow	23.99
3	green	17.50
4	yellow, blue	9.99
5	red	29.99

This table is not in first normal form because the [Color] column can contain multiple values. For example, the first row includes values "red" and "green."

To bring this table to first normal form, we split the table into two tables and now we have the resulting tables:

TABLE_PRODUCT_PRICE	
Product ID	Price
1	15.99
2	23.99
3	17.50
4	9.99
5	29.99

TABLE_PRODUCT_Color	
Product ID	Color
1	red
1	green
2	yellow
3	green
4	yellow
4	blue
5	red

Now first normal form is satisfied, as the columns on each table all hold just one value.

Second Normal Form

A database is in second normal form if it satisfies the following conditions:

- It is in first normal form.

- All non-key attributes are fully functional dependent on the primary key.

In a table, if attribute B is functionally dependent on A, but is not functionally dependent on a proper subset of A, then B is considered fully functional dependent on A. Hence, in a 2NF table, all non-key attributes cannot be dependent on a subset of the primary key. Note that if the primary key is not a composite key, all non-key attributes are always fully functional dependent on the primary key. A table that is in 1st normal form and contains only a single key as the primary key is automatically in 2nd normal form.

2nd Normal Form Example

Consider the following example:

TABLE_PURCHASE_DETAIL		
Customer ID	Store ID	Purchase Location
1	1	Los Angeles
1	3	San Francisco
2	1	Los Angeles
3	2	New York
4	3	San Francisco

This table has a composite primary key [Customer ID, Store ID]. The non-key attribute is [Purchase Location]. In this case, [Purchase Location] only depends on [Store ID], which is only part of the primary key. Therefore, this table does not satisfy second normal form.

To bring this table to second normal form, we break the table into two tables, and now we have the following:

TABLE_PURCHASE	
Customer ID	Store ID
1	1

1	3
2	1
3	2
4	3

TABLE_STORE	
Store ID	Purchase Location
1	Los Angeles
2	New York
3	San Francisco

What we have done is to remove the partial functional dependency that we initially had. Now, in the table [TABLE_STORE], the column [Purchase Location] is fully dependent on the primary key of that table, which is [Store ID].

Third Normal Form

A relation is in third normal form if it is in 2NF and no non key attribute is transitively dependent on the primary key.

A bank uses the following relation:

Vendor(ID, Name, Account_No, Bank_Code_No, Bank)

The attribute ID is the identification key. All attributes are single valued (1NF). The table is also in 2NF.

The following dependencies exist:

- Name, Account_No, Bank_Code_No are functionally dependent on ID (ID □ Name, Account_No, Bank_Code_No).

- Bank is functionally dependent on Bank_Code_No (Bank_Code_No □ Bank).

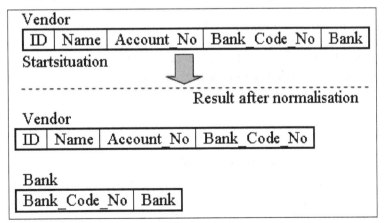

The table in this example is in 1NF and in 2NF. But there is a transitive dependency between Bank_Code_No and Bank, because Bank_Code_No is not the primary key of this relation. To get to the third normal form (3NF), we have to put the bank name in a separate table together with the clearing number to identify it.

BCNF

BCNF was developed by Raymond Boyce and E.F. Codd; the latter is widely considered the father of relational database design.

BCNF is really an extension of 3rd Normal Form (3NF). For this reason it is frequently termed 3.5NF. 3NF states that all data in a table must depend only on that table's primary key, and not on any other field in the table. At first glance it would seem that BCNF and 3NF are the same thing. However, in some rare cases it does happen that a 3NF table is not BCNF-compliant. This may happen in tables with two or more overlapping composite candidate keys.

Data Type and Size

All the languages in computer world support datatypes. Datatypes defines the domain of the columns in the table or variables in the code. They define whether the column or variable contains numbers, alphabets, boolean values etc. This is very much important because, it controls the misuse of column – if anyone is trying to insert alphabets into numeric column, it does not allow. If the datatypes of column is not defined, we can store any data in any column, hence making the jumble. Any table needs to be well defined and well structured. Datatypes is to help to create a clean database.

There are six types of inbuilt datatypes:

- Scalar data types: Used to store scalar values like numbers, decimals etc.

- Composite data types: It is combination of other datatypes usually scalar datatypes.

- Reference data types: Used to store the information about another datatype. It can be referred as pointers in C.

- LOB data types: Used to store large objects like images, videos etc.

- Unknown Column types: When column types are not known, this datatype is used.

- User Define data types: These datatypes are defined by the developer while coding using the above base datatypes. They define new datatypes to ease their coding. This is can be considered as composite datatype too.

Scalar Data Types

These datatypes are used to store the numeric column values or numeric variables. Suppose we have a column AGE in a table. This column can have only numbers in it. We cannot insert any date or alphabets into it. Hence we declare this column as NUMBER. This restricts the user while they try to insert any other values other than number. This is one of the mechanisms to maintain the domain constraint of a column.

There are four types of Scalar datatypes – Character, Numeric, Date/Time and Boolean.

Character Data type: This type of datatype is used to store alpha-numeric values like alphabets as well as numbers and special characters. There are different subtypes in this character datatype depending on the storage space and length of the data to be stored.

While creating a table:

```
CREATE TABLE STUDENT (STD_NAME CHAR (15), ADDRESS VARCHAR2 (50));
```

In PL/SQL:

```
DECLARE

        v_name VARCHAR2 (30);

BEGIN ….
```

Datatype	Sub-Datatype	Description			Storage
Character Data Type	CHAR	Used to store fixed length of string or value.			32767 bytes
	CHARACTER	This is same as CHAR, and both are used alternatively. CHAR is most commonly used.			32767 bytes
	VARCHAR2	This is also similar to CHAR, where strings are stored. This datatype will define fixed length but the actual length of the string will be the length of the value i.e.; if VARCHAR2(10) is defined on column NAME and if NAME has one value 'James', then the length of that column value is 5, instead of 10. In the case of CHAR, it will be always 10; the space after the names will be filled with NULLS.			32767 bytes
		VARCHAR2 Subtypes: Following sub type defines same length value.			
		Sub Data types	Description		
		STRING	they are similar to VARCHAR2, only the name difference		
		VARCHAR			
	NCHAR	Stores National Character data (Unicode) within the specified length.			32767 bytes
	NVARCHAR2	This is similar to VARCHAR2, but used to store unicode values.			32767 bytes
	RAW	This datatype is used for such data like music, video, graphics etc where conversion of datatype between different systems is not required. They are representing in bits and bytes.			32767 bytes
	LONG	Used to store variable length of strings with backward compatibility. We can store very large data in it. But it is usually recommended to use LOB when there is a need for LONG. Because LOB has less restriction on storage and conversions, and have more features added when there is a new release. LONG columns are preferred in SELCT or UPDATE statements than tables.			32760 bytes
	LONG RAW	This is combination of LONG and RAW datatypes.			32760 bytes
	ROWID	The ROWID data type represents the actual storage address of a row. And table index identities as a logical ROWID. This data type used to store backward compatibility.			
	UROWID[(size)]	The UROWID data type identifies as universal ROWID, same as ROWID data type. Use UROWID data type for developing newer applications.			4000 bytes

Numeric Datatypes: - Stores different types of numeric data – numbers, decimals etc. Depending on the type we have different sub types of numeric datatypes.

While creating a table:

```
CREATE TABLE STUDENT (

STD_ID NUMBER (8), ADDRESS VARCHAR2 (50));
```

In PL/SQL:

```
DECLARE

          v_total PLS_INTEGER;

BEGIN …
```

Datatype	Sub-Datatype	Description			Storage
NUMERIC DATA Types	NUMBER (p, s)	NUMBER data type used to store numeric data. Storage Range : Precision range(p) : 1 to 38 and Scale range(s) : -84 to 127			
		NUMBER Subtypes: This sub type defines different types storage range.			
		Sub Data types	Description		Max Precision
		INTEGER	This data types are used to store fixed decimal points. You can use based on your requirements.		38 digits
		INT			38 digits
		SMALLINT			38 digits
		DEC			38 digits
		DECIMAL			38 digits
		NUMERIC			38 digits
		REAL			63 binary digits
		DOUBLE PRECISION			126 binary digits
		FLOAT			126 binary digits
	BINARY_INTEGER	BINARY_INTEGER data type store positive and negative values. They require less storage space compare of NUMBER data type values. Storage Range: from -2147483647 to 2147483647.			
		Sub Data types	Description		
		NATURAL	Only Positive values are stored.		
		POSITIVE			
		NATURALN	NULL values are not stored in this datatype. Only non-null positive values are allowed.		
		POSITIVEN			
		SIGNTYPE	SIGNTYPE allow only -1, 0, and 1 value.		
	PLS_INTEGER	PLS_INTEGER data type used to store signed integers data. They require less storage space compare of NUMBER data type value. Storage Range: from -2147483647 to 2147483647. PLS_INTEGER data type gives better performance on the data. PLS_INTEGER perform arithmetic operation faster than NUMBER / BINARY_INTEGER data type.			

Date/Time Datatypes: These datatypes are used to store date and timestamps in the columns and variables.

Datatype	Sub-Datatype	Description		
Date / Time Datatype	DATE	DATE data type stores valid date-time format with fixed length. Starting date from Jan 1, 4712 BC to Dec 31, 9999 AD.		
	TIMESTAMP	Stores valid date with year, month, day and time with hour, minute, second		
		Type	TIMESTAMP Type	
		1	Syntax: TIMESTAMP [(fractional_seconds_precision)] fractional_seconds_precision optionally specifies the number of digits in the fractional part of the second precision. Range from 0 to 9. The default is 6.	
			Example: TIMESTAMP '2014-04-13 18:10:52.124'	
		2	Syntax: TIMESTAMP [(fractional_seconds_precision)] WITH TIME ZONE	
			Example: TIMESTAMP '2014-04-13 18:10:52.124 +05:30'	
			WITH TIME ZONE specify the UTC time zone. Following two values represent the same instant in UTC.	
			TIMESTAMP '1999-04-15 8:00:00 -8:00' (8.00 AM Pacific Standard Time) or	
			TIMESTAMP '1999-04-15 11:00:00 -5:00' (11:00 AM Eastern Standard Time) both are same.	
		3	Syntax: TIMESTAMP [(fractional_seconds_precision)] WITH LOCAL TIME ZONE	
			Example: COL_NAME TIMESTAMP(3) WITH LOCAL TIME ZONE;	
			WITH LOCAL TIME ZONE specifies when you insert values into the database column, value is stored with the time zone of the database.	
			The time-zone displacement is not stored in the column. When you retrieve value from Oracle database, returns it according to your UTC local time zone.	

Boolean Datatypes: - It is used to store boolean values – TRUE or FALSE. It can also store NULL and is considered as unsigned boolean variable. We cannot compare boolean columns of two tables.

```
SELECT * FROM EMP

 WHERE IS_EMPLOYED = (SELECT IS_EMPLOYEED

                              FROM EMP WHERE EMP_NAME = 'John'); -- this query
is not valid
```

Composite Data Types or User Define Data Types

Depending upon the need of the program, the developer combines one or more datatype variables into form a one variable. This type of variables will have multiple same or different base datatypes defined in it. These types of variables are used while coding. This type of datatypes is known as composite or user defined datatypes.

Record is one of the composite datatypes. It can have any number of datatypes within it. One can imagine this as an array with different types of data or as a table itself. Most of the time scalar datatypes are used to create records.

In order to declare a variable as a composite datatype, we have to define the composite datatype according our necessity. Then that datatype can be assigned to other variables to have such records.

```
TYPE record_type_name IS RECORD

(Column1 DATATYPE, Column2 DATATYPE... ColumnN DATATYPE);

TYPE rc_emp IS RECORD

(emp_id NUMBER, emp_name VARCHAR2 (15), date_of_birth DATE); -- An employee re-
cord rc_emp with datatypes number, varchar2 and Date is created.
```

Here rc_emp is the name of the composite datatype. Above is the syntax for creating the composite datatype. Once it is created, it can be assigned to variable in two methods:

- vr_emp_record rc_emp; -- Declares a variable 'vr_emp_record' with three columns of different datatypes. This variable now can hold an array or table of data. Each column inside this variable can be referred as vr_emp_record.emp_id, vr_emp_record.emp_name and vr_emp_record.date_of_birth.

- Another method is to create individual variables for each column in the record type.

```
rc_emp_id vr_emp_record.emp_id%TYPE;

rc_emp_name vr_emp_record.emp_name%TYPE;

rc_date_of_birth vr_emp_record. date_of_birth %TYPE; -- vr_emp_record is a re-
cord type
```

This method of declaration is useful while we have to assign the datatypes of existing table columns. In such case no need to create record types, we can directly use tables to assign the datatypes like below. This will help the developer to automatically assign the datatype of the table columns, and he need not check the datatype of each columns. Also, if there are any changes to datatype or length of the columns, then it will be automatically reflected in the code. No need to change the code in such cases.

```
rc_emp_id EMPLOYEE.emp_id%TYPE;

rc_emp_name EMPLOYEE.emp_name%TYPE;

rc_date_of_birth EMPLOYEE. date_of_birth %TYPE; -- Where EMPLOYEE is a table.
```

Let us consider an example to understand it better.

```
DECLARE

 TYPE rc_emp IS RECORD

        (emp_id NUMBER,

        emp_name VARCHAR2 (15),

        date_of_birth DATE); -- Declaring a record type with user defined columns
```

```
      vr_emp_record rc_emp; -- Declaring a variable of datatype rc_emp
BEGIN

      DBMS_OUTPUT.PUT_LINE ('EMPLOYEE RECORD');

      DBMS_OUTPUT.PUT_LINE ('-------------------------');

      -- Accessing the columns of datatype rc_emp

      DBMS_OUTPUT.PUT_LINE ('Employee ID:' || vr_emp_record.emp_id);

      DBMS_OUTPUT.PUT_LINE ('Employee NAME:' || vr_emp_record.emp_name);

      DBMS_OUTPUT.PUT_LINE ('Employee Date Of Birth:' || vr_emp_record.date_
of_birth);

END;

DECLARE

      rc_emp EMPLOYEE%ROWTYPE; -- Declaring a table record type

      rv_emp_name EMPLOYEE.emp_name%TYPE; --declaring a variable with table
column type

BEGIN

      DBMS_OUTPUT.PUT_LINE ('EMPLOYEE RECORD');

      DBMS_OUTPUT.PUT_LINE ('-------------------------');

      -- Accessing the columns of datatype rc_emp

      DBMS_OUTPUT.PUT_LINE ('Employee ID:' || rc_emp.emp_id);

      DBMS_OUTPUT.PUT_LINE ('Employee NAME:' || rc_emp.emp_name);

      DBMS_OUTPUT.PUT_LINE ('Employee Date Of Birth:' || rc_emp.date_of_birth);

END;
```

Here both the block of codes is same and gives the same output (imagine EMPLOYEE table has only three columns as we defined first). The first block of code uses user defined column datatypes in the record variable whereas second block of code uses table and its column to define the variable datatypes.

Advantage of ROWTYPE	Disadvantage of ROWTYPE
Need not explicitly define the column datatypes. They will be automatically retrieved from the tables.	When a record is created using ROWTYPE, whole of the columns are assigned to the record variable. Memory will be used to create the datatypes of all the columns. The developer might need only few of the columns to code, but other columns are also unnecessarily created in the record.
When table is altered for some column datatypes or column length, it will be automatically reflected in the code. No need to modify the code when there is table change.	

This is how we create a datatype. But it will not have any values of the columns of the table. We have to explicitly assign the values to them. In above blocks of code, we have not assigned any values and it will display nothing. That example was just to demonstrate how to declare and access record variables. We can assign and retrieve values of a record type as follows:

Syntax	Usage
record_name.col_name := value;	To directly assign a value to a specific column of a record or to directly assign value to a specific column of record which is declared using %ROWTYPE.
SELECT col1, col2 INTO record_name.col_name1, record_name.col_name2 FROM table_name [WHERE clause];	To assign the values of each columns to the record columns.
SELECT * INTO record_name FROM table_name [WHERE clause];	To assign the values of each columns or the whole table to a record.
Variable_name := record_name.col_name;	To get a value from a record column and assigning it to a variable.

```
DECLARE

        rc_emp EMPLOYEE%ROWTYPE; -- Declaring a table record type

        rv_emp_name EMPLOYEE.emp_name%TYPE; --declaring a variable with table
column type

BEGIN

        rc_emp.emp_id: = 100; -- Assigning the values

        rc_emp.emp_name: = 'John';

        DBMS_OUTPUT.PUT_LINE ('EMPLOYEE RECORD');

        DBMS_OUTPUT.PUT_LINE ('-------------------------');

        -- Accessing the columns of datatype rc_emp

        DBMS_OUTPUT.PUT_LINE ('Employee ID:' || rc_emp.emp_id);

        DBMS_OUTPUT.PUT_LINE ('Employee NAME:' || rc_emp.emp_name);

END;
```

Similar to Records, we have one more composite datatype called collections. It is similar to arrays and it will have same datatypes. There are three types of collections.

Associative Array or Index by Table: These are two dimensional array with (key, value) pair. Key is a position identifier of each value. The key can be integer or character/string here. We can have any number of (key, value) pair in it. There is no limit for the number of data in this array, hence unbounded. This is the most frequently used type of collections.

```
TYPE index_table IS TABLE OF value_datatype [NOT NULL] INDEX BY key_datatype;

v_ index_table index_table;
```

Above syntax creates a collection with name index_table with values of value_datatype and key with key_datatype. Once the collection is created, collection variable v_index_table is created.

```
DECLARE

TYPE salary_col IS TABLE OF NUMBER INDEX BY VARCHAR2 (20);

 v_salary_list salary_col;

v_name VARCHAR2 (25);

BEGIN

 -- Assigning the data to tables

 salary_list ('Sophia'):= 45000;

 salary_list ('John'):= 75000;

v_name:= salary_list. FIRST; -- Retrieving the first data

DBMS_OUTPUT.PUT_LINE ('Salary of '|| v_name || 'is '|| salary_list (v_name));
--it will display output as 'Salary of Sophia is 45000. It will not display
John's detail. In order to get his details, we have to reassign v_name:= sala-
ry_list. Next and then display

END;
```

Nested Tables: These are like one dimensional array, but we can have any number of records in it. The size of this type increases dynamically as and when we get records. Records are added one after the other in a sequence, but when we delete any record from it, the space for deleted record is not deleted. Hence this type of tables will be dense while inserting the data, and gradually becomes sparse. Nested tables can be used as a column in the table as well as can be used in PL/SQL code.

Syntax for this is as below:

```
TYPE nt_name IS TABLE OF record_datatype [NOT NULL];

table_name nt_name;
```

where record_datatype can be an any DBMS datatypes or it can be any column type of a table.

E.g.; TYPEnt_salary IS TABLE OF NUMBER;

OR TYPE nt_salary IS TABLE OF EMPLOYEE.SALARY%TYPE;

Below program shows how to declare, create and access nested tables:

```
DECLARE

TYPE nt_salary IS TABLE OF NUMBER;

TYPE nt_empname IS TABLE OF VARCHAR2 (20);

 nt_salary_list nt_salary;

 nt_emp_list nt_empname;

BEGIN
```

```
-- Assigning the data to nested tables

nt_emp_list: = nt_empname ('Sophia', 'James', 'Bryan');

nt_salary_list: = nt_salary (20000, 40000, 60000);

-- Retrieving the records of nested table

FOR i IN 1... nt_emp_list.count LOOP -- nt_emp_list.countwill give total number
of records in the nested table

  DBMS_OUTPUT.PUT_LINE ('Salary For '||nt_emp_list (i) || ': '||nt_salary_list
(i));

END LOOP;

END;
```

The Output would be:

- Salary for Sophia: 20000

- Salary for James: 40000

- Salary for Bryan: 60000

Variable array (varray): This is also similar to nested array and can be considered as one dimensional array, provided it has fixed number of records. Unlike nested tables, we have to declare the number of records in this array in advance and can be used in the program. In addition, we cannot delete the individual records of the array. Because of these features, developers are less likely to use this array. They prefer associative array or nested tables in their programs.

Syntax for Varray is:

```
TYPE varray_name IS VARRAY (index) OF DATATYPE;
```

E.g.: - TYPE va_salary IS VARRAY (4) OF NUMBER;

va_salary_list va_salary;

Below program shows how to declare, create and access varray.

```
DECLARE

             TYPE va_salary IS VARRAY (4) OF NUMBER;

             TYPE va_empname IS VARRAY (4) OF VARCHAR2 (20);


va_salary_list va_salary;

va_emp_list va_empname;

BEGIN

-- Assigning the data to varray
```

```
 va_emp_list: = va_empname ('Sophia', 'James', 'Bryan');

va_salary_list: = va_salary (20000, 40000, 60000);

-- Retrieving the records of varray

FOR i IN 1... va_emp_list.count LOOP -- va_emp_list.countwill give total number
of records in the varray

 DBMS_OUTPUT.PUT_LINE ('Salary For '||va_emp_list (i) || ': '||va_salary_list
(i));

END LOOP;

END;
```

The Output would be:

- Salary for Sophia: 20000

- Salary for James: 40000

- Salary for Bryan: 60000

Comparison of three types of collections is given below:

Collection Type	Number of Records	Key Type	Dense or Sparse	Where Created	Can Be Object Type Attribute
Associative array (or index-by table)	Unbounded	String or integer	Either	Only in PL/SQL block	No
Nested table	Unbounded	Integer	Starts dense, can become sparse	Either in PL/SQL block or at schema level	Yes
Variable-size array (Varray)	Bounded	Integer	Always dense	Either in PL/SQL block or at schema level	Yes

Reference Data Types

This datatype refers to the existing data in the program. It acts like pointers to the variable. One of the examples of reference datatype is refcursor. They are the cursor variables used to reference and access the static cursor. We can pass this variable to procedures/functions and get the values from function as a refcursor. In short it acts a variable, but reference to the query defined at the runtime.

```
DECLARE

 TYPE rc_cursor is ref cursor;

       CURSOR c_course IS

              SELECT * FROM COURSE;

 l_cursor rc_cursor;

 n_ID NUMBER;

BEGIN
```

```
    IF n_ID = 10 THEN

    -- Dynamically opens the cursor for student ids less than 10

            Open l_cursor FOR 'SELECT * FROM STUDENT WHERE STD_ID<= 10';

    ELSE

    -- Dynamically opens the cursor for student ids greater than 10

            OPEN l_cursor FOR 'SELECT * FROM STUDENT WHERE STD_ID > 10';

      END IF;

    -- Opens static cursor c_course

      OPEN c_course;

END;
```

LOB Data Types

These types of datatypes are used to store very large amount of data in a column / variable. It can store file like music, graphics etc. We have following types of LOB datatypes:

Datatype	Sub-Datatype	Description	Storage
LOB Data type	BFILE	Used to store large binary objects into Operating System file. BFILE stores full file locator's path which are points to a stored binary object with in server. BFILE data type is read only, you can't modify them.	Size: up to 4GB (232 - 1 bytes)
			Directory name: 30 character
			File name: 255 characters
	BLOB	It is same as BFILE, used to store unstructured binary object into Operating System file. BLOB type fully supported transactions are recoverable and replicated.	Size: 8 TB to 128 TB
			(4GB - 1) * DB_BLOCK_SIZE
	CLOB	Large blocks of character data are stored into Database using this datatype. Store single byte and multi byte character data. CLOB types are fully supported transactions, and are recoverable and replicated.	Size: 8 TB to 128 TB
			(4GB - 1) * DB_BLOCK_SIZE
	NCLOB	NCLOB data type to store large blocks of NCHAR data into Database. Store single byte and multi byte character data. NCLOB type fully supported transactions are recoverable and replicated.	Size: 8 TB to 128 TB
			(4GB - 1) * DB_BLOCK_SIZE

Unknown Column Types

We have seen this in the user defined datatypes to declare the variables. This is called unknown columns because this type of datatypes is not base datatypes and is defined by the user or tables. The developer does not predict the datatype of it just by seeing name or declaration. He has to see the definition of record datatype to understand it.

Datatype	Sub-Datatype	Description	
Unknown Column Datatypes	%TYPE	Used to store single column with unknown datatype. Column is identified by %TYPE data type.	
		E.g. EMP.ENO%TYPE	
	%ROWTYPE	Stores the datatype of all the columns in a table. All columns are identified by %ROWTYPE datatype.	
		E.g. EMP%ROWTYPE--> a table will be assigned with the EMP table's entire column datatypes.	
	%ROWID	ROWID is data type. ROWID is two type extended or restricted. Extended ROWID return 0 and restricted ROWID return 1 otherwise return the row number.	
		Some functions are defined on ROWID and are defined in DBMS_ROWID package.	
		Function ROWID	Description
		ROWID_VERIFY	Verifies that if the ROWID can be extended.
		ROWID_TYPE	0 = ROWID, 1 = extended.
		ROWID_BLOCK_NUMBER	Block number that contain the record return 1.
		ROWID_OBJECT	Number of the object that are in the record.
		ROWID_RELATIVE_FNUMBER	Returns the Relative file number that contains record.
		ROWID_ROW_NUMBER	Row number of the Record.
		ROWID_TO_ABSOLUTE_FNUMBER	Return the absolute file number.
		ROWID_TO_EXTENDED	Converts the ROWID to extended format.
		ROWID_TO_RESTRICTED	Converts the ROWID to restricted format.

Variables

Variables are used to store the data temporarily in a program. They act as an intermediary place holder to hold the results while manipulating the data in the program. Each variable will have datatype depending on the kind of data that we are going to store. Datatypes will be same as column datatypes that we saw above.

Syntax for declaring a variable is,

Variable_name DATATYPE;

We can even assign default value to the variable. When a variable is declared as NOT NULL, default value has to be assigned.

```
Variable_name DATATYPE: = value;

Variable_name DATATYPE NOT NULL: = value;

n_age NUMBER NOT NULL: = 18;

v_name VARCHAR2 (25);
```

In a program, we can either directly assign value to a variable or we can use it in a query to get the value of columns into it.

```
n_age: = 20;                          SELECT NAME, AGE
                          OR            INTO v_name, n_
v_name: = 'Sophia';                   FROM PERSON
                                       WHERE SSN=12343;
```

Scope of Variables

In a PL/SQL program, we can have multiple blocks i.e.; it has multiple BEGIN – END blocks one inside another. When variables are declared in these blocks, they act with respect to their blocks.

A variable declared inside a block is accessible to that block alone. Such variables are called local variables. They cannot be accessed by any outer blocks. When we have inner blocks, then we can access the variables declared by its outer blocks. Such variables are called global variables.

```
DECLARE

        n_age NUMBER; -- Global Variable

BEGIN

        SELECT AGE INTO n_age FROM PERSON WHERE SSN = 323234;

        DECLARE

        v_name VARCHAR2 (30); -- Local Variable, accessible only inside this
block

        BEGIN

                SELECT PERS_NAME

                        INTO v_name

                 FROM PERSON WHERE SSN = 323234;

                DBMS_OUTPUT.PUT_LINE ('Name of the Person is '|| v_name);

        END;

DBMS_OUTPUT.PUT_LINE ('Age of the Person is '|| v_name);

END;
```

Constants

As the name suggests, they are constant in the program. They are variables with literal value and their remains unchanged throughout the program. These are used to reduce the use of actual values again and again in the program. Declaring a constant and assigning a value once at the beginning, and then using constant throughout the program, makes program clean and understandable.

Also, if there is any change to the constant value, we have to change only at one place rather than changing all the code till the end.

Syntax for constant is:

```
constant_name CONSTANT DATATYPE: = value; -- value has to be assigned without
fail, since it is a constant

        pi CONSTANT NUMBER (2, 2): = 3.14;

        incr_percentage CONSTANT NUMBER: = 10;

        declared_holiday CONSTANT VARCHAR2 (7): = 'SUNDAY';
```

In a program these constants are used as any regular variable. Only difference from variable is that we cannot change the value of the constant.

Database Accessing

When a transaction is executed, then different memory blocks are assigned to the transaction to hold the data. The data residing in the database are stored in the physical memory like hard disk. The data location in the physical memory is called as physical blocks. When a transaction retrieves the data from these physical blocks, the same is copied to the main memory and are stored in buffer blocks. These are temporary storage blocks and are helpful in accessing the data again and again. This reduces the access to physical blocks and hence time/cost are also reduced.

Let B be a block in the memory. Then input (B) implies transferring the data from the physical block B to the buffer block in the main memory. Output (B) implies transferring the data from buffer block to main memory for permanently updating it in the database. In addition some memory blocks are assigned to each transaction in the main memory to in which it can hold the data items temporarily. This memory blocks are called as work area of the transactions. This is depicted in below diagram.

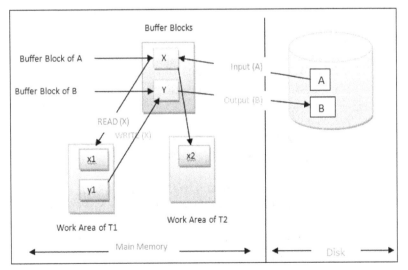

We can observe in above diagram that, when a transaction T1 wants to access the data item A, it is retrieved from the physical memory (input (A)) into buffer block X in the main memory. Then the local copy of it is created, x1 and assigned to the work area of T1. Similarly, result of transaction T1

is stored in the local variable y1 and is transferred to buffer block, Y. It is then updated to disk by output (B). This is how data items are transferred when a transaction is being processed.

Data Structure

A data structure is a specialized format for organizing, processing, retrieving and storing data. While there are several basic and advanced structure types, any data structure is designed to arrange data to suit a specific purpose so that it can be accessed and worked with in appropriate ways.

In computer programming, a data structure may be selected or designed to store data for the purpose of working on it with various algorithms. Each data structure contains information about the data values, relationships between the data and functions that can be applied to the data.

Characteristics of Data Structures

Data structures are often classified by their characteristics. Possible characteristics are:

- Linear or non-linear: This characteristic describes whether the data items are arranged in chronological sequence, such as with an array, or in an unordered sequence, such as with a graph.

- Homogeneous or non-homogeneous: This characteristic describes whether all data items in a given repository are of the same type or of various types.

- Static or dynamic: This characteristic describes how the data structures are compiled. Static data structures have fixed sizes, structures and memory locations at compile time. Dynamic data structures have sizes, structures and memory locations that can shrink or expand depending on the use.

Types of Data Structures

Data structure types are determined by what types of operations are required or what kinds of algorithms are going to be applied. These types include:

- Arrays: An array stores a collection of items at adjoining memory locations. Items that are the same type get stored together so that the position of each element can be calculated or retrieved easily. Arrays can be fixed or flexible in length.

- Stacks: A stack stores a collection of items in the linear order that operations are applied. This order could be last in first out (LIFO) or first in first out (FIFO).

- Queues: A queue stores a collection of items similar to a stack; however, the operation order can only be first in first out.

- Linked lists: A linked list stores a collection of items in a linear order. Each element, or node, in a linked list contains a data item as well as a reference, or link, to the next item in the list.

- Trees: A tree stores a collection of items in an abstract, hierarchical way. Each node is linked to other nodes and can have multiple sub-values, also known as children.

- Graphs: A graph stores a collection of items in a non-linear fashion. Graphs are made up of a finite set of nodes, also known as vertices, and lines that connect them, also known as edges. These are useful for representing real-life systems such as computer networks.

- Tries: A trie, or keyword tree, is a data structure that stores strings as data items that can be organized in a visual graph.

- Hash tables: A hash table, or a hash map, stores a collection of items in an associative array that plots keys to values. A hash table uses a hash function to convert an index into an array of buckets that contain the desired data item.

These are considered complex data structures as they can store large amounts of interconnected data. Examples of primitive, or basic, data structures are integers, floats, Booleans and characters.

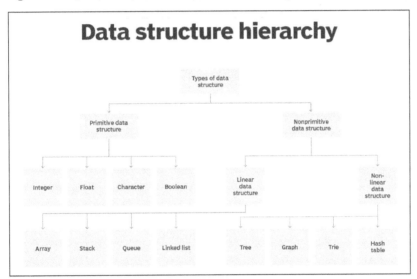

Uses of Data Structures

In general, data structures are used to implement the physical forms of abstract data types. This can be translated into a variety of applications, such as displaying a relational database as a binary tree.

In programming languages, data structures are used to organize code and information in a digital space. For example, Python lists and dictionaries or JavaScript array and objects are common coding structures used for storing and retrieving information. Data structures are also a crucial part of designing efficient software.

Importance of Data Structures

Data structures are essential for managing large amounts of data, such as information kept in databases or indexing services, efficiently. Proper maintenance of data systems requires the identification of memory allocation, data interrelationships and data processes, all of which data structures help with.

Additionally, it is not only important to use data structures but it is important to choose the proper data structure for each task. Choosing an ill-suited data structure could result in slow runtimes or unresponsive code. A few factors to consider when picking a data structure include what kind of information will be stored, where should existing data be placed, how should data be sorted and how much memory should be reserved for the data.

Database Schema

A database schema represents the logical configuration of all or part of a relational database. It can exist both as a visual representation and as a set of formulas known as integrity constraints that govern a database. These formulas are expressed in a data definition language, such as SQL. As part of a data dictionary, a database schema indicates how the entities that make up the database relate to one another, including tables, views, stored procedures, and more.

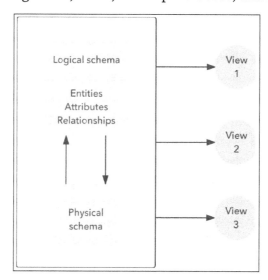

Typically, a database designer creates a database schema to help programmers whose software will interact with the database. The process of creating a database schema is called data modeling. When following the three-schema approach to database design, this step would follow the creation of a conceptual schema. Conceptual schemas focus on an organization's informational needs rather than the structure of a database.

There are two main kinds of database schema:

- A logical database schema conveys the logical constraints that apply to the stored data. It may define integrity constraints, views, and tables.

- A physical database schema lays out how data is stored physically on a storage system in terms of files and indices.

At the most basic level, a database schema indicates which tables or relations make up the database, as well as the fields included on each table. Thus, the terms schema diagram and entity-relationship diagram are often interchangeable.

Schema in Oracle Database System

In the Oracle database system, the term database schema, which is also known as "SQL schema," has a different meaning. Here, a database can have multiple schemas (or "schemata," if you're feeling fancy). Each one contains all the objects created by a specific database user. Those objects may include tables, views, synonyms, and more. Some objects cannot be included in a schema, such as users, contexts, roles, and directory objects.

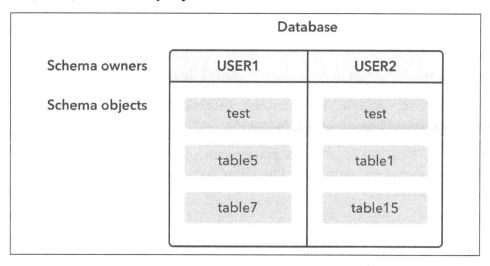

Users can be granted access to log into individual schemas on a case-by-case basis, and ownership is transferable. Since each object is associated with a particular schema, which serves as a kind of namespace, it's helpful to give some synonyms, which allows other users to access that object without first referring to the schema it belongs to.

These schemas do not necessarily indicate the ways that the datafiles are stored physically. Instead, schema objects are stored logically within a tablespace. The database administrator can specify how much space to assign to a particular object within a datafile.

Finally, schemas and tablespaces don't necessarily line up perfectly: objects from one schema can be found in multiple tablespaces, while a tablespace can include objects from several schemas.

Schema Integration Requirements

It can be useful to integrate multiple sources into a single schema. Make sure these requirements are met for a seamless transition:

Overlap Preservation

Every overlapping element in the schemas you are integrating should be in a database schema table.

Extended Overlap Preservation

Elements that only appear in one source, but that are associated with overlapping elements, should be copied to the resulting database schema.

Normalization

Independent relationships and entities should not be lumped together in the same table in the database schema.

Minimality

It's ideal if none of the elements in any of the sources are lost.

Types of Database schema

Certain patterns have developed in designing database schema.

The widely used star schema is also the simplest. In it, one or more fact tables are linked to any number of dimensional tables. It's best for handling simple queries.

The related snowflake schema is also used to represent a multidimensional database. In this pattern, however, dimensions are normalized into lots of separate tables, creating the expansive effect of a snowflake-like structure.

Database Instance

The term "database instance" means different things to different vendors. Its most frequently used in connection with Oracle database implementations.

General Meaning of a Database Instance

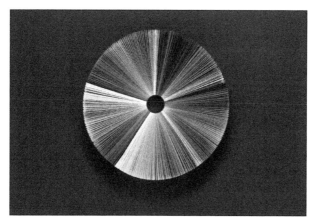

In general, a database instance describes a complete database environment, including the RDBMS software, table structure, stored procedures, and other functionality. Database administrators might create multiple instances of the same database for different purposes.

For example, an organization with an employee's database might have three different instances: production (used to contain live data), pre-production (used to test new functionality prior to release into production) and development (used by database developers to create new functionality).

Oracle Database Instances

If you have an Oracle database, you know that a database instance means a very specific thing.

While the database itself includes all the application data and metadata stored in physical files on a server, an instance is a combination of the software and memory used to access that data.

For example, if you sign in to an Oracle database, your login session is an instance. If you log off or shut down your computer, your instance disappears, but the database and all your data remain intact. An Oracle instance can access only one database at a time, while an Oracle database can be accessed by multiple instances.

SQL Server Instances

A SQL Server instance usually means a specific installation of SQL Server. It is not the database itself; rather, it is the software used to create the database. Maintaining multiple instances might be useful when managing server resources because each instance can be configured for memory and CPU usage, which is something you can't do for individual databases within a SQL Server instance.

Database Scheme vs. Database Instance

It may also be useful to think of an instance in context with a database scheme. The scheme is the metadata that defines the database design and how the data will be organized. This includes its tables and their columns and any rules that govern the data. For instance, an employee table in a database might have columns for name, address, employee ID and job descriptions. This is the structure, or scheme, of the database.

An instance of the database is a snapshot of the actual content at any given time, including the data itself and its relationship to other data in the database.

Entity-relationship Data Model

The ER or (Entity Relational Model) is a high-level conceptual data model diagram. Entity-Relation model is based on the notion of real-world entities and the relationship between them.

ER modeling helps you to analyze data requirements systematically to produce a well-designed database. So, it is considered a best practice to complete ER modeling before implementing your database.

ER Diagrams

Entity relationship diagram displays the relationships of entity set stored in a database. In other words, we can say that ER diagrams help you to explain the logical structure of databases. At first look, an ER diagram looks very similar to the flowchart. However, ER Diagram includes many specialized symbols, and its meanings make this model unique.

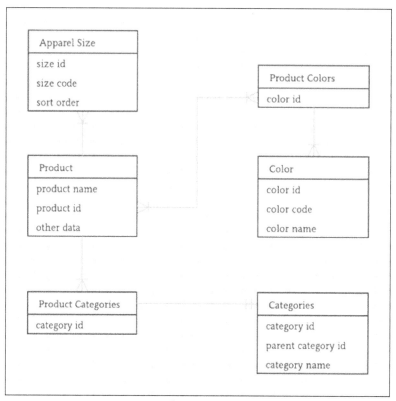

Sample ER Diagram.

Facts about ER Diagram Model

- ER model allows you to draw Database Design.

- It is an easy to use graphical tool for modeling data.

- Widely used in Database Design.

- It is a GUI representation of the logical structure of a Database.

- It helps you to identify the entities which exist in a system and the relationships between those entities.

Reason for using ER Diagrams

Here, are prime reasons for using the ER Diagram:

- Helps you to define terms related to entity relationship modeling.

- Provide a preview of how all your tables should connect, what fields are going to be on each table.

- Helps to describe entities, attributes, relationships.

- ER diagrams are translatable into relational tables which allow you to build databases quickly.

- ER diagrams can be used by database designers as a blueprint for implementing data in specific software applications.

- The database designer gains a better understanding of the information to be contained in the database with the help of ERP diagram.

- ERD is allowed you to communicate with the logical structure of the database to users.

Components of the ER Diagram

This model is based on three basic concepts:

- Entities,

- Attributes,

- Relationships.

Example:

For example, in a University database, we might have entities for Students, Courses, and Lecturers. Students entity can have attributes like Rollno, Name, and DeptID. They might have relationships with Courses and Lecturers.

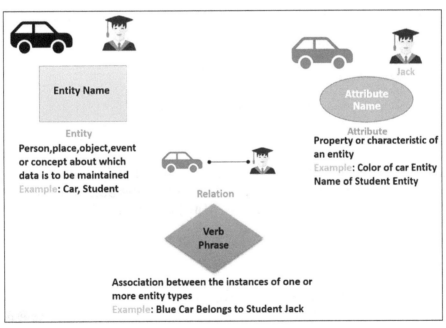

Entity

An entity is an object in the real world with an independent existence that can be differentiated from other objects. An entity might be:

- An object with physical existence (e.g., a lecturer, a student, a car).

- An object with conceptual existence (e.g., a course, a job, a position).

Entities can be classified based on their strength. An entity is considered weak if its tables are existence dependent.

- That is, it cannot exist without a relationship with another entity.

- Its primary key is derived from the primary key of the parent entity.

  ○ The Spouse table, in the COMPANY database, is a weak entity because its primary key is dependent on the Employee table. Without a corresponding employee record, the spouse record would not exist.

An entity is considered strong if it can exist apart from all of its related entities.

- Kernels are strong entities.

- A table without a foreign key or a table that contains a foreign key that can contain nulls is a strong entity.

Another term to know is entity type which defines a collection of similar entities.

An entity set is a collection of entities of an entity type at a particular point of time. In an entity relationship diagram (ERD), an entity type is represented by a name in a box.

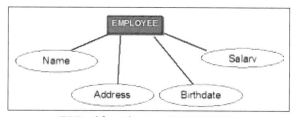

ERD with entity type EMPLOYEE.

Existence Dependency

An entity's existence is dependent on the existence of the related entity. It is existence-dependent if it has a mandatory foreign key (i.e., a foreign key attribute that cannot be null). For example, in the COMPANY database, a Spouse entity is existence -dependent on the Employee entity.

Kinds of Entities

You should also be familiar with different kinds of entities including independent entities, dependent entities and characteristic entities.

Independent Entities

Independent entities, also referred to as kernels, are the backbone of the database. They are what other tables are based on. Kernels have the following characteristics:

- They are the building blocks of a database.

- The primary key may be simple or composite.

- The primary key is not a foreign key.

- They do not depend on another entity for their existence.

Dependent Entities

Dependent entities, also referred to as derived entities, depend on other tables for their meaning. These entities have the following characteristics:

- Dependent entities are used to connect two kernels together.

- They are said to be existence dependent on two or more tables.

- Many to many relationships become associative tables with at least two foreign keys.

- They may contain other attributes.

- The foreign key identifies each associated table.

- There are three options for the primary key:

  ◦ Use a composite of foreign keys of associated tables if unique.

  ◦ Use a composite of foreign keys and a qualifying column.

  ◦ Create a new simple primary key.

Characteristic Entities

Characteristic entities provide more information about another table. These entities have the following characteristics:

- They represent multivalued attributes.

- They describe other entities.

- They typically have a one to many relationships.

- The foreign key is used to further identify the characterized table.

- Options for primary key are as follows:

  ◦ Use a composite of foreign key plus a qualifying column.

  ◦ Create a new simple primary key. In the COMPANY database, these might include:

    ▪ Employee (EID, Name, Address, Age, Salary) – EID is the simple primary key.

    ▪ Employee Phone (EID, Phone) – EID is part of a composite primary key. Here, EID is also a foreign key.

Relationship

A relationship is an association that exists between two entities. For example, Instructor teaches

Class or Student attends Class. Most relationships can also be stated inversely. For example, Class is taught by Instructor.

The relationships on an Entity-Relationship Diagram are represented by lines drawn between the entities involved in the association. The name of the relationship is placed either above, below, or beside the line.

Relationships between Entities

There can be a simple relationship between two entities. For example, Student attends a Class.

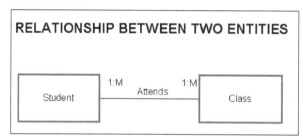

Some relationships involve only one entity. For example, Employee reports to Employee.

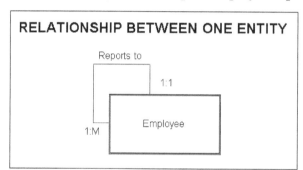

This type of relationship is called a recursive relationship.

There can be a number of different relationships between the same two entities. For example:

- Employee is assigned to a Project,

- Employee bills to a Project.

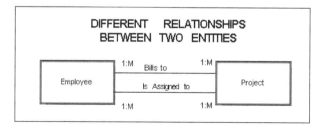

One entity can participate in a number of different relationships involving different entities. For example:

- Project Manager manages a Project,

- Project Manager reports to Project Director,

- Project Manager approves Employee Time.

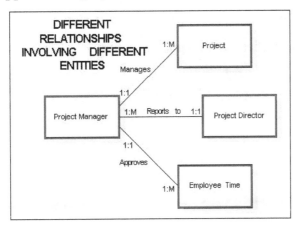

Characteristics of Relationships

A relationship may be depicted in a variety of ways to improve the accuracy of the representation of the real world. The major aspects of a relationship are:

Relationship Title

Naming the Relationship

Place a name for the relationship on the line representing the relationship on the E-R diagram. Use a simple but meaningful action verb (e.g., buys, places, takes) to name the relationship. Assign relationship names that are significant to the business or that are commonly understood in every-day language.

Bi-directional Relationships

Whenever possible, use the active form of the verb to name the relationship. Note that all relationships are bi-directional. In one direction, the active form of the verb applies. In the opposite direction, the passive form applies.

For example, the relationship Employee operates Machine is named using the active verb operates:

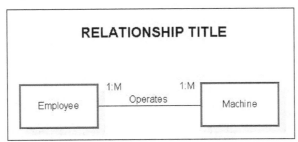

However, the relationship Machine is operated by Employee also applies. This is the passive form of the verb.

By convention, the passive form of the relationship name is not included on the E-R diagram. This helps avoid clutter on the diagram.

Relationship Cardinality

Relationship cardinality identifies the maximum number of instances in which an entity participates in a relationship.

There are three types of relationship cardinality:

- One-to-one,
- One-to-many,
- Many-to-many.

One-to-One (1:1)

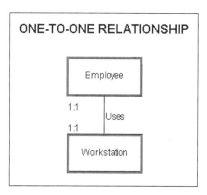

A one-to-one relationship between two entities indicates that each occurrence of one entity in the relationship is associated with a single occurrence in the related entity. There is a one-to-one mapping between the two, such that knowing the value of one entity gives you the value of the second. For example, in this relationship an Employee uses a maximum of one Workstation.

One-to-Many (1:M), Many-to-One (M:1)

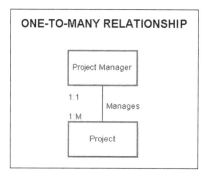

A one-to-many or a many-to-one relationship between two entities indicates that a single occurrence of one entity is associated with one or more occurrences of the related entity. The example indicates that there is one Project Manager associated with each Project, and that each Project Manager may be associated with more than one Project.

Many-to-Many (M:M)

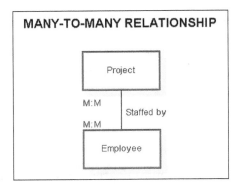

A many-to-many relationship between two entities indicates that either entity participating in the relationship may occur one or several times. The example indicates that there may be more than one Employee associated with each Project, and that each Employee may be associated with more than one Project at a time. That is, projects may share employees.

It is appropriate to identify and illustrate many-to-many relationships at the conceptual level of detail. Such relationships are broken down to one-to-many relationships at the logical level of detail. For example, at the logical level the many-to-many relationship above is better represented by introducing a new entity such as Assignment and splitting the many-to-many into two one-to-many relationships. The new entity Assignment contains the primary keys of Project and Employee.

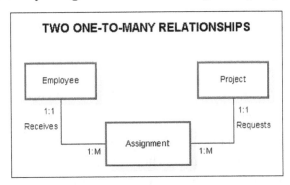

In this manner, useful data regarding a specific employee's contribution to a specific project is accommodated in the Assignment entity.

This refinement is a normal part of entity analysis leading to the discovery of new entities. Many-to-many relationships must be decomposed into one-to-many relationships to implement the physical data model. An associative entity is created to record the relationship between the two entities.

Foreign Keys

To relate one entity to another, make the primary key of one entity an attribute of the other entity (foreign key).

In a one-to-one relationship the foreign key may be placed in either of the entities. In a one-to-many or many-to-one relationship the foreign key is placed in the entity that has the many relationship.

Relationship Dependency

Types of Relationship Dependencies

Three relationship dependencies are possible:

- Mandatory,

- Optional,

- Contingent.

Relationship dependencies may be of different degrees. Each relationship dependency is illustrated differently.

Mandatory Relationship

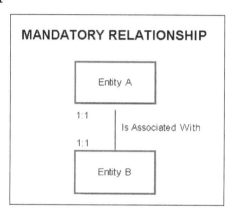

A mandatory relationship indicates that for every occurrence of entity A there must exist an entity B, and vice versa.

When specifying a relationship as being mandatory one-to-one, you are imposing requirements known as integrity constraints. For example, there is one Project Manager associated with each Project, and each Project Manager is associated with one Project at a time. A Project Manager may not be removed if the removal causes a Project to be without a Project Manager. If a Project Manager must be removed, its corresponding project must also be removed. A Project may not be removed if it leaves a Project Manager without a Project. A new project may be added if it can be managed by an existing Project Manager. If there is no Project Manager to manage the Project, a Project Manager must be added with the addition of a new Project.

When specifying a relationship as being mandatory one-to-many or many-to-one, you are imposing integrity constraints. For example, an Employee is assigned one too many tasks and a task is assigned to one and only one Employee. There would not be a Task without an Employee, and there would not be an Employee without a Task. Similarly, if an Employee is added, Task must be added.

Some relationships are naturally or inherently mandatory. For example, consider the relationship Mother has Child. There would not be a Child without a Mother, nor would there be a Mother without a Child.

Other relationships are mandatory due to legislative or business rules, such as "a project is not considered to exist until it has been assigned a budget." This type of mandatory relationship should be analyzed to assess whether or not the rule is a temporary or unnecessary restriction.

Optional Relationship

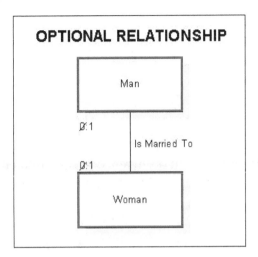

An optional relationship between two entities indicates that it is not necessary for every entity occurrence to participate in the relationship. In other words, for both entities the minimum number of instances in which each participates, in each instance of the relationship is zero (o).

As an example, consider the relationship Man is married to Woman. Both entities may be depicted in an Entity-Relationship Model because they are of interest to the organization. However, not every man, or woman, is necessarily married. In this relationship, if an employee is not married to another employee in the organization, the relationship could not be shown.

The optional relationship is useful for depicting changes over time where relationships may exist one day but not the next. For example, consider the relationship "Employee attends Training Seminar." There is a period of time when an Employee is not attending a Training Seminar or a Training Seminar may not be held.

Optional relationships may be unnecessary if an entity can be subdivided into subtypes or entirely different entities. For example, the entity Person could represent both employees and dependents in a superannuation system. In the wider aspects of a personnel system, an optional relationship would be necessary to link Person to Job. However, breaking down the Person entity into the separate entities Employee (which would have a mandatory relationship to Job), and Dependent (which would not be involved in such a relationship), provides a clearer representation.

Contingent Relationship

A contingent relationship represents an association which is mandatory for one of the involved entities, but optional for the other. In other words, for one of the entities the minimum number of instances that it participates in each instance of the relationship is one (1), the mandatory association, and for the other entity the minimum number of instances that it participates in each instance of the relationship is zero (o), the optional association.

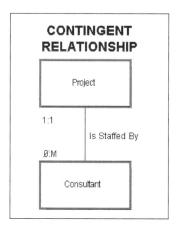

For example, consider the relationship Man fathers Child. Not all occurrences of the entity Man will have produced a child. However, if an occurrence of the Child entity exists, it must be related to a Man entity. This is an inherent or natural contingent relationship.

Contingent relationships may exist due to business rules, such as Project is staffed by Consultant.

In this case, a Project may or may not be staffed by a Consultant. However, if a Consultant is registered in the system, a business rule may state that a Consultant must be associated with a Project.

Relationship Combinations with other Relationships

Types of Relationship Combinations

Entities are often involved in a variety of relationships. Optional relationships are often affected by the existence of another relationship.

Clarify the nature of two or more relationships concerned with a particular entity by one of the following combinations:

- Inclusive OR (either or both),

- Exclusive OR (either, but not both),

- AND (both must exist).

Inclusive OR

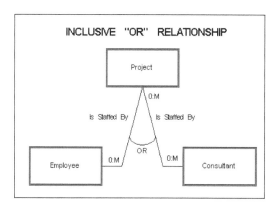

An inclusive OR relationship indicates that entity A is related to either entity B or entity C or both B and C.

In the example, the project team may be composed of employees, consultants, or both.

Exclusive OR

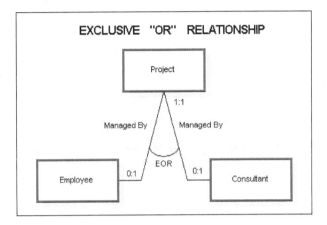

An exclusive OR relationship indicates that entity A is related to either entity B or entity C but not both B and C.

In the example, a project can only be managed by one person, either an employee or a consultant.

AND

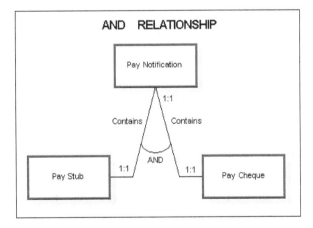

An AND relationship indicates that entity A is related to both entity B and entity C.

In the example, the pay notification contains both the stub and the cheque. Note that this is a different situation to identifying entity subtypes in that the cheque is not simply one type of notification.

Attribute

Attributes are the properties which define the entity type. For example, Roll_No, Name, DOB, Age, Address, Mobile_No are the attributes which defines entity type Student. In ER diagram, attribute is represented by an oval.

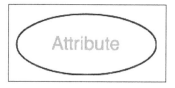

Key Attribute

The attribute which uniquely identifies each entity in the entity set is called key attribute. For example, Roll_No will be unique for each student. In ER diagram, key attribute is represented by an oval with underlying lines.

Composite Attribute

An attribute composed of many other attribute is called as composite attribute. For example, Address attribute of student Entity type consists of Street, City, State, and Country. In ER diagram, composite attribute is represented by an oval comprising of ovals.

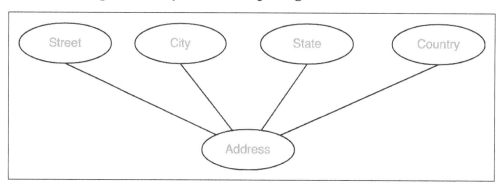

Multivalued Attribute

An attribute consisting more than one value for a given entity. For example, Phone_No (can be more than one for a given student). In ER diagram, multivalued attribute is represented by double oval.

Derived Attribute

An attribute which can be derived from other attributes of the entity type is known as derived attribute. e.g.; Age (can be derived from DOB). In ER diagram, derived attribute is represented by dashed oval.

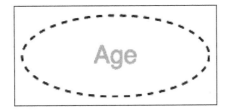

The complete entity type Student with its attributes can be represented as:

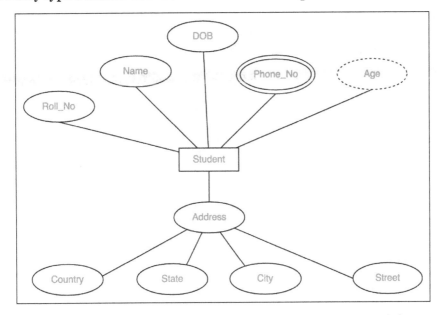

Cardinality

Cardinality defines the possible number of occurrences in one entity which is associated with the number of occurrences in another. For example, ONE team has MANY players. When present in an ERD, the entity Team and Player are inter-connected with a one-to-many relationship. In an ER diagram, cardinality is represented as a crow's foot at the connector's ends. The three common cardinal relationships are one-to-one, one-to-many, and many-to-many.

Types of Cardinality Ratios

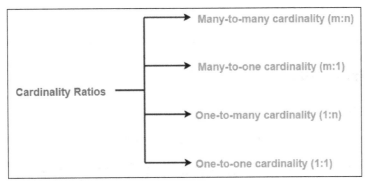

There are four types of cardinality ratios:

- Many-to-Many cardinality (m:n).

- Many-to-One cardinality (m:1).

- One-to-Many cardinality (1:n).

- One-to-One cardinality (1:1).

Many-to-Many Cardinality

By this cardinality constraint,

- An entity in set A can be associated with any number (zero or more) of entities in set B.

- An entity in set B can be associated with any number (zero or more) of entities in set A.

Symbol used:

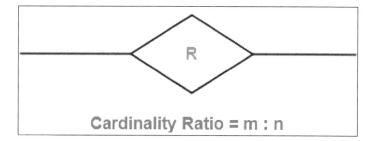

Example:

Consider the following ER diagram:

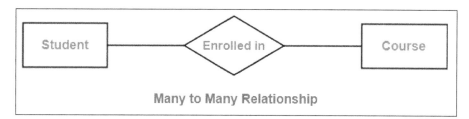

here,

- One student can enroll in any number (zero or more) of courses.

- One course can be enrolled by any number (zero or more) of students.

Many-to-One Cardinality

By this cardinality constraint,

- An entity in set A can be associated with at most one entity in set B.

- An entity in set B can be associated with any number (zero or more) of entities in set A.

Symbol used:

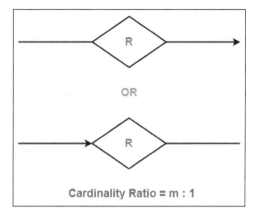

Example:

Consider the following ER diagram:

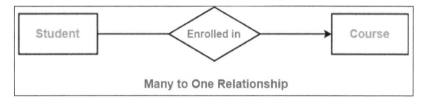

here,

- One student can enroll in at most one course.

- One course can be enrolled by any number (zero or more) of students.

One-to-Many Cardinality

By this cardinality constraint:

- An entity in set A can be associated with any number (zero or more) of entities in set B.

- An entity in set B can be associated with at most one entity in set A.

Symbol used:

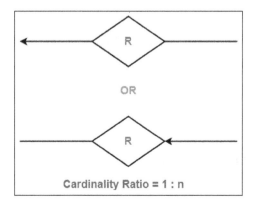

Example:

Consider the following ER diagram:

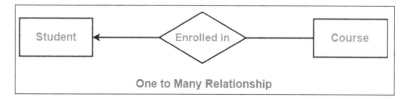

One to Many Relationship

here:

- One student can enroll in any number (zero or more) of courses.

- One course can be enrolled by at most one student.

One-to-One Cardinality

By this cardinality constraint:

- An entity in set A can be associated with at most one entity in set B.

- An entity in set B can be associated with at most one entity in set A.

Symbol used:

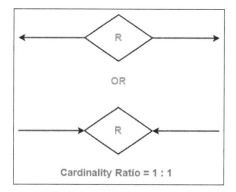

Cardinality Ratio = 1 : 1

Example:

Consider the following ER diagram:

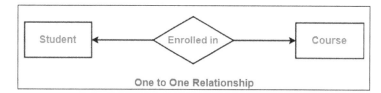

One to One Relationship

here:

- One student can enroll in at most one course.

- One course can be enrolled by at most one student.

Enhanced Entity-relationship Model

Today's time the complexity of the data is increasing so it becomes more and more difficult to use the traditional ER model for database modeling. To reduce this complexity of modeling we have to make improvements or enhancements were made to the existing ER model to make it able to handle the complex application in a better way.

Enhanced entity-relationship diagrams are advanced database diagrams very similar to regular ER diagrams which represents requirements and complexities of complex databases.

It is a diagrammatic technique for displaying the Sub Class and Super Class; Specialization and Generalization; Union or Category; Aggregation etc.

Generalization and Specialization

These are very common relationship found in real entities. However this kind of relationships was added later as enhanced extension to classical ER model. Specialized class are often called as sub-class while generalized class are called superclass, probably inspired by object oriented programming. A sub-class is best understood by "IS-A analysis". Following statements hopefully makes some sense to your mind "Technician IS-A Employee", "Laptop IS-A Computer".

An entity is specialized type/class of other entity. For example, Technician is special Employee in a university system Faculty is special class of Employee. We call this phenomenon as generalization/specialization. In the example here Employee is generalized entity class while Technician and Faculty are specialized class of Employee.

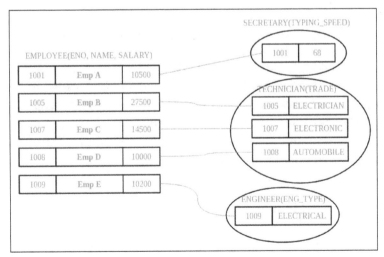

Example – This example instance of "sub-class" relationships. Here we have four sets employee: Secretary, Technician, and Engineer. Employee is super-class of rest three set of individual sub-class is subset of Employee set.

An entity belonging to a sub-class is related with some super-class entity. For instance emp no 1001 is a secretary, and his typing speed is 68. Emp no 1009 is engineer (sub-class) and her trade is "Electrical", so forth.

Sub-class entity "inherits" all attributes of super-class; for example employee 1001 will have attributes eno, name, salary, and typing speed.

Enhanced ER Model of above Example

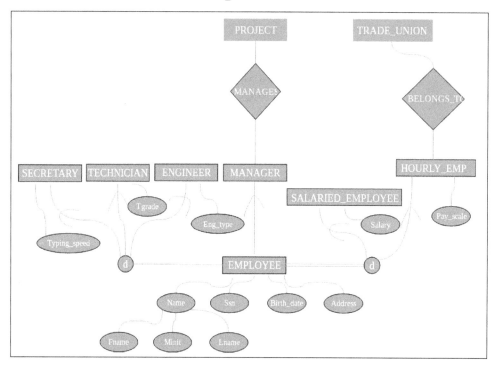

Constraints

There are two types of constraints on "Sub-class" relationship:

- Total or Partial: A sub-classing relationship is total if every super-class entity is to be associated with some sub-class entity, otherwise partial. Sub-class "job type based employee category" is partial sub-classing – not necessary every employee is one of (secretary, engineer, and technician), i.e. union of these three types is proper subset of all employees. Whereas other sub-classing "Salaried Employee AND Hourly Employee" is total; union of entities from sub-classes is equal to total employee set, i.e. every employee necessarily has to be one of them.

- Overlapped or Disjoint: If an entity from super-set can be related (can occur) in multiple sub-class sets, then it is overlapped sub-classing, otherwise disjoint. Both the examples: job-type based and salaries/hourly employee sub-classing are disjoint.

These constraints are independent of each other: can be "overlapped and total or partial" or "disjoint and total or partial". Also sub-classing has transitive property.

Multiple Inheritances (Sub-class of Multiple Super Classes)

An entity can be sub-class of multiple entity types; such entities are sub-class of multiple entities and have multiple super-classes; Teaching Assistant can subclass of Employee and Student both.

A faculty in a university system can be sub-class of Employee and Alumnus both. In multiple inheritance, attributes of sub-class is union of attributes of all super-classes.

Union

- Set of Library Members is UNION of Faculty, Student, and Staff. A union relationship indicates either of type; for example: a library member is either Faculty or Staff or Student.

- Below are two examples shows how UNION can be depicted in ERD – Vehicle Owner is UNION of PERSON and Company, and RTO Registered Vehicle is UNION of Car and Truck.

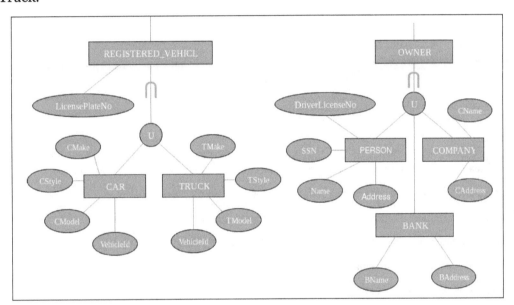

You might see some confusion in Sub-class and UNION; consider example in above figure Vehicle is super-class of CAR and Truck; this is very much the correct example of subclass as well but here use it different we are saying RTO Registered vehicle is UNION of Car and Vehicle, they do not inherit any attribute of Vehicle, attributes of car and truck are altogether independent set, where is in sub-classing situation car and truck would be inheriting the attribute of vehicle class.

Semantic Data Model

The semantic data model is a method of structuring data in order to represent it in a specific logical way. It is a conceptual data model that includes semantic information that adds a basic meaning to the data and the relationships that lie between them. This approach to data modeling and data organization allows for the easy development of application programs and also for the easy maintenance of data consistency when data is updated.

The semantic data model is a relatively new approach that is based on semantic principles that result in a data set with inherently specified data structures. Usually, singular data or a word does not convey any meaning to humans, but paired with a context this word inherits more meaning.

In a database environment, the context of data is often defined mainly by its structure, such as its properties and relationships with other objects. So, in a relational approach, the vertical structure of the data is defined by explicit referential constraints, but in semantic modeling this structure is defined in an inherent way, which is to say that a property of the data itself may coincide with a reference to another object.

A semantic data model may be illustrated graphically through an abstraction hierarchy diagram, which shows data types as boxes and their relationships as lines. This is done hierarchically so that types that reference other types are always listed above the types that they are referencing, which makes it easier to read and understand.

Abstractions used in a semantic data model:

- Classification - "instance_of" relations.

- Aggregation - "has_a" relations.

- Generalization - "is_a" relations.

References

- Database-design-phase-2-conceptual-design: mariadb.com, Retrieved 02 June, 2019

- Concepts-of-database-architecture: medium.com, Retrieved 07 May, 2019

- Datatypes-variables, dbms: tutorialcup.com, Retrieved 08 March, 2019

- Data-structure: searchsqlserver.techtarget.com, Retrieved 25 February, 2019

- Database-schema, database-diagram: lucidchart.com, Retrieved 20 June, 2019

- Database-instance-1019612: lifewire.com, Retrieved 15 July, 2019

- Er-diagram-tutorial-dbms: guru99.com, Retrieved 15 May, 2019

- Understanding-relationships-in-e-r-diagrams-020607: it.toolbox.com, Retrieved 16 August, 2019

- Enhanced-er-model: geeksforgeeks.org, Retrieved 22 April, 2019

Database Application Development

Database application development is used for inserting and retrieving data from a computerized database. Rule wizard framework, user interface design and format, and form creation are some aspects that fall under its domain. This chapter discusses in detail these concepts related to database application development.

Database applications are software programs designed to collect, manage and disseminate information efficiently. Many home and small business owners create simple databases such as customer contact and mailing lists with easy to use software such as Microsoft "Access" and "FileMaker Pro." "Oracle," "SQL Server," and "FoxPro" are examples of advanced database applications with programming languages that can be used to build custom business solutions in networked environments.

Database applications are used to search, sort, calculate, report and share information. Databases can also contain code to perform mathematical and statistical calculations on the data to support queries submitted by users. Database applications provide security by restricting access to data based upon user names and passwords. Most database applications are customized with a database programming language to automate specific types of work.

Accounting Applications

An accounting system is a custom database application used to manage financial data. Custom forms are used to record assets, liabilities, inventory and the transactions between customers and suppliers. The income statements, balance sheets, purchase orders and invoices generated are custom reports based upon information that is entered into the database. Accounting applications can run on a single computer suitable for a small business or in a networked shared environment to accommodate the needs of multiple departments and locations in larger organizations. "Microsoft Money," "Quicken," "QuickBooks" and "Peachtree" are accounting systems built upon database applications.

CRM Applications

A customer relationship management system (CRM) is another example of a database application that has been customized to manage the marketing, sales, and support relationships between a business and its customers. The ultimate goal is to maximize sales, minimize costs and foster strategic customer relationships. Simple contact management programs such as "ACT," or the task manager in Microsoft's "Outlook" can be customized to suit the needs of individuals and small businesses. "SAP," "Salesforce.com," and Oracle's "Siebel" are robust CRM database applications suitable for larger enterprises.

Web Applications

Many contemporary web sites are built using several database applications simultaneously as core components. Most retail store Web sites including "Bestbuy.com," and "Amazon.com" use database systems to store, update and present data about products for sale. These Web sites also combine an accounting database system to record sales transactions and a CRM database application to incorporate feedback and drive a positive customer experience. The popular Web-based "Facebook" application is essentially a database built upon the "MySQL" database system and is an indication of the increasing usage of database applications as foundations for Web-based applications.

Using the Rule Wizard Framework

The Rule Wizard Framework facilitates building the wizards that generate rule files for solving a specific business problem. A wizard is a sequence of pages which guides users through defining a rule while they enter data. After data is entered, a rule module addressing the specific business problem is generated. To define a wizard, you must define the data structures required to hold the parameters, the GUI, and the code generation—all contained in a rule template in XML format.

When deciding to build a rule wizard for a specific task, consider the following input components:

- The business problem to solve along with its solution using rules.

- The parameters leading to variations in the rules module which solves the problem.

- The GUI requirements which allow the user to specify values for the parameters.

The rule wizard Framework facilitates wizard building by:

- Making possible the building of the wizard GUI without any Java code in some cases or by designing simple components in other cases.

- Providing a powerful macro language (Velocity) in which the rule template writer can express variations of the rules according to the parameters.

After defining the business problem and its solution using parameterized rules, the rule template writer completes the following tasks:

- Design the data structures or macros holding the parameters.

- Design the GUI.

- Write the code generation portion.

The following example illustrates this process without generating valid rule language code, but uses only the data entered by the user. The rule template follows, using the simplest data structure available—a string:

```
<?xml version="1.0" encoding="UTF-8"?>

<!DOCTYPE template SYSTEM "resources/ruleTemplate.dtd" >

<template name="ex1">

<screen number="10">

 <editor macro="text" label="Text"/>

</screen>

<macro name="text" type="varname"/>

<text>

Hello, you entered $text.

</text>

</template>
```

Now run the Rule Wizard using this rule template as input:

```
RuleWizard -t ex1.rtu
```

where -t option is used for specifying the RuleTemplate file name.

The RuleWizard.cmd file is located in the OEBPS_HOME\bin directory. Assume that the OEBPS_HOME\bin directory is in your PATH and that the sample code is saved in the file ex1.rtu. The extension .rtu stands for "rule template unit."

The <template> tag describes the rule template unit. The <screen> tag represents a step in the wizard. The <macro> tag is the only data structure used in this rule template. Rule Wizard provides some predefined macro types. A macro type defines the data type and also specifies a default editor. For example, the type varname specifies the need for a string conforming to the variable name restriction in the Java language. The editor is a simple JTextField.

The <editor> tag appears in the first step of the wizard, as it is contained on the first screen of the template. A label is specified—in the example, "Text"—and displayed beside the editor requesting the user to enter the required information.

Click Finish to verify the `varname` type of the macro you specified as well as the validations performed. If you type a legal value, such as `Example` and click `Finish` again, then the following message appears on the console:

```
Hello, you entered Example.
```

Notice that, in the code generation portion within the <text> tag, you can retrieve the value of the text macro by writing `$text`.

To add more steps to the wizard, repeat the process by duplicating the tags shown in the first example. Macro names must be unique in a template, editors must be associated to a macro, and pages are ordered according to the values in their `number` attribute.

In the case of Schedule Wizard, you can specify the application name while invoking RuleWizard.

For example,

```
%OEBPS_HOME%\bin>RuleWizard

-t %OEBPS_HOME\templates\Schedule.rtu -a Assignment

-e %OEBPS_HOME%\ebmsapps\%app%\rules\SC_instancename_param.rtp.
```

where,

-t option is used for specifying RuleTemplate file name.

-a option is used for specifying application name.

-e option is used for specifying the ruletemplate parameter file name.

User Interface Design and Format

User interface (UI) design is the process of making interfaces in software or computerized devices with a focus on looks or style. Designers aim to create designs users will find easy to use and pleasurable. UI design typically refers to graphical user interfaces but also includes others, such as voice-controlled ones.

Designing GUIs for User Delight

User interfaces are the access points where users interact with designs. Graphical user interfaces (GUIs) are designs' control panels and faces; voice-controlled interfaces involve oral-auditory interaction, while gesture-based interfaces witness users engaging with 3D design spaces via bodily motions. User interface design is a craft that involves building an essential part of the user experience; users are very swift to judge designs on usability and likeability. Designers focus on building interfaces users will find *highly usable* and *efficient*. Thus, a thorough understanding of the contexts users will find themselves in when making those judgments is crucial. You should create the illusion that users aren't interacting with a device so much as they're trying to attain goals *directly* and as effortlessly as possible. This is in line with the intangible nature of software – instead of depositing icons on a screen; you should aim to make the interface effectively invisible, offering users portals through which they can interact directly with the reality of their tasks. Focus on sustaining this "magic" by letting users find their way about the interface intuitively – the less they notice they must use controls, the more they'll immerse themselves. This dynamic applies to another dimension of UI design: Your design should have as many enjoyable features as are appropriate.

UI vs. UX Design

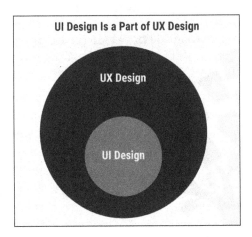

Often confused with UX design, UI design is more concerned with the surface and overall feel of a design, whereas the latter covers the entire spectrum of the user experience. One analogy is to picture UX design as a vehicle with UI design as the driving console. In GUIs, you should create pleasing aesthetics and animations that convey your organization's values and maximize usability.

How to Make Great UIs

To deliver impressive GUIs, remember – users are humans, with needs such as comfort and low cognitive loads. Follow these guidelines:

- Make elements such as buttons and other common elements perform predictably (including responses such as pinch = zoom) so users can unconsciously use them everywhere. Form should follow function.

- Maintain high discoverability. Clearly label icons and include well-indicated affordances.

- Keep interfaces simple and create an "invisible" feel. Every element must serve a purpose.

- Respect the user's eye and attention regarding layout; focus on hierarchy and readability:

  ○ Alignment – minimize your number of alignment lines (think justified text); typically choose edge (over center) alignment.

  ○ Draw attention to key features using:

    ▪ Color, brightness and contrast. Avoid including colors or buttons excessively.

    ▪ Text via font sizes, bold type/weighting, italics, capitals and distance between letters. Users should pick up meanings just by scanning.

- Minimize the number of actions for performing tasks but focus on one chief function per page; guide users by indicating preferred actions. Ease complex tasks by using progressive disclosure.

- Put controls near objects users want to control.

- Keep users informed vis-à-vis system responses/actions with feedback.

- Consider defaults to reduce user burdens (e.g., pre-fill forms).

- Use reusable design patterns to guide behavior regarding navigation and search functions.

- Concentrate on maintaining brand consistency.

Graphical User Interface

We have many database management systems available in the market, many of them with friendly Graphical User Interfaces, using which the users can execute queries and handle tables and other objects. However, the GUIs provided by each database server are exclusive to its own database. Moreover, a person with little technical knowledge will find it difficult to use one.

Limitations of the Existing System

- GUIs provided by most of the database is exclusive to its own database.

- Working with different databases through a single friendly interface is impossible.

- The features and functionality provided by each GUIs differ from one RDBMS to another.

- A GUI that provides a friendly environment to a user with little knowledge of SQL in such a way that he can work with more than one type of databases is hard to find.

The RDBMS uses a collection of tables to represent both data and the relationships among those data. Each table has multiple columns and each column has unique name and fixed data type. Each table in the database has a unique name assigned to it.

The software is developed using Java as front end using MSSQL Server, MS Access and Oracle. The software is developed with the keen intention of creating a Graphical User Interface for 3 Relational Database Management System.

 The product entitled GUI for RDBMS is developed with the keen intention of creating a Graphical User Interface for commonly used Relational Database Management System like MSSQL Server, Oracle etc. This is a general-level GUI, which can be connected to more than one database residing on the system. As a result, any database manipulation can be performed using a single product. Moreover, the queries can be executed very easily, since the user need not type any queries, but can simply select the appropriate options according to their requirements. Thus, this product can be used by a person with no knowledge of SQL.

- Database Creation: In case of MS SQL Server, by clicking on the corresponding icon, a new database can be created.

- Database Login: Once a database is created, a user can login to his/her database and, after which he/she can work with the objects in the database. In case of Oracle, we are always automatically logged into the default database of Oracle and we can login into the same as different users.

- Database Rename: A database in MSSQL server can be renamed by selecting the corresponding option.

- Database Drop: There is an option provided for dropping an already existing database when the GUI is connected to the MSSQL Server.

- Database Profile: The user can monitor and view the database properties, like name, owner, and size, date of creation, status and contents.

- Objects: The user can access the opened database through a Graphical User Interface. Through this interface, the user can view and work with the database objects like tables, queries and reports.

- Create Table: The user can create tables in the selected database. A design view is provided, through which the user can simply enter the field name, select the data type from a select list. There are separate options for setting a field as primary, unique, or not null. There is also an option for adding checking constraint on a field or a default value in a field.

- View Table: This option enables the user to view the contents (rows) in a table.

- Execute Queries: The user can execute any query on the database using the user-friendly graphical interface. All the tables in the database are listed, from which the user can select the one in which he/she has to execute the query. The user can select the type of query to be executed (like select, update, make-table and delete). The fields in the tables in which the query has to be executed can be selected from a list and the conditions can be input, all using the graphical interface. The conditions can include sorting (ascending, descending or none), fields to be displayed, criteria and any other specification, if any. The result of the query action is exhibited.

- Select: User can first select a table, and then execute select queries on it. Select query can be executed in different ways:

    ◦ Specific fields or all fields in a table can be displayed.

    ◦ Only distinct fields can be displayed if required.

    ◦ Aggregate function can be applied to a field selected.

    ◦ Field or fields satisfying a specific condition can be selected.

    ◦ Selection can also be made using Order by or Group by clause.

- Alter: Any alteration on the table can be made on a selected table using this option. Alterations that can be made include the following:

    ◦ Alter the data type of an existing field in the selected table.

    ◦ Altering the selected table by adding a new field to the table.

    ◦ Altering the selected table by dropping an existing field in the table.

    ◦ Altering the selected table by adding a constraint to a field in the table.

    ◦ Altering the selected table by dropping a constraint specified on the field in the table.

- Update: This option is used for making any updating on a selected table. Any condition for updating can also be specified if required.

- Delete: This option is used for deleting rows from a selected table. Deletion can also be performed by specifying condition so that only rows satisfying that condition is deleted.

- Drop: This option allows a user to drop an already existing table from a database

- Insert: Using this option the user can insert rows into an existing table.

- SQL query analyzer: If required, the user can execute queries in SQL mode, not using the graphical interface. A separate workspace is provided, where the query can be typed and executed.

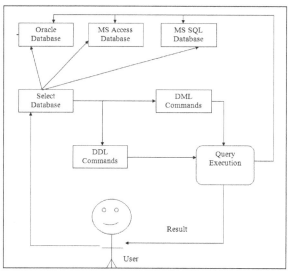

System design.

User selects appropriate database system such as Oracle, MS access, MS SQL server. After selecting database system user will perform either DDL or DML commands. Query execution unit will execute a query and make changes to databases. Query execution unit will also provide result to user.

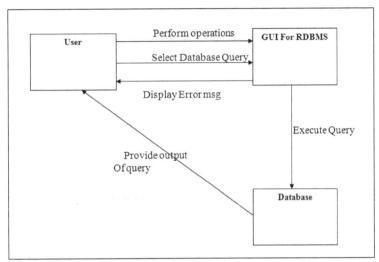

User Interface Design.

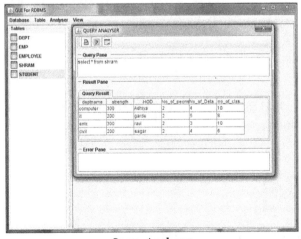

Connecting dialog.

In GUI for RDBMS, there is a dialog box for user using which he/she can select the database system such as Oracle, SQL Server, and MS Access.

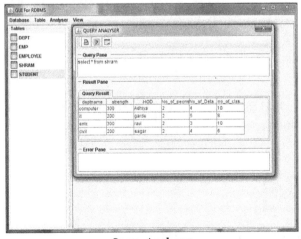

Query Analyzer.

In GUI for RDBMS, there is an option for Query Analyzer using which user can type and execute different queries if he/she is having knowledge of SQL (Structured Query Language).

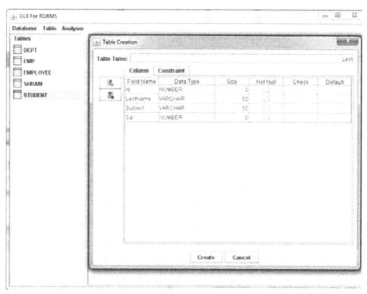

Table create.

In GUI for RDBMS, there in an option for a user to create table. In this user have to specify the name of table, columns and can apply constraints.

Edit Table.

In GUI for RDBMS, there in an option for a user to edit table. In this user can insert new row, delete an existing row and modify row.

Creating Forms

Creating Forms without Form Wizard

A form is a database object that you can use to enter, edit, or display data from a table or a query. You can use forms to control access to data, such as which fields of data are displayed. For example, certain users may not need to see all of the fields in a table. Providing those users with a form that contains just the necessary fields makes it easier for them to use the database.

Think of forms as windows through which people see and reach the database. An effective form speeds the use of the database, because people don't have to search for what they need. A visually attractive form makes working with the database more pleasant and more efficient, and it can also help prevent incorrect data from being entered. While data can be entered directly into a table, the larger the table, the harder it is to be sure that the data is in the right field and record.

Getting Started

Access gives you three main ways to create a form: with a single mouse click, with the Form Wizard, or in Design view. Once you understand all three ways, you can choose the method or methods that will be best for your purposes.

There are three types of forms that can be created with a single mouse click: Simple Form, Split Form, and Multiple Items Form. You can begin using the new form immediately, or you can modify it in Layout view or Design view to better suit your needs.

To create a form with a single click:

- Open the table or query upon which you want to base the form.

- To create a form on which all fields from the underlying table or query are placed, displaying one record at a time, on the Create tab, click Form.

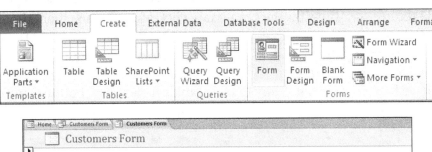

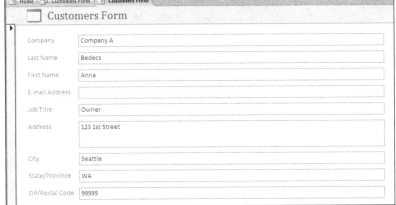

- To create a split form on the Create tab, click More Forms, and then Split Form. The two views are connected to the same data source and are synchronized with each other at all times. Selecting a field in one part of the form selects the same field in the other part of the form. You can add, edit, or delete data from either part.

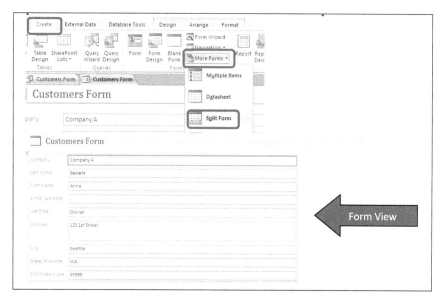

- To create a form on which all fields from the underlying table or query are placed, displaying multiple records at a time, on the Create tab, click More Forms, then Multiple Items. The form that Access creates resembles a datasheet. The data is Form View Datasheet View Information Technology Services, UIS 3 arranged in rows and columns, and you see more than one record at a time. However, a Multiple Items form gives you more customization options than a datasheet, such as the ability to add graphical elements, buttons, and other controls.

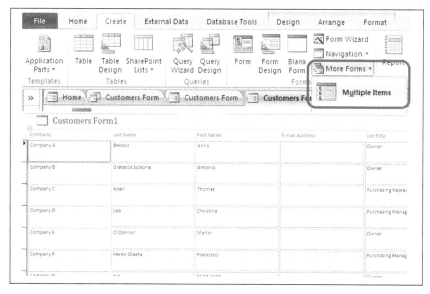

To be more selective about which fields appear on your form, you can use the Form Wizard.

You can also use fields from more than one table or query, provided that you specified the relationships between the tables and queries beforehand. You will need to tell the wizard:

- The table or query on which to base the form.

- Which fields to use on the form.

- Which form layout to apply.

- Which visual style to apply.

To use the Form Wizard,

- On the Create tab, click Form Wizard.

- Follow the onscreen steps.

- Additional customization can be done in Design view.

Design view is the best way to create a form when you want full control and complete freedom.

The challenge is that you are on your own, without the prearrangements of the Form Wizard.

However, you can also create a form by other methods, and then change its details in Design view.

To create a form in Design view:

- On the Create tab, click Form Design.

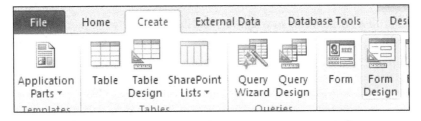

- Click the Add Existing Fields button on the Design tab, if necessary, to see a list of tables and their fields. Then simply drag the desired fields onto the form.

- You can also create a form from scratch in Layout view instead of Design view. From the Create tab, click Blank Form.

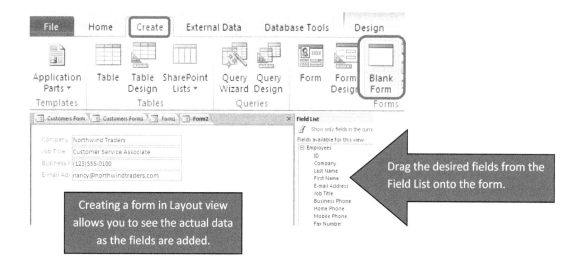

Customizing the Form

Once you know how to create forms, it is time to start making those forms look and act the way you want. To do that, you need to know your way around the parts of a form.

Controls are the parts of forms that most users see and work with. They are objects that display data, perform actions, and let you view and work with information. Controls make forms easier and more interesting to use.

Some controls are bound. A bound control is attached directly to a specific field in a selected table or query. When someone enters or changes data in a bound form control, that new data or changed data is immediately updated in the table. Similarly, data viewed in a bound control will change in the form whenever it changes in the table.

A control that doesn't have a source of data is called an unbound control. Unbound controls are used to display information, lines, rectangles, and pictures.

A control whose source of data is an expression, rather than a field, is called a calculated control. For example, if a table contains fields for unit price and quantity sold, a calculated control can be created to determine total price (unit price * quantity sold).

Controls can be added through the Controls group on the Design tab.

Calculated controls are created by writing an expression. For example, we will calculate the order total based on the unit price and quantity ordered fields.

Add a text box to the form by using the Text Box control on the Design tab.

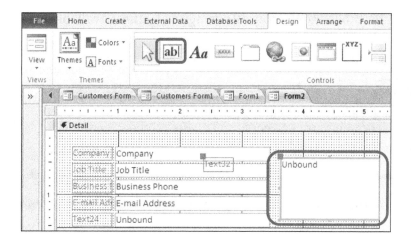

1. Click the Property Sheet button to display the properties, if necessary.

To select a control, click it with your mouse. You can then use the selection handles to move or resize it. Multiple controls can be selected in several ways:

- Hold Shift while you click them.

- Draw a lasso around them with your mouse.

- Click in the ruler to select all intersecting controls.

Controls can also be resized and/or moved.

- To resize a control, point the mouse at a handle. The mouse will look like a two-headed arrow.

- To move a control, point the mouse to the box surrounding the control. The mouse will look like a four-headed arrow.

- To move a bound control without its label (or vice versa), point the mouse to the larger selection handle in the upper left corner.

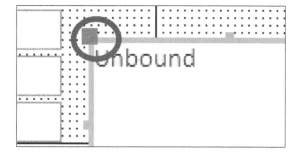

- Controls can also be moved by using the arrow keys on the keyboard.

Text formatting can be applied to the controls using the features available in Themes group on the Design tab.

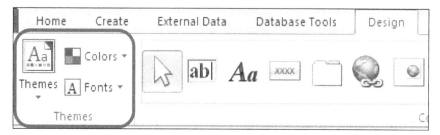

The tools available on the Arrange tab are especially helpful for arranging controls with a precise look.

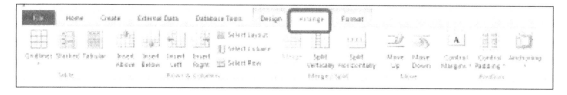

Sections of the Form

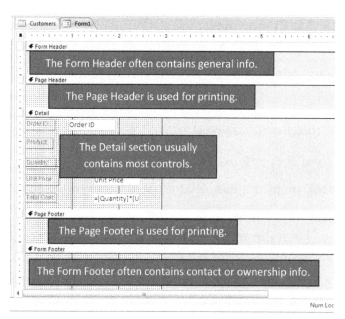

Sections can be resized by clicking and dragging the edge of the section bar.

Adjusting Tab Order

Some people use the Tab key to move through a form, from one control to another, as they enter or view data. It is important that the tab order be logical and easy to work with.

To change the tab order:

- Switch to Design view, if necessary.

- From the Arrange tab, click Tab Order.

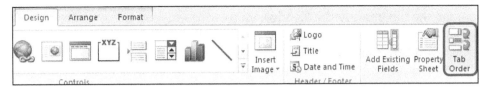

- Under Section, click the name of the form section for which you want to change the tab Order.

- Drag the control names up or down in the Custom Order list.

- The Auto Order button will set the tab order to a left-to-right, top-to-bottom order.

Using Tab Control

Tab controls are the easiest way to create a multi-page form. They are also useful if you want to avoid scrolling.

To add a tab control to the form:

- From the Design tab, click the Tab Control button.

- Click the form at the desired location of the tab control. The form will automatically adjust its size to accommodate the tab control.

- Drag fields onto the tab control. Format the controls as desired.

- To rename the tab, modify the Caption on the property sheet.

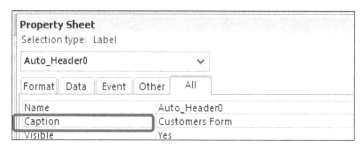

- To add more tabs, right-click and choose Insert and then the location.

- The completed tab control looks like this:

Creating Forms with Form Wizard

You can include a variety of different types of forms in your applications. You can include forms that enable users to update just a single row in a table or multiple rows at once. Application Builder includes a number of wizards you can use to create forms automatically, or you can create forms manually.

Topics in this topic include:

- Creating a Form using a Wizard.

- Creating a Tabular Form.

- Creating a Master Detail Form.

- Creating a Form Manually.

- Validating User Input in Forms.

Creating a Form using a Wizard

The easiest way to create a form is to use a wizard. For example, the Form on Table or View Wizard creates one item for each column in a table. It also includes the necessary buttons and processes required to insert, update, and delete rows from the table using a primary key. Each region has a defined name and display position; all other attributes are items, buttons, processes, and branches.

To create a form using a wizard:

- On the Workspace home page, click the Application Builder icon.

- Select an application.

- Click Create Page.

- Select Form and click Next.

- Under Forms, select a type of form page,

Forms Page Types

- Form on a Procedure: Builds a form based on stored procedure arguments. Use this approach when you have implemented logic or data manipulation language (DML) in a stored procedure or package.

- Form on a Table or View: Creates a form that enables users to update a single row in a database table.

- Form on a Table with Report: Creates two pages. One page displays a report. Each row provides a link to the second page to enable users to update each record.

- This wizard does not support tables having more than 127 columns. Selecting more than 127 columns generates an error.

- Master Detail Form: Creates a form that displays a master row and multiple detail rows within a single HTML form. With this form, users can query, insert, update, and delete values from two tables or views.

- Tabular Form: Creates a form in which users can update multiple rows in a database.

- Form on a SQL Query: Creates a form based on the columns returned by a SQL query such as an EQUIJOIN.

- Summary Page: Creates a read-only version of a form. Typically used to provide a confirmation page at the end of a wizard.

- Form on Web Service: Creates a page with items based on a Web service definition. This wizard creates a user input form, a process to call the Web service, and a submit button.

- Form and Report on Web Service: Creates a page with items based on a Web service definition. This wizard creates a user input form, a process to call the Web service, a submit button, and displays the results returned in a report.

Creating a Tabular Form

A tabular form enables users to update multiple rows in a table. The Tabular Form Wizard creates a form to perform update, insert, and delete operations on multiple rows in a database table.

To create a tabular form:

- On the Workspace home page, click the Application Builder icon.

- Select an application.

- Click Create Page.

- Select Form and click Next.

- Select Tabular Form and click Next.

The Tabular Form Wizard appears.

- For Table/View Owner:

  - Specify the table or view owner on which you want to base your tabular form.

  - Select the operations to be performed on the table (for example, Update, Insert and Delete).

  - Click Next.

- For Table/View Name, select a table and click Next.

- For Displayed Columns:

  - Select the columns (updatable and nonupdatable) to include in the form.

  - Note that you can modify the column order or your SQL query after you create the page.

  - Click Next.

- For Primary Key, select the Primary Key column and a secondary Primary Key column (if applicable) and click Next.

- For Primary Key Source, select a source type for the primary key column and click Next.

Valid options include:

- ○ Existing trigger - Select this option if a trigger is defined for the table. You can also select this option if you plan on specifying the primary key column source later after completing the form.

- ○ Custom PL/SQL function - Select this option if you want to provide a PL/SQL function to generate returning key value.

- ○ Existing sequence - Select this option if you want to pick the sequence from a list of sequences available in the selected schema.

- On Updatable Columns, select which columns should be updatable and click Next.

- On Page and Region Attributes:

  - ○ Specify page and region information.

  - ○ Select a region template.

  - ○ Select a report template.

  - ○ Click Next.

- On Tab, specify a tab implementation for this page and click Next.

- On Button Labels, enter the display text to appear for each button and click Next.

- On Branching, specify the pages to branch to after the user clicks the Submit and Cancel buttons and click Next.

- Click Finish.

Creating Sub-Forms

A subform is a form that is inserted in another form. The primary form is called the main form, and the form that is enclosed in form is called the subform. A form/subform combination is sometimes referred to as a hierarchical form, a master/detail form, or a parent/child form.

Subforms are especially effective when you want to show data from tables or queries that have a one-to-many relationship. A one-to-many relationship is an association between two tables in which the primary key value of each record in the primary table corresponds to the value in the matching field or fields of many records in the related table. For example, you can create a form that displays employee data, and contains a subform that displays each employee's orders. The data in the Employees table is the "one" side of the relationship. The data in the Orders table is the "many" side of the relationship — each employee can have more than one order.

A form that contains a subform:

1. The main form shows data from the "one" side of the relationship.

2. The subform shows data from the "many" side of the relationship.

The main form and subform in this kind of form are linked so that the subform displays only records that are related to the current record in the main form. For example, when the main form displays Nancy Freehafer's information, the subform displays only her orders. If the form and subform were unlinked, the subform would display all the orders, not just Nancy's.

The following table defines some of the terminology that is associated with subforms. Access will handle most of the details if you use the procedures, but it is helpful to know what is occurring behind the scenes if you need to make modifications later.

- Subform control: The control that embeds a form into a form. You can think of the subform control as a "view" of another object in your database, whether it is another form, a table, or a query. The subform control provides properties which allow you to link the data displayed in the control to the data on the main form.

- Source Object property: The property of the subform control that determines what object is displayed in the control.

- Datasheet: A simple display of data in rows and columns, much like a spreadsheet. The subform control displays a datasheet when its source object is a table or query, or when its source object is a form whose Default View property is set to Datasheet. In these cases, the subform is sometimes referred to as a datasheet or subdatasheet instead of as a subform.

- Link Child Fields property: The property of the subform control that specifies which field or fields in the subform link the subform to the main form.

- Link Master Fields property: The property of the subform control that specifies which field or fields on the main form link the main form to the subform.

Create or Add a Subform

Use the following table to determine which procedure is most appropriate for your situation:

Scenario	Recommended procedure
You want Access to create both a main form and a subform, and to link the subform to the main form.	Create a form that contains a subform by using the Form Wizard.
You want to use an existing form as the main form, but you want Access to create a new subform and add it to the main form.	Add one or more subforms to an existing form by using the Subform Wizard.
You want to use an existing form as the main form, and you want to add one or more existing forms to that form as subforms.	Create a subform by dragging one form onto another.

Create a Form that Contains a Subform by using the Form Wizard

This procedure creates a new form and subform combination by using the Form Wizard. This is also the quickest way to get started if you have not already created the forms that you want to use as the main form or the subform.

- On the Create tab, in the Forms group, click Form Wizard.

- On the first page of the wizard, in the Tables/Queries drop-down list, select a table or query. For this example, to create an Employees form that displays orders for each employee in a subform, we will select Table: Employees (the "one" side of the one-to-many relationship).

- Double-click the fields that you want to include from this table or query.

- On the same page of the wizard, in the Tables/Queries drop-down list, select another table or query from the list. For this example, we will select the Orders table (the "many" side of the one-to-many relationship).

- Double-click the fields that you want to include from this table or query.

- When you click Next, assuming that you set up the relationships correctly before you started the wizard, the wizard asks How do you want to view your data? — that is, by which table or query. Select the table on the "one" side of the one-to-many relationship. For this example, to create the Employees form, we will click by Employees. The wizard displays a small diagram of a form. The page should resemble the following illustration:

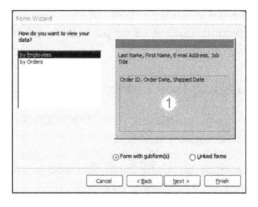

- At the bottom of the wizard page, select Form with subforms, and then click Next.

- On the What layout would you like for your subform? page, click the layout option that you want, and then click Next. Both layout styles arrange the subform data in rows and columns, but a tabular layout is more customizable. You can add color, graphics, and other formatting elements to a tabular subform, whereas a datasheet is more compact, like the datasheet view of a table.

- On the next page of the wizard, select a formatting style for the form, and then click Next. If you chose Tabular on the previous page, the formatting style you choose will also be applied to the subform.

- On the last page of the wizard, type the titles that you want for the forms. Access names the forms based on the titles that you type, and labels the subform based on the title that you type for the subform.

- Specify whether you want to open the form in Form view, so that you can view or enter information, or in Design view, so that you can modify its design, and then click Finish.

Access creates two forms — one for the main form that contains the subform control, and one for the subform itself.

Add One or more Subforms to an Existing Form by using the Subform Wizard

Use this procedure to add one or more subforms to an existing form. For each subform, you can choose to have Access create a new form or use an existing form as the subform.

- Right-click the existing form in the Navigation Pane, and then click Design View.

- On the Design tab, in the Controls group, click the down-arrow to display the Controls gallery, and ensure that Use Control Wizards is selected.

- On the Design tab, in the Controls group, click the Subform/Subreport button.

- Click on the form where you want to place the subform.

- Follow the directions in the wizard.

When you click Finish, Access adds a subform control to your form. If you chose to have Access create a new form for the subform instead of using an existing form, Access creates the new form object and adds it to the Navigation Pane.

Create a Subform by Dragging One Form onto Another

Use this procedure if you want to use an existing form as a main form, and you want to add one or more existing forms to that form as subforms.

- In the Navigation Pane, right-click the form that you want to use as the main form, and then click Layout View.

- Drag the form that you want to use as the subform from the Navigation Pane onto the main form.

Access adds a subform control to the main form and binds the control to the form that you dragged from the Navigation Pane. Access also tries to link the subform to the main form, based on the relationships that have been defined in your database.

- Repeat this step to add any additional subforms to the main form.

- To verify that the linking was successful, on the Home tab, in the Views group, click View, click Form View, and then use the main form's record selector to advance through several records. If the subform filters itself correctly for each employee, then the procedure is complete.

If the previous test does not work, Access was unable to determine how to link the subform to the main form, and the Link Child Fields and Link Master Fields properties of the subform control are blank. You must set these properties manually by doing the following:

- Right-click the main form in the Navigation Pane, and then click Design View.

- Click the subform control one time to select it.

- If the Property Sheet task pane is not displayed, press F4 to display it.

- In the Property Sheet, click the Data tab.

- Click the Build button Builder button next to the Link Child Fields property box. The Subform Field Linker dialog box appears.

- In the Master Fields and Child Fields drop-down lists, select the fields that you want to link the forms with, and then click OK. If you are not sure which fields to use, click Suggest to have Access try to determine the linking fields.

- Save the main form, switch to Form view, and then verify that the form works as expected.

Open a Subform in a New Window in Design View

If you want to make design changes to a subform while you are working on its main form in Design view, you can open the subform in its own window:

- Click the subform to select it.

- On the Design tab, in the Tools group, click Subform in New Window.

Change the Default View of a Subform

When you add a subform to a form, the subform/subreport control displays the subform according to the subform's Default View property. This property can be set to the following values:

- Single Form,

- Continuous Forms,

- Datasheet,

- Split Form.

When you first create a subform, this property may be set to Continuous Forms or perhaps Single Form. However, if you set the Default View property of a subform to Datasheet, then the subform will display as a datasheet on the main form.

To set the Default View property of a subform:

- Close any open objects.

- In the Navigation Pane, right-click the subform and then click Design View.

- If the Property Sheet is not already displayed, press F4 to display it.

- In the drop-down list at the top of the Property Sheet, make sure Form is selected.

- On the Format tab of the Property Sheet, set the Default View property to the view you want to use.

- Save and close the subform, and then open the main form to check the results.

Add Related Data to a Form without Creating a Subform

It is not always necessary to create a separate form object to display related data. For example, if you are working on a form in Layout view or Design view and you drag a table or query from the Navigation Pane to the form, Access creates a subform/subreport control that displays the data in that object. The object's Default View property determines how the data is displayed. Usually, this is set to Datasheet view, but you can also set the Default View property of a table or query to Single Form, Split Form, or Continuous Forms, giving you more flexibility in displaying related data on forms.

References

- What-are-database-applications: techwalla.com, Retrieved 14 May, 2019

- Ui-design: interaction-design.org, Retrieved 15 April, 2019

- Design-and-Implementation-of-Graphical-User-Interface-for-Relational-Database-Management-System-4948292: academia.edu, Retrieved 06 May, 2019

- DesigningFormsinAccess2010, informationtechnologyservices: uis.edu, Retrieved 03 January, 2019

- Create-a-form-that-contains-a-subform-a-one-to-many-form: support.office.com, Retrieved 12 March, 2019

Data Analysis Services

Data analysis services are integral part of database management. It performs services such as cleaning, inspecting, and modeling of data and sound decision making. Data warehouse, data transformation, online analytical processing are some of the area covered in this subject. This chapter closely examines these areas of data analysis services to provide an extensive understanding of the subject.

Data Warehouse

A Data Warehousing (DW) is process for collecting and managing data from varied sources to provide meaningful business insights. A Data warehouse is typically used to connect and analyze business data from heterogeneous sources. The data warehouse is the core of the BI system which is built for data analysis and reporting.

It is a blend of technologies and components which aids the strategic use of data. It is electronic storage of a large amount of information by a business which is designed for query and analysis instead of transaction processing. It is a process of transforming data into information and making it available to users in a timely manner to make a difference.

The decision support database (Data Warehouse) is maintained separately from the organization's operational database. However, the data warehouse is not a product but an environment. It is an architectural construct of an information system which provides users with current and historical decision support information which is difficult to access or present in the traditional operational data store.

You many know that a 3NF-designed database for an inventory system many have tables related to each other. For example, a report on current inventory information can include more than 12 joined conditions. This can quickly slow down the response time of the query and report. A data warehouse provides a new design which can help to reduce the response time and helps to enhance the performance of queries for reports and analytics.

Data warehouse system is also known by the following name:

- Decision Support System (DSS),

- Executive Information System,

- Management Information System,

- Business Intelligence Solution,

- Analytic Application,

- Data Warehouse.

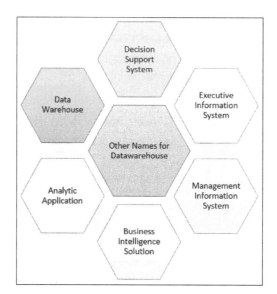

A Data Warehouse works as a central repository where information arrives from one or more data sources. Data flows into a data warehouse from the transactional system and other relational databases.

Data may be:

- Structured,

- Semi-structured,

- Unstructured data.

The data is processed, transformed, and ingested so that users can access the processed data in the Data Warehouse through Business Intelligence tools, SQL clients, and spreadsheets. A data warehouse merges information coming from different sources into one comprehensive database.

By merging all of this information in one place, an organization can analyze its customers more holistically. This helps to ensure that it has considered all the information available. Data warehousing makes data mining possible. Data mining is looking for patterns in the data that may lead to higher sales and profits.

Types of Data Warehouse

Three main types of Data Warehouses are:

- Enterprise Data Warehouse: Enterprise Data Warehouse is a centralized warehouse. It provides decision support service across the enterprise. It offers a unified approach for organizing and representing data. It also provides the ability to classify data according to the subject and give access according to those divisions.

- Operational Data Store: Operational Data Store, which is also called ODS, are nothing but data store required when neither Data warehouse nor OLTP systems support organizations reporting needs. In ODS, Data warehouse is refreshed in real time. Hence, it is widely preferred for routine activities like storing records of the Employees.

- Data Mart: A data mart is a subset of the data warehouse. It specially designed for a particular line of business, such as sales, finance, sales or finance. In an independent data mart, data can collect directly from sources.

General Stages of Data Warehouse

Earlier, organizations started relatively simple use of data warehousing. However, over time, more sophisticated use of data warehousing begun.

The following are general stages of use of the data warehouse:

- Offline Operational Database: In this stage, data is just copied from an operational system to another server. In this way, loading, processing, and reporting of the copied data do not impact the operational system's performance.

- Offline Data Warehouse: Data in the Data warehouse is regularly updated from the Operational Database. The data in Data warehouse is mapped and transformed to meet the Data warehouse objectives.

- Real time Data Warehouse: In this stage, Data warehouses are updated whenever any transaction takes place in operational database. For example, Airline or railway booking system.

- Integrated Data Warehouse: In this stage, Data Warehouses are updated continuously when the operational system performs a transaction. The Data warehouse then generates transactions which are passed back to the operational system.

Components of Data Warehouse

Four components of Data Warehouses are:

- Load manager: Load manager is also called the front component. It performs with all the operations associated with the extraction and load of data into the warehouse. These operations include transformations to prepare the data for entering into the Data warehouse.

- Warehouse Manager: Warehouse manager performs operations associated with the management of the data in the warehouse. It performs operations like analysis of data to ensure consistency, creation of indexes and views, generation of denormalization and aggregations, transformation and merging of source data and archiving and baking-up data.

- Query Manager: Query manager is also known as backend component. It performs all the operation operations related to the management of user queries. The operations of these Data warehouse components are direct queries to the appropriate tables for scheduling the execution of queries.

- End-user access tools: This is categorized into five different groups like 1. Data Reporting 2. Query Tools 3. Application development tools 4. EIS tools, 5. OLAP tools and data mining tools.

Data Warehouse Users

Data warehouse is needed for all types of users like:

- Decision makers who rely on mass amount of data.

- Users who use customized, complex processes to obtain information from multiple data sources.

- It is also used by the people who want simple technology to access the data.

- It also essential for those people who want a systematic approach for making decisions.

- If the user wants fast performance on a huge amount of data which is a necessity for reports, grids or charts, then Data warehouse proves useful.

- Data warehouse is a first step if you want to discover 'hidden patterns' of data-flows and groupings.

Purpose of a Data Warehouse

Here, are most common sectors where Data warehouse is used:

- Airline: In the Airline system, it is used for operation purpose like crew assignment, analyses of route profitability, frequent flyer program promotions, etc.

- Banking: It is widely used in the banking sector to manage the resources available on desk effectively. Few banks also used for the market research, performance analysis of the product and operations.

- Healthcare: Healthcare sector also used Data warehouse to strategize and predict outcomes, generate patient's treatment reports, share data with tie-in insurance companies, medical aid services, etc.

- Public sector: In the public sector, data warehouse is used for intelligence gathering. It helps government agencies to maintain and analyze tax records, health policy records, for every individual.

- Investment and Insurance sector: In this sector, the warehouses are primarily used to analyze data patterns, customer trends, and to track market movements.

- Retain chain: In retail chains, Data warehouse is widely used for distribution and marketing. It also helps to track items, customer buying pattern, promotions and also used for determining pricing policy.

- Telecommunication: A data warehouse is used in this sector for product promotions, sales decisions and to make distribution decisions.

- Hospitality Industry: This Industry utilizes warehouse services to design as well as estimate their advertising and promotion campaigns where they want to target clients based on their feedback and travel patterns.

Steps to Implement Data Warehouse

The best way to address the business risk associated with a Data warehouse implementation is to employ a three-prong strategy as below:

- Enterprise strategy: Here we identify technical including current architecture and tools. We also identify facts, dimensions, and attributes. Data mapping and transformation is also passed.

- Phased delivery: Data warehouse implementation should be phased based on subject areas. Related business entities like booking and billing should be first implemented and then integrated with each other.

- Iterative Prototyping: Rather than a big bang approach to implementation, the Data warehouse should be developed and tested iteratively.

Here, are key steps in Data warehouse implementation along with its deliverables.

Step	Tasks	Deliverables
1	Need to define project scope	Scope Definition
2	Need to determine business needs	Logical Data Model
3	Define Operational Data store requirements	Operational Data Store Model
4	Acquire or develop Extraction tools	Extract tools and Software
5	Define Data Warehouse Data requirements	Transition Data Model
6	Document missing data	To Do Project List
7	Maps Operational Data Store to Data Warehouse	D/W Data Integration Map
8	Develop Data Warehouse Database design	D/W Database Design
9	Extract Data from Operational Data Store	Integrated D/W Data Extracts
10	Load Data Warehouse	Initial Data Load
11	Maintain Data Warehouse	On-going Data Access and Subsequent Loads

Best Practices to Implement a Data Warehouse

- Decide a plan to test the consistency, accuracy, and integrity of the data.

- The data warehouse must be well integrated, well defined and time stamped.

- While designing Data warehouse make sure you use right tool, stick to life cycle, take care about data conflicts and ready to learn you're your mistakes.

- Never replace operational systems and reports.

- Don't spend too much time on extracting, cleaning and loading data.

- Ensure to involve all stakeholders including business personnel in Data warehouse. implementation process. Establish that Data warehousing is a joint/team project. You don't want to create Data warehouse that is not useful to the end users.

- Prepare a training plan for the end users.

Advantages and Disadvantages of a Data Warehouse

Advantages of Data Warehouse

- Data warehouse allows business users to quickly access critical data from some sources all in one place.

- Data warehouse provides consistent information on various cross-functional activities. It is also supporting ad-hoc reporting and query.

- Data Warehouse helps to integrate many sources of data to reduce stress on the production system.

- Data warehouse helps to reduce total turnaround time for analysis and reporting.

- Restructuring and Integration make it easier for the user to use for reporting and analysis.

- Data warehouse allows users to access critical data from the number of sources in a single place. Therefore, it saves user's time of retrieving data from multiple sources.

- Data warehouse stores a large amount of historical data. This helps users to analyze different time periods and trends to make future predictions.

Disadvantages of Data Warehouse

- Not an ideal option for unstructured data.

- Creation and Implementation of Data Warehouse is surely time confusing affair.

- Data Warehouse can be outdated relatively quickly.

- Difficult to make changes in data types and ranges, data source schema, indexes, and queries.

- The data warehouse may seem easy, but actually, it is too complex for the average users.

- Despite best efforts at project management, data warehousing project scope will always increase.

- Sometime warehouse users will develop different business rules.

- Organizations need to spend lots of their resources for training and Implementation purpose.

Components of Data Warehouse

Overall Architecture

The data warehouse architecture is based on a relational database management system server that functions as the central repository for informational data. Operational data and processing is completely separated from data warehouse processing. This central information repository is surrounded by a number of key components designed to make the entire environment functional, manageable and accessible by both the operational systems that source data into the warehouse and by end-user query and analysis tools.

Typically, the source data for the warehouse is coming from the operational applications. As the data enters the warehouse, it is cleaned up and transformed into an integrated structure and format.

The transformation process may involve conversion, summarization, filtering and condensation of data. Because the data contains a historical component, the warehouse must be capable of holding and managing large volumes of data as well as different data structures for the same database over time.

Data Warehouse Database

The central data warehouse database is the cornerstone of the data warehousing environment. This database is almost always implemented on the relational database management system (RDBMS) technology. However, this kind of implementation is often constrained by the fact that traditional RDBMS products are optimized for transactional database processing. Certain data warehouse attributes, such as very large database size, ad hoc query processing and the need for flexible user view creation including aggregates, multi-table joins and drill-downs have become drivers for different technological approaches to the data warehouse database. These approaches include:

- Parallel relational database designs for scalability that include shared-memory, shared disk, or shared-nothing models implemented on various multiprocessor configurations (symmetric multiprocessors or SMP, massively parallel processors or MPP, and/or clusters of uni- or multiprocessors).

- An innovative approach to speed up a traditional RDBMS by using new index structures to bypass relational table scans.

- Multidimensional databases (MDDBs) that are based on proprietary database technology; conversely, a dimensional data model can be implemented using a familiar RDBMS. Multi-dimensional databases are designed to overcome any limitations placed on the warehouse by the nature of the relational data model. MDDBs enable on-line analytical processing (OLAP) tools that architecturally belong to a group of data warehousing components jointly categorized as the data query, reporting, analysis and mining tools.

Sourcing, Acquisition, Cleanup and Transformation Tools

A significant portion of the implementation effort is spent extracting data from operational systems and putting it in a format suitable for informational applications that run off the data warehouse.

The data sourcing, cleanup, transformation and migration tools perform all of the conversions, summarizations, key changes, structural changes and condensations needed to transform disparate data into information that can be used by the decision support tool. They produce the programs and control statements, including the COBOL programs, MVS job-control language (JCL), UNIX scripts, and SQL data definition language (DDL) needed to move data into the data warehouse for multiple operational systems. These tools also maintain the meta data. The functionality includes:

- Removing unwanted data from operational databases.

- Converting to common data names and definitions.

- Establishing defaults for missing data.

- Accommodating source data definition changes.

The data sourcing, cleanup, extract, transformation and migration tools have to deal with some significant issues including:

- Database heterogeneity: DBMSs are very different in data models, data access language, data navigation, operations, concurrency, integrity, recovery etc.

- Data heterogeneity: This is the difference in the way data is defined and used in different models – homonyms, synonyms, unit compatibility (U.S. vs metric), different attributes for the same entity and different ways of modeling the same fact.

These tools can save a considerable amount of time and effort. However, significant shortcomings do exist. For example, many available tools are generally useful for simpler data extracts.

Frequently, customized extract routines need to be developed for the more complicated data extraction procedures.

Meta Data

Meta data is data about data that describes the data warehouse. It is used for building, maintaining, managing and using the data warehouse. Meta data can be classified into:

- Technical meta data, which contains information about warehouse data for use by warehouse designers and administrators when carrying out warehouse development and management tasks.

- Business meta data, which contains information that gives users an easy-to-understand perspective of the information stored in the data warehouse.

Equally important, meta data provides interactive access to users to help understand content and find data. One of the issues dealing with meta data relates to the fact that many data extraction tool capabilities to gather meta data remain fairly immature. Therefore, there is often the need to create a meta data interface for users, which may involve some duplication of effort.

Meta data management is provided via a meta data repository and accompanying software. Meta data repository management software, which typically runs on a workstation, can be used to map the source data to the target database; generate code for data transformations; integrate and transform the data; and control moving data to the warehouse.

As user's interactions with the data warehouse increase, their approaches to reviewing the results of their requests for information can be expected to evolve from relatively simple manual analysis for trends and exceptions to agent-driven initiation of the analysis based on user-defined thresholds. The definition of these thresholds, configuration parameters for the software agents using them, and the information directory indicating where the appropriate sources for the information can be found are all stored in the meta data repository as well.

Access Tools

The principal purpose of data warehousing is to provide information to business users for strategic decision-making. These users interact with the data warehouse using front-end tools. Many of these tools require an information specialist, although many end users develop expertise in the tools. Tools fall into four main categories: query and reporting tools, application development tools, online analytical processing tools, and data mining tools.

Query and Reporting tools can be divided into two groups: reporting tools and managed query tools. Reporting tools can be further divided into production reporting tools and report writers.

Production reporting tools let companies generate regular operational reports or support high-volume batch jobs such as calculating and printing paychecks. Report writers, on the other hand, are inexpensive desktop tools designed for end-users.

Managed query tools shield end users from the complexities of SQL and database structures by inserting a metalayer between users and the database. These tools are designed for easy-to-use, point-and-click operations that either accept SQL or generate SQL database queries.

Often, the analytical needs of the data warehouse user community exceed the built-in capabilities of query and reporting tools. In these cases, organizations will often rely on the tried-and-true approach of in-house application development using graphical development environments such as PowerBuilder, Visual Basic and Forte. These application development platforms integrate well with popular OLAP tools and access all major database systems including Oracle, Sybase, and Informix.

OLAP tools are based on the concepts of dimensional data models and corresponding databases, and allow users to analyze the data using elaborate, multidimensional views. Typical business applications include product performance and profitability, effectiveness of a sales program or marketing campaign, sales forecasting and capacity planning. These tools assume that the data is organized in a multidimensional model.

A critical success factor for any business today is the ability to use information effectively. Data mining is the process of discovering meaningful new correlations, patterns and trends by digging into large amounts of data stored in the warehouse using artificial intelligence, statistical and mathematical techniques.

Data Marts

The concept of a data mart is causing a lot of excitement and attracts much attention in the data warehouse industry. Mostly, data marts are presented as an alternative to a data warehouse that takes significantly less time and money to build. However, the term data mart means different things to different people. A rigorous definition of this term is a data store that is subsidiary to a data warehouse of integrated data. The data mart is directed at a partition of data (often called a subject area) that is created for the use of a dedicated group of users. A data mart might, in fact, be a set of denormalized, summarized, or aggregated data. Sometimes, such a set could be placed on the data warehouse rather than a physically separate store of data. In most instances, however, the data mart is a physically separate store of data and is resident on separate database server, often a local area network serving a dedicated user group. Sometimes the data mart simply comprises relational OLAP technology which creates highly denormalized dimensional model (e.g., star schema) implemented on a relational database. The resulting hypercubes of data are used for analysis by groups of users with a common interest in a limited portion of the database.

These types of data marts, called dependent data marts because their data is sourced from the data warehouse, have a high value because no matter how they are deployed and how many different enabling technologies are used, different users are all accessing the information views derived from the single integrated version of the data.

Unfortunately, the misleading statements about the simplicity and low cost of data marts sometimes result in organizations or vendors incorrectly positioning them as an alternative to the data warehouse. This viewpoint defines independent data marts that in fact, represent fragmented point solutions to a range of business problems in the enterprise. This type of implementation should be rarely deployed in the context of an overall technology or applications architecture. Indeed, it is missing the ingredient that is at the heart of the data warehousing concept — that of data integration. Each independent data mart makes its own assumptions about how to consolidate the data, and the data across several data marts may not be consistent.

Moreover, the concept of an independent data mart is dangerous — as soon as the first data mart is created, other organizations, groups, and subject areas within the enterprise embark on the task of building their own data marts. As a result, you create an environment where multiple operational systems feed multiple non-integrated data marts that are often overlapping in data content, job scheduling, connectivity and management. In other words, you have transformed a complex many-to-one problem of building a data warehouse from operational and external data sources to a many-to-many sourcing and management nightmare.

Data Warehouse Administration and Management

Data warehouses tend to be as much as 4 times as large as related operational databases, reaching terabytes in size depending on how much history needs to be saved. They are not synchronized in real time to the associated operational data but are updated as often as once a day if the application requires it.

In addition, almost all data warehouse products include gateways to transparently access multiple enterprise data sources without having to rewrite applications to interpret and utilize the data.

Furthermore, in a heterogeneous data warehouse environment, the various databases reside on disparate systems, thus requiring inter-networking tools. The need to manage this environment is obvious.

Managing data warehouses includes security and priority management; monitoring updates from the multiple sources; data quality checks; managing and updating meta data; auditing and reporting data warehouse usage and status; purging data; replicating, subsetting and distributing data; backup and recovery and data warehouse storage management.

Information Delivery System

The information delivery component is used to enable the process of subscribing for data warehouse information and having it delivered to one or more destinations according to some user-specified scheduling algorithm. In other words, the information delivery system distributes warehouse-stored data and other information objects to other data warehouses and end-user products such as spreadsheets and local databases. Delivery of information may be based on time of day or on the completion of an external event. The rationale for the delivery systems component is based on the fact that once the data warehouse is installed and operational, its users don't have to be aware of its location and maintenance. All they need is the report or an analytical view of data at a specific point in time. With the proliferation of the Internet and the World Wide Web such a delivery system may leverage the convenience of the Internet by delivering warehouse-enabled information to thousands of end-users via the ubiquitous worldwide network.

In fact, the Web is changing the data warehousing landscape since at the very high level the goals of both the Web and data warehousing are the same: easy access to information. The value of data warehousing is maximized when the right information gets into the hands of those individuals who need it, where they need it and they need it most. However, many corporations have struggled with complex client/server systems to give end users the access they need. The issues become even more difficult to resolve when the users are physically remote from the data warehouse location. The Web removes a lot of these issues by giving users universal and relatively inexpensive access to data. Couple this access with the ability to deliver required information on demand and the result is a web-enabled information delivery system that allows users dispersed across continents to perform a sophisticated business-critical analysis and to engage in collective decision-making.

Development Tools for Data Warehouse

The first data warehouse solutions were on-premise, and, while those remain, there is also a proliferation of *cloud-native* solutions which have entered the space.

The functionality for data warehouses is the same for on-prem and cloud native, although one can expect on-prem solutions to contain specific functionality for installation, sharding, replication, scaling and configuration that is absent from the cloud versions, as the latter solutions are generally managed. Data warehouses all:

- Store a large repository of integrated data imported from one or many disparate sources, for a single source of truth across an organization;

- Require (and in some cases, enable) data cleansing, deduplication, or schema adjustments to be done on imported data;

- Enable machine learning or AI to be run on large datasets to identify trends, discover hidden relationships and/or predict future events;

- Enable data to be queried into different formats for consumption by different stakeholders, or exported into different systems or visualization frameworks;

- Allow the generation of custom reports or ad-hoc analysis;

- Facilitate data mining;

- Serve data scientists, analysts, and other data consumers.

On-premise Data Warehouses

Using an on-prem solution naturally involves purchasing, installing, and maintaining your own hardware for storing the contents of your data warehouse, in addition to managing the data it stores.

For certain companies with large, established data warehousing infrastructure, or companies with major concerns over accessibility (millisecond response times) or data-security, on-prem solutions may still be the best option.

Cloud-native Data Warehouses

Cloud-native data warehouses involve purchasing a solution hosted in the cloud, and funneling data to it, usually through an API or some other means. Because of the advantages cloud-native solutions provide, nearly all providers of traditionally on-prem solutions have a cloud offering. Cloud-based data warehouses are cost-effective, quick and easy to prepare, can scale without any extra effort, have security built in, and support multi-tenancy.

What's more, cloud native users benefit from delegating maintenance and management of their DWs to third parties. In addition to the labor that's freed up (for analytics or other activities), users need neither outlay an initial hardware cost nor worry about what to do with excess hardware when scaling down.

ETL Tools

ETL stands for "Extract, Transform, and Load" and consists of the tools and processes used for pulling data from one store, transforming it for placement, and finally, loading it into another (often aggregate) store. Just as with data warehouses, ETL tools have progressed over time from self-administered to cloud-native offerings.

Batch Run/Incumbent ETL Tools

Remember when you used to see your bank account updated a day after your most recent financial transaction? That's because historically, many organizations used free compute and storage resources to perform nightly batches of ETL jobs. Some organizations and processes still work this way.

Open Source ETL Tools

These solutions are the evolutionary middle step between incumbent batch-based tools and fully managed cloud-based solutions. They solve some of the problems that batch run tools do not, for example, handling real-time streaming data.

Open source ETL tools have some drawbacks, but are generally a good choice when a customer isn't seeking a commercial solution.

Cloud-Native ETL Tools

Today's ETL tools are cloud-based and run in real time. Cloud-based means your ETL solution is managed and you need not worry about hardware costs, scaling, replication, or security, because these are usually built-in.

Real-Time ETL Tools

The demand for real-time support has moved the model from batch processing to one based on message queues and streams. Kafka has become the leading distributed message queue, and companies like Alooma have built SaaS or on-prem ETL solutions atop it.

Batch processing of ETL work makes little sense if your data (or insights from it) are needed instantly. And many applications work this way today — a tweet or social media update goes live immediately, not tomorrow.

BI Tools

BI and Analytics tools are about everything you do with the data to get insights once you've captured it. These include tools for visualization, data science analysis, analytics and KPIs.

Data Warehouse Design

Data warehouse design is data from multiple sources that support analytical reporting and data analysis. A poorly designed data warehouse can result in acquiring and using inaccurate source data that negatively affect the productivity and growth of your organization.

Requirements Gathering

Gathering requirements is step one of the data warehouse design process. The goal of the requirements gathering phase is to determine the criteria for a successful implementation of the data warehouse. An organization's long-term business strategy should be just as important as the current business and technical requirements. User analysis and reporting requirements must be identified as well as hardware, development, testing, implementation, and user training.

Once the business and technical strategy has been decided the next step is to address how the organization will back up the data warehouse and how it will recover if the system fails. Developing a disaster recovery plan while gathering requirements, ensures that the organization is prepared to respond quickly to direct and indirect threats to the data warehouse.

Physical Environment Setup

Once the business requirements are set, the next step is to determine the physical environment for the data warehouse. At a minimum, there should be separate physical application and database servers as well as separate ETL/ELT, OLAP, cube, and reporting processes set up for development, testing, and production. Building separate physical environments ensure that all changes can be tested before moving them to production, development, and testing can occur without halting the production environment, and if data integrity becomes suspect, the IT staff can investigate the issue without negatively impacting the production environment.

Data Modeling

Once requirements gathering and physical environments have been defined, the next step is to define how data structures will be accessed, connected, processed, and stored in the data warehouse. This process is known as data modeling. During this phase of data warehouse design, is where data sources are identified. Knowing where the original data resides and just as importantly, the availability of that data, is crucial to the success of the project. Once the data sources have been identified, the data warehouse team can begin building the logical and physical structures based on established requirements.

ETL

The ETL process takes the most time to develop and eats up the majority of implementation. Identifying data sources during the data modeling phase may help to reduce ETL development time. The goal of ETL is to provide optimized load speeds without sacrificing quality. Failure at this stage of the process can lead to poor performance of the ETL process and the entire data warehouse system.

OLAP Cube Design

On-Line Analytical Processing (OLAP) is the answer engine that provides the infrastructure for ad-hoc user query and multi-dimensional analysis. OLAP design specification should come from those who will query the data. Documentation specifying the OLAP cube dimensions and measures should be obtained during the beginning of data warehouse design process. The three critical elements of OLAP design include:

Grouping measures - Numerical values you want to analyze such as revenue, number of customers, how many products customers purchase, or average purchase amount.

Dimension - Where measures are stored for analysis such as geographic region, month, or quarter. Granularity - The lowest level of detail that you want to include in the OLAP dataset.

During development, make sure the OLAP cube process is optimized. A data warehouse is usually not a nightly priority run, and once the data warehouse has been updated, there little time left to update the OLAP cube. Not updating either of them in a timely manner could lead to reduced system performance. Taking the time to explore the most efficient OLAP cube generation path can reduce or prevent performance problems after the data warehouse goes live.

Front End Development

At this point, business requirements have been captured, physical environment complete, data model decided, and ETL process has been documented. The next step is to work on how users will access the data warehouse. Front end development is how users will access the data for analysis and run reports. There are many options available, including building your front end in-house or purchasing an off the shelf product. Either way, there are a few considerations to keep in mind to ensure the best experience for end users.

Secure access to the data from any device - desktop, laptop, tablet, or phone should be the primary consideration. The tool should allow your development team to modify the backend structure as enterprise level reporting requirements change. It should also provide a Graphical User Interface (GUI) that enables users to customize their reports as needed. The OLAP engine and data can be the best in class, but if users are not able to use the data, the data warehouse becomes an expensive and useless data repository.

Report Development

For most end users, the only contact they have with the data warehouse is through the reports they generate. Users' ability to select their report criteria quickly and efficiently is an essential feature for data warehouse report generation. Delivery options are another consideration. Along with receiving reports through a secure web interface, users may want or need reports sent as an email attachment, or spreadsheet. Controlling the flow and visibility of data is another aspect of report development that must be addressed. Developing user groups with access to specific data segments should provide data security and control. Reporting will and should change well after the initial implementation. A well-designed data warehouse should be able to handle the new reporting requests with little to no data warehouse system modification.

Performance Tuning

The recommendation was to create separate development and testing environments. Doing so allows organizations to provide system performance tuning on ETL, query processing, and report delivery without interrupting the current production environment. Make sure the development and testing environments-hardware and applications mimic the production environment so that the performance enhancements created in development will work in the live production environment.

Testing

Once the data warehouse system has been developed according to business requirements, the next step is to test it. Testing, or quality assurance, is a step that should not be skipped because it will allow the data warehouse team to expose and address issues before the initial rollout. Failing to complete the testing phase could lead to implementation delays or termination of the data warehouse project.

Implementation

Deciding to make the system available to everyone at once or perform a staggered release, will depend on the number of end users and how they will access the data warehouse system. Another important aspect of any system implementation and one that is often skipped, is end-user training. No matter how "intuitive" the data warehouse team and developers think the GUI is, if the actual end users finds the tool difficult to use, or do not understand the benefits of using the data warehouse for reporting and analysis, they will not engage.

Data Transformation

Data transformation is the process of converting data from one format or structure into another format or structure. Data transformation is critical to activities such as data integration and data management. Data transformation can include a range of activities: you might convert data types, cleanse data by removing nulls or duplicate data, enrich the data, or perform aggregations, depending on the needs of your project.

Typically, the process involves two stages.

In the first stage, you:

- Perform data discovery where you identify the sources and data types.

- Determine the structure and data transformations that need to occur.

- Perform data mapping to define how individual fields are mapped, modified, joined, filtered, and aggregated.

In the second stage, you:

- Extract data from the original source: The range of sources can vary, including structured sources, like databases, or streaming sources, such as telemetry from connected devices, or log files from customers using your web applications.

- Perform transformations: You transform the data, such as aggregating sales data or converting date formats, editing text strings or joining rows and columns.

- Send the data to the target store: The target might be a database or a data warehouse that handles structured and unstructured data.

You might want to transform your data for a number of reasons. Generally, businesses want to transform data to make it compatible with other data, move it to another system, join it with other data, or aggregate information in the data.

For example, consider the following scenario: your company has purchased a smaller company, and you need to combine information for the Human Resources departments. The purchased company uses a different database than the parent company, so you'll need to do some work to ensure that these records match. Each of the new employees has been issued an employee ID, so this can serve as a key. But, you'll need to change the formatting for the dates, you'll need to remove any duplicate rows, and you'll have to ensure that there are no null values for the Employee ID field so that all employees are accounted for. All these critical functions are performed in a staging area before you load the data to the final target.

Other common reasons to transform data include:

- You are moving your data to a new data store; for example, you are moving to a cloud data warehouse and you need to change the data types.

- You want to join unstructured data or streaming data with structured data so you can analyze the data together.

- You want to add information to your data to enrich it, such as performing lookups, adding geolocation data, or adding timestamps.

- You want to perform aggregations, such as comparing sales data from different regions or totaling sales from different regions.

How is Data Transformed

There are a few different ways to transform data:

- Scripting: Some companies perform data transformation via scripts using SQL or Python to write the code to extract and transform the data.

- On-premise ETL tools: ETL (Extract, Transform, Load) tools can take much of the pain out of scripting the transformations by automating the process. These tools are typically hosted on your company's site, and may require extensive expertise and infrastructure costs.

- Cloud-based ETL tools: These ETL tools are hosted in the cloud, where you can leverage the expertise and infrastructure of the vendor.

Data Transformation Challenges

Data transformation can be difficult for a number of reasons:

- Time-consuming: You may need to extensively cleanse the data so you can transform or migrate it. This can be extremely time-consuming, and is a common complaint amongst data scientists working with unstructured data.

- Costly: Depending on your infrastructure, transforming your data may require a team of experts and substantial infrastructure costs.

- Slow: Because the process of extracting and transforming data can be a burden on your system, it is often done in batches, which means you may have to wait up to 24 hours for the next batch to be processed. This can cost you time in making business decisions.

Data Extraction

Extraction is the operation of extracting data from a source system for further use in a data warehouse environment. This is the first step of the ETL process. After the extraction, this data can be transformed and loaded into the data warehouse.

The source systems for a data warehouse are typically transaction processing applications. For example, one of the source systems for a sales analysis data warehouse might be an order entry system that records all of the current order activities.

Designing and creating the extraction process is often one of the most time-consuming tasks in the ETL process and, indeed, in the entire data warehousing process. The source systems might be very complex and poorly documented, and thus determining which data needs to be extracted can be difficult. The data has to be extracted normally not only once, but several times in a periodic manner to supply all changed data to the warehouse and keep it up-to-date. Moreover, the source system typically cannot be modified, nor can its performance or availability be adjusted, to accommodate the needs of the data warehouse extraction process.

These are important considerations for extraction and ETL in general.

Designing this process means making decisions about the following two main aspects:

- Which extraction method do I choose? This influences the source system, the transportation process, and the time needed for refreshing the warehouse.

- How do we provide the extracted data for further processing? This influences the transportation method, and the need for cleaning and transforming the data.

Extraction Methods in Data Warehouse

The extraction method you should choose is highly dependent on the source system and also from the business needs in the target data warehouse environment. Very often, there's no possibility to add additional logic to the source systems to enhance an incremental extraction of data due to the performance or the increased workload of these systems. Sometimes even the customer is not allowed to add anything to an out-of-the-box application system.

The estimated amount of the data to be extracted and the stage in the ETL process (initial load or maintenance of data) may also impact the decision of how to extract, from a logical and a physical perspective. Basically, you have to decide how to extract data logically and physically.

Logical Extraction Methods

There are two kinds of logical extraction:

- Full Extraction,

- Incremental Extraction.

Full Extraction

The data is extracted completely from the source system. Since this extraction reflects all the data currently available on the source system, there's no need to keep track of changes to the data source since the last successful extraction. The source data will be provided as-is and no additional logical information (for example, timestamps) is necessary on the source site. An example for a full extraction may be an export file of a distinct table or a remote SQL statement scanning the complete source table.

Incremental Extraction

At a specific point in time, only the data that has changed since a well-defined event back in history will be extracted. This event may be the last time of extraction or a more complex business event like the last booking day of a fiscal period. To identify this delta change there must be a possibility to identify all the changed information since this specific time event. This information can be either provided by the source data itself like an application column, reflecting the last-changed timestamp or a change table where an appropriate additional mechanism keeps track of the changes besides the originating transactions. In most cases, using the latter method means adding extraction logic to the source system.

Many data warehouses do not use any change-capture techniques as part of the extraction process. Instead, entire tables from the source systems are extracted to the data warehouse or staging area, and these tables are compared with a previous extract from the source system to identify the changed data. This approach may not have significant impact on the source systems, but it clearly can place a considerable burden on the data warehouse processes, particularly if the data volumes are large.

Physical Extraction Methods

Depending on the chosen logical extraction method and the capabilities and restrictions on the source side, the extracted data can be physically extracted by two mechanisms. The data can either be extracted online from the source system or from an offline structure. Such an offline structure might already exist or it might be generated by an extraction routine.

There are the following methods of physical extraction:

- Online Extraction,

- Offline Extraction,

- Online Extraction.

The data is extracted directly from the source system itself. The extraction process can connect directly to the source system to access the source tables themselves or to an intermediate system that stores the data in a preconfigured manner (for example, snapshot logs or change tables). Note that the intermediate system is not necessarily physically different from the source system.

With online extractions, you need to consider whether the distributed transactions are using original source objects or prepared source objects.

Offline Extraction

The data is not extracted directly from the source system but is staged explicitly outside the original source system. The data already has an existing structure (for example, redo logs, archive logs or transportable tablespaces) or was created by an extraction routine.

You should consider the following structures:

- Flat filesData in a defined, generic format. Additional information about the source object is necessary for further processing.

- Dump filesOracle-specific format. Information about the containing objects is included.

- Redo and archive logsInformation is in a special, additional dump file.

- Transportable tablespaces.

Change Data Capture

An important consideration for extraction is incremental extraction, also called Change Data Capture. If a data warehouse extracts data from an operational system on a nightly basis, then the data warehouse requires only the data that has changed since the last extraction (that is, the data that has been modified in the past 24 hours).

When it is possible to efficiently identify and extract only the most recently changed data, the extraction process (as well as all downstream operations in the ETL process) can be much more efficient, because it must extract a much smaller volume of data. Unfortunately, for many source systems, identifying the recently modified data may be difficult or intrusive to the operation of the system. Change Data Capture is typically the most challenging technical issue in data extraction.

Because change data capture is often desirable as part of the extraction process and it might not be possible to use Oracle's Change Data Capture mechanism - timestamps, partitioning and triggers.

These techniques are based upon the characteristics of the source systems, or may require modifications to the source systems. Thus, each of these techniques must be carefully evaluated by the owners of the source system prior to implementation.

Each of these techniques can work in conjunction with the data extraction technique discussed previously. For example, timestamps can be used whether the data is being unloaded to a file or accessed through a distributed query.

Timestamps

The tables in some operational systems have timestamp columns. The timestamp specifies the time and date that a given row was last modified. If the tables in an operational system have columns containing timestamps, then the latest data can easily be identified using the timestamp columns. For example, the following query might be useful for extracting today's data from an order table:

```
SELECT * FROM orders WHERE TRUNC(CAST(order_date AS date),'dd') = TO_

DATE(SYSDATE,'dd-mon-yyyy');
```

If the timestamp information is not available in an operational source system, you will not always be able to modify the system to include timestamps. Such modification would require, first, modifying the operational system's tables to include a new timestamp column and then creating a trigger to update the timestamp column following every operation that modifies a given row.

Partitioning

Some source systems might use Oracle range partitioning, such that the source tables are partitioned along a date key, which allows for easy identification of new data. For example, if you are extracting from an order table, and the order table is partitioned by week, then it is easy to identify the current week's data.

Triggers

Triggers can be created in operational systems to keep track of recently updated records. They can then be used in conjunction with timestamp columns to identify the exact time and date when a given row was last modified. You do this by creating a trigger on each source table that requires change data capture. Following each DML statement that is executed on the source table, this trigger updates the timestamp column with the current time. Thus, the timestamp column provides the exact time and date when a given row was last modified.

A similar internalized trigger-based technique is used for Oracle materialized view logs. These logs are used by materialized views to identify changed data, and these logs are accessible to end users. A materialized view log can be created on each source table requiring change data capture. Then, whenever any modifications are made to the source table, a record is inserted into the materialized view log indicating which rows were modified. If you want to use a trigger-based mechanism, use change data capture.

Materialized view logs rely on triggers, but they provide an advantage in that the creation and maintenance of this change-data system is largely managed by Oracle.

However, Oracle recommends the usage of synchronous Change Data Capture for trigger based change capture, since CDC provides an externalized interface for accessing the change information and provides a framework for maintaining the distribution of this information to various clients

Trigger-based techniques affect performance on the source systems, and this impact should be carefully considered prior to implementation on a production source system.

Data Warehousing Extraction Examples

You can extract data in two ways:

- Extraction Using Data Files.

- Extraction via Distributed Operations.

Extraction using Data Files

Most database systems provide mechanisms for exporting or unloading data from the internal database format into flat files. Extracts from mainframe systems often use COBOL programs, but many databases, as well as third-party software vendors, provide export or unload utilities.

Data extraction does not necessarily mean that entire database structures are unloaded in flat files. In many cases, it may be appropriate to unload entire database tables or objects. In other cases, it may be more appropriate to unload only a subset of a given table such as the changes on the source system since the last extraction or the results of joining multiple tables together. Different extraction techniques vary in their capabilities to support these two scenarios.

When the source system is an Oracle database, several alternatives are available for extracting data into files:

- Extracting into Flat Files Using SQL*Plus.

- Extracting into Flat Files Using OCI or Pro*C Programs.

- Exporting into Oracle Export Files Using Oracle's Export Utility.

Extracting into Flat Files using SQL*Plus

The most basic technique for extracting data is to execute a SQL query in SQL*Plus and direct the output of the query to a file. For example, to extract a flat file, country_city.log, with the pipe sign as delimiter between column values, containing a list of the cities in the US in the table's countries and customers, the following SQL script could be run:

```
SET echo off SET pagesize 0

SPOOL country_city.log

SELECT distinct t1.country_name ||'|'|| t2.cust_city

FROM countries t1, customers t2

WHERE t1.country_id = t2.country_id

AND t1.country_name= 'United States of America';

SPOOL off
```

The exact format of the output file can be specified using SQL*Plus system variables.

This extraction technique offers the advantage of being able to extract the output of any SQL statement. The example previously extracts the results of a join.

This extraction technique can be parallelized by initiating multiple, concurrent SQL*Plus sessions, each session running a separate query representing a different portion of the data to be extracted. For example, suppose that you wish to extract data from an orders table, and that the orders table has been range partitioned by month, with partitions orders_jan1998, orders_feb1998 and so on. To extract a single year of data from the orders table, you could initiate 12 concurrent SQL*Plus sessions, each extracting a single partition. The SQL script for one such session could be:

```
SPOOL order_jan.dat
SELECT * FROM orders PARTITION (orders_jan1998);
SPOOL OFF
```

These 12 SQL*Plus processes would concurrently spool data to 12 separate files. You can then concatenate them if necessary (using operating system utilities) following the extraction. If you are planning to use SQL*Loader for loading into the target, these 12 files can be used as is for a parallel load with 12 SQL*Loader sessions.

Even if the orders table is not partitioned, it is still possible to parallelize the extraction either based on logical or physical criteria. The logical method is based on logical ranges of column values, for example:

```
SELECT ... WHERE order_date

BETWEEN TO_DATE('01-JAN-99') AND TO_DATE('31-JAN-99');
```

The physical method is based on a range of values. By viewing the data dictionary, it is possible to identify the Oracle data blocks that make up the orders table. Using this information, you could then derive a set of rowid-range queries for extracting data from the orders table:

```
SELECT * FROM orders WHERE rowid BETWEEN value1 and value2;
```

Parallelizing the extraction of complex SQL queries is sometimes possible, although the process of breaking a single complex query into multiple components can be challenging. In particular, the coordination of independent processes to guarantee a globally consistent view can be difficult.

Extracting into Flat Files using OCI or Pro*C Programs

OCI programs (or other programs using Oracle call interfaces, such as Pro*C programs), can also be used to extract data. These techniques typically provide improved performance over the SQL*Plus approach, although they also require additional programming. Like the SQL*Plus approach, an OCI program can extract the results of any SQL query. Furthermore, the parallelization techniques described for the SQL*Plus approach can be readily applied to OCI programs as well.

When using OCI or SQL*Plus for extraction, you need additional information besides the data itself. At minimum, you need information about the extracted columns. It is also helpful to know the extraction format, which might be the separator between distinct columns.

Exporting into Oracle Export Files using Oracle's Export Utility

Oracle's Export utility allows tables (including data) to be exported into Oracle export files. Unlike the SQL*Plus and OCI approaches, which describe the extraction of the results of a SQL statement, Export provides a mechanism for extracting database objects. Thus, Export differs from the previous approaches in several important ways:

- The export files contain metadata as well as data. An export file contains not only the raw data of a table, but also information on how to re-create the table, potentially including any indexes, constraints, grants, and other attributes associated with that table.

- A single export file may contain a subset of a single object, many database objects, or even an entire schema.

- Export cannot be directly used to export the results of a complex SQL query. Export can be used only to extract subsets of distinct database objects.

- The output of the Export utility must be processed using the Oracle Import utility.

Oracle provides a direct-path export, which is quite efficient for extracting data. However, in Oracle8i, there is no direct-path import, which should be considered when evaluating the overall performance of an export-based extraction strategy.

Extraction via Distributed Operations

Using distributed-query technology, one Oracle database can directly query tables located in various different source systems, such as another Oracle database or a legacy system connected with the Oracle gateway technology. Specifically, a data warehouse or staging database can directly access tables and data located in a connected source system. Gateways are another form of distributed-query technology. Gateways allow an Oracle database (such as a data warehouse) to access database tables stored in remote, non-Oracle databases. This is the simplest method for moving data between two Oracle databases because it combines the extraction and transformation into a single step, and requires minimal programming. However, this is not always feasible.

Continuing our example, suppose that you wanted to extract a list of employee names with department names from a source database and store this data into the data warehouse. Using an Oracle Net connection and distributed-query technology, this can be achieved using a single SQL statement:

```
CREATE TABLE country_city

AS

SELECT distinct t1.country_name, t2.cust_city

FROM countries@source_db t1, customers@source_db t2

WHERE t1.country_id = t2.country_id

AND t1.country_name='United States of America';
```

This statement creates a local table in a data mart, country_city and populates it with data from the countries and customers tables on the source system.

This technique is ideal for moving small volumes of data. However, the data is transported from the source system to the data warehouse through a single Oracle Net connection. Thus, the scalability of this technique is limited. For larger data volumes, file-based data extraction and transportation techniques are often more scalable and thus more appropriate.

Data Cleaning

Data cleaning, also called data cleansing or scrubbing, deals with detecting and removing errors and inconsistencies from data in order to improve the quality of data. Data quality problems are present in single data collections, such as files and databases, e.g., due to misspellings during data entry, missing information or other invalid data. When multiple data sources need to be integrated, e.g., in data warehouses, federated database systems or global web-based information systems, the need for data cleaning increases significantly. This is because the sources often contain redundant data in different representations. In order to provide access to accurate and consistent data, consolidation of different data representations and elimination of duplicate information become necessary.

Data warehouses require and provide extensive support for data cleaning. They load and continuously refresh huge amounts of data from a variety of sources so the probability that some of the sources contain "dirty data" is high. Furthermore, data warehouses are used for decision making, so that the correctness of their data is vital to avoid wrong conclusions. For instance, duplicated or missing information will produce incorrect or misleading statistics ("garbage in, garbage out"). Due to the wide range of possible data inconsistencies and the sheer data volume, data cleaning is considered to be one of the biggest problems in data warehousing. During the so-called ETL process (extraction, transformation, loading), illustrated in figure further data transformations deal with schema/data translation and integration, and with filtering and aggregating data to be stored in the warehouse. As indicated in figure, all data cleaning is typically performed in a separate data staging area before loading the transformed data into the warehouse. A large number of tools of varying functionality is available to support these tasks, but often a significant portion of the cleaning and transformation work has to be done manually or by low-level programs that are difficult to write and maintain.

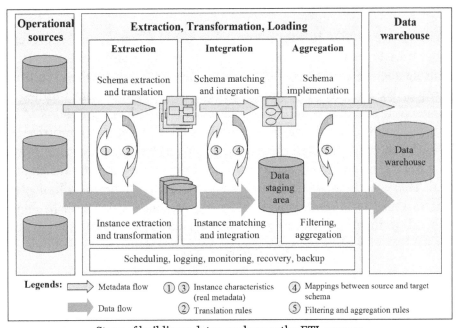

Steps of building a data warehouse: the ETL process.

Federated database systems and web-based information systems face data transformation steps similar to those of data warehouses. In particular, there is typically a wrapper per data source for extraction and a mediator for integration. So far, these systems provide only limited support for data cleaning, focusing instead on data transformations for schema translation and schema integration. Data is not reintegrated as for data warehouses but needs to be extracted from multiple sources, transformed and combined during query runtime. The corresponding communication and processing delays can be significant, making it difficult to achieve acceptable response times. The effort needed for data cleaning during extraction and integration will further increase response times but is mandatory to achieve useful query results.

A data cleaning approach should satisfy several requirements. First of all, it should detect and remove all major errors and inconsistencies both in individual data sources and when integrating multiple sources. The approach should be supported by tools to limit manual inspection and programming effort and be extensible to easily cover additional sources. Furthermore, data cleaning should not be performed in isolation but together with schema-related data transformations based on comprehensive metadata. Mapping functions for data cleaning and other data transformations should be specified in a declarative way and be reusable for other data sources as well as for query processing. Especially for data warehouses, a workflow infrastructure should be supported to execute all data transformation steps for multiple sources and large data sets in a reliable and efficient way.

While a huge body of research deals with schema translation and schema integration, data cleaning has received only little attention in the research community. A number of authors focused on the problem of duplicate identification and elimination. Some research groups concentrate on general problems not limited but relevant to data cleaning, such as special data mining approaches and data transformations based on schema matching. More recently, several research efforts propose and investigate a more comprehensive and uniform treatment of data cleaning covering several transformation phases, specific operators and their implementation.

Data Cleaning Problems

Data transformations are needed to support any changes in the structure, representation or content of data. These transformations become necessary in many situations, e.g., to deal with schema evolution, migrating a legacy system to a new information system, or when multiple data sources are to be integrated. We roughly distinguish between single-source and multi-source problems and between schema- and instance-related problems. Schema-level problems of course are also reflected in the instances; they can be addressed at the schema level by an improved schema design (schema evolution), schema translation and schema integration. Instance-level problems, on the other hand, refer to errors and inconsistencies in the actual data contents which are not visible at the schema level. They are the primary focus of data cleaning. Figure also indicates some typical problems for the various cases. While not shown in figure, the single-source problems occur (with increased likelihood) in the multi-source case, too, besides specific multi-source problems.

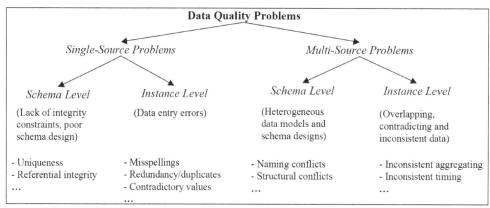

Classification of data quality problems in data sources.

Single-Source Problems

The data quality of a source largely depends on the degree to which it is governed by schema and integrity constraints controlling permissible data values. For sources without schema, such as files, there are few restrictions on what data can be entered and stored, giving rise to a high probability of errors and inconsistencies. Database systems, on the other hand, enforce restrictions of a specific data model (e.g., the relational approach requires simple attribute values, referential integrity, etc.) as well as application-specific integrity constraints. Schema-related data quality problems thus occur because of the lack of appropriate model-specific or application-specific integrity constraints, e.g., due to data model limitations or poor schema design, or because only a few integrity constraints were defined to limit the overhead for integrity control. Instance-specific problems relate to errors and inconsistencies that cannot be prevented at the schema level (e.g., misspellings).

Table: Examples for single-source problems at schema level (violated integrity constraints).

Scope/Problem		Dirty Data	Reasons/Remarks
Attribute	Illegal values	bdate=30.13.70	values outside of domain range
Record	Violated attribute dependencies	age=22, bdate=12.02.70	age = (current date – birth date) should hold
Record type	Uniqueness violation	emp1=(name="John Smith", SSN="123456") emp2=(name="Peter Miller", SSN="123456")	Uniqueness for SSN (social security number) violated
Source	Referential integrity violation	emp=(name="John Smith", deptno=127)	Referenced department (127) not defined

For both schema- and instance-level problems we can differentiate different problem scopes: attribute (field), record, record type and source; examples for the various cases are shown in tables. Note that uniqueness constraints specified at the schema level do not prevent duplicated instances, e.g., if information on the same real world entity is entered twice with different attribute values.

Table: Examples for single-source problems at instance level.

Scope/Problem		Dirty Data	Reasons/Remarks
Attribute	Missing values	phone=9999-999999	Unavailable values during data entry (dummy values or null)
	Misspellings	city="Liipzig"	Usually typos, phonetic errors
	Cryptic values, Abbreviations	experience="B"; occupation="DB Prog."	
	Embedded values	name="J. Smith 12.02.70 New York"	Multiple values entered in one attribute (e.g. in a free-form field)
	Misfielded values	city="Germany"	
Record	Violated attribute dependencies	city="Redmond", zip=77777	City and zip code should correspond
Record type	Word transpositions	$name_1$= "J. Smith", $name_2$="-Miller P."	usually in a free-form field
	Duplicated records	emp_1=(name="John Smith"); emp_2=(name="J. Smith")	Same employee represented twice due to some data entry errors
	Contradicting records	emp_1=(name="John Smith", bdate=12.02.70); emp_2=(name="John Smith", bdate=12.12.70)	The same real world entity is described by different values
Source	Wrong references	emp=(name="John Smith", deptno=17)	Referenced department (17) is defined but wrong

Given that cleaning data sources is an expensive process, preventing dirty data to be entered is obviously an important step to reduce the cleaning problem. This requires an appropriate design of the database schema and integrity constraints as well as of data entry applications. Also, the discovery of data cleaning rules during warehouse design can suggest improvements to the constraints enforced by existing schemas.

Multi-source Problems

The problems present in single sources are aggravated when multiple sources need to be integrated. Each source may contain dirty data and the data in the sources may be represented differently, overlap or contradict. This is because the sources are typically developed, deployed and maintained independently to serve specific needs. This results in a large degree of heterogeneity w.r.t. data management systems, data models, schema designs and the actual data.

At the schema level, data model and schema design differences are to be addressed by the steps of schema translation and schema integration, respectively. The main problems w.r.t. schema designs are naming and structural conflicts. Naming conflicts arise when the same name is used for different objects (homonyms) or different names are used for the same object (synonyms). Structural conflicts occur in many variations and refer to different representations of the same object in different sources, e.g., attribute vs. table representation, different component structure, different data types, different integrity constraints, etc.

In addition to schema-level conflicts, many conflicts appear only at the instance level (data conflicts). All problems from the single-source case can occur with different representations in different sources (e.g., duplicated records, contradicting records, etc.). Furthermore, even when there are the same attribute names and data types, there may be different value representations (e.g., for marital status) or different interpretation of the values (e.g., measurement units Dollar vs. Euro) across sources. Moreover, information in the sources may be provided at different aggregation levels (e.g., sales per product vs. sales per product group) or refer to different points in time (e.g. current sales as of yesterday for source 1 vs. as of last week for source 2).

A main problem for cleaning data from multiple sources is to identify overlapping data, in particular matching records referring to the same real-world entity (e.g., customer). This problem is also referred to as the object identity problem, duplicate elimination or the merge/purge problem. Frequently, the information is only partially redundant and the sources may complement each other by providing additional information about an entity. Thus duplicate information should be purged out and complementing information should be consolidated and merged in order to achieve a consistent view of real world entities.

Customer (Source 1)

CID	Name	Street	City	Sex
11	Kristen Smith	2 Hurley Pl	South Fork, MN 48503	0
24	Christian Smith	Hurley St 2	S Fork MN	1

Client (Source 2)

Cno	LastName	FirstName	Gender	Address	Phone/Fax
24	Smith	Christoph	M	23 Harley St, Chicago IL, 60633-2394	333-222-6542/333-222-6599
493	Smith	Kris L.	F	2 Hurley Place, South Fork MN, 48503-5998	444-555-6666

Customers (Integrated Target with Cleaned Data)

No	LName	FName	Gender	Street	City	State	ZIP	Phone	Fax	CID	Cno
1	Smith	Kristen L.	F	2 Hurley Place	South Fork	MN	48503-5998	444-555-6666		11	493
2	Smith	Chris-tian	M	2 Hurley Place	South Fork	MN	48503-5998			24	
3	Smith	Chris-toph	M	23 Harley Street	Chicago	IL	60633-2394	333-222-6542	333-222-6599		24

The two sources in the example of figure are both in relational format but exhibit schema and data conflicts. At the schema level, there are name conflicts (synonyms Customer/Client, Cid/ Cno, Sex/Gender) and structural conflicts (different representations for names and addresses). At the instance level, we note that there are different gender representations ("0"/"1" vs. "F"/"M") and presumably a duplicate record. The latter observation also reveals that while Cid/Cno is both source-specific identifiers, their contents are not comparable between the sources; different numbers (11/493) may refer to the same person while different persons can have the same number. Solving these problems requires both schema integration and data cleaning; the third table shows a possible solution. The schema conflicts should be resolved first to allow data cleaning, in particular detection of duplicates based on a uniform representation of names and addresses, and matching of the Gender/Sex values.

Data Cleaning Approaches

In general, data cleaning involves several phases:

- Data analysis: In order to detect which kinds of errors and inconsistencies are to be removed, a detailed data analysis is required. In addition to a manual inspection of the data or data samples, analysis programs should be used to gain metadata about the data properties and detect data quality problems.

- Definition of transformation workflow and mapping rules: Depending on the number of data sources, their degree of heterogeneity and the "dirtiness" of the data, a large number of data transformation and cleaning steps may have to be executed. Sometime, a schema translation is used to map sources to a common data model; for data warehouses, typically a relational representation is used. Early data cleaning steps can correct single-source instance problems and prepare the data for integration. Later steps deal with schema/data integration and cleaning multi-source instance problems, e.g., duplicates. For data warehousing, the control and data flow for these transformation and cleaning steps should be specified within a workflow that defines the ETL process.

The schema-related data transformations as well as the cleaning steps should be specified by a declarative query and mapping language as far as possible, to enable automatic generation of the transformation code. In addition, it should be possible to invoke user-written cleaning code and special purpose tools during a data transformation workflow. The transformation steps may request user feedback on data instances for which they have no built-in cleaning logic.

- Verification: The correctness and effectiveness of a transformation workflow and the transformation definitions should be tested and evaluated, e.g., on a sample or copy of the source data, to improve the definitions if necessary. Multiple iterations of the analysis, design and verification steps may be needed, e.g., since some errors only become apparent after applying some transformations.

- Transformation: Execution of the transformation steps either by running the ETL workflow for loading and refreshing a data warehouse or during answering queries on multiple sources.

- Backflow of cleaned data: After (single-source) errors are removed, the cleaned data should also replace the dirty data in the original sources in order to give legacy applications the improved data too and to avoid redoing the cleaning work for future data extractions. For data warehousing, the cleaned data is available from the data staging area.

The transformation process obviously requires a large amount of metadata, such as schemas, instance-level data characteristics, transformation mappings, workflow definitions, etc. For consistency, flexibility and ease of reuse, this metadata should be maintained in a DBMS-based repository. To support data quality, detailed information about the transformation process is to be recorded, both in the repository and in the transformed instances, in particular information about the completeness and freshness of source data and lineage information about the origin of transformed objects and the changes applied to them. For instance, in figure, the derived table Customers contains the attributes CID and Cno, allowing one to trace back the source records.

Data Analysis

Metadata reflected in schemas is typically insufficient to assess the data quality of a source, especially if only a few integrity constraints are enforced. It is thus important to analyses the actual instances to obtain real (reengineered) metadata on data characteristics or unusual value patterns. This metadata helps finding data quality problems. Moreover, it can effectively contribute to identify attribute correspondences between source schemas (schema matching), based on which automatic data transformations can be derived.

There are two related approaches for data analysis, data profiling and data mining. Data profiling focuses on the instance analysis of individual attributes. It derives information such as the data type, length, value range, discrete values and their frequency, variance, uniqueness, occurrence of null values, typical string pattern (e.g., for phone numbers), etc., providing an exact view of various quality aspects of the attribute. Table shows examples of how this metadata can help detecting data quality problems.

Table: Examples for the use of reengineered metadata to address data quality problems.

Problems	Metadata	Examples/Heuristics
Illegal values	cardinality	e.g., cardinality (gender) > 2 indicates problem.
	max, min	Max, min should not be outside of permissible range.
	variance, deviation	Variance, deviation of statistical values should not be higher than threshold.
Misspellings	attribute values	Sorting on values often brings misspelled values next to correct values.
Missing values	null values	Percentage/number of null values.
	attribute values + default values	Presence of default value may indicate real value is missing.
Varying value representations	attribute values	Comparing attribute value set of a column of one table against that of a column of another table.
Duplicates	cardinality + uniqueness	Attribute cardinality = # rows should hold.
	attribute values	Sorting values by number of occurrences; more than 1 occurrence indicates duplicates.

Data mining helps discover specific data patterns in large data sets, e.g., relationships holding between several attributes. This is the focus of so-called descriptive data mining models including clustering, summarization, association discovery and sequence discovery. Integrity constraints among attributes such as functional dependencies or application-specific "business rules" can be derived, which can be used to complete missing values, correct illegal values and identify duplicate records across data sources. For example, an association rule with high confidence can hint to data quality problems in instances violating this rule. So a confidence of 99% for rule "total=quantity*unit price" indicates that 1% of the records do not comply and may require closer examination.

The data transformation process typically consists of multiple steps where each step may perform schema and instance-related transformations (mappings). To allow a data transformation and cleaning system to generate transformation code and thus to reduce the amount of self-programming it is necessary to specify the required transformations in an appropriate language, e.g., supported by a graphical user interface. Various ETL tools offer this functionality by supporting proprietary rule languages. A more general and flexible approach is the use of the standard query language SQL to perform the data transformations and utilize the possibility of application-specific language extensions, in particular user defined functions (UDFs) supported in SQL:99. UDFs can be implemented in SQL or a general purpose programming language with embedded SQL statements. They allow implementing a wide range of data transformations and support easy reuse for different transformation and query processing tasks. Furthermore, their execution by the DBMS can reduce data access cost and thus improve performance.

Finally, UDFs are part of the SQL:99 standard and should (eventually) be portable across many platforms and DBMSs:

```
CREATE VIEW Customer2 (LName, FName, Gender, Street, City, State, ZIP, CID) AS
```

SELECT LastNameExtract (Name), FirstNameExtract (Name), Sex, Street, CityExtract (City),

StateExtract (City), ZIPExtract (City), CID

FROM Customer

Figure shows a transformation step specified in SQL:99. The example refers to figure and covers part of the necessary data transformations to be applied to the first source. The transformation defines a view on which further mappings can be performed. The transformation performs a schema restructuring with additional attributes in the view obtained by splitting the name and address attributes of the source. The required data extractions are achieved by UDFs (shown in boldface). The UDF implementations can contain cleaning logic, e.g., to remove misspellings in city names or provide missing zip codes.

UDFs may still imply a substantial implementation effort and do not support all necessary schema transformations. In particular, simple and frequently needed functions such as attribute splitting or merging are not generically supported but need often to be re-implemented in application-specific variations. More complex schema restructurings (e.g., folding and unfolding of attributes) are not supported at all. To generically support schema-related transformations, language extensions such as the SchemaSQL proposal are required. Data cleaning at the instance level can also benefit from special language extensions such as a Match operator supporting "approximate joins". System support for such powerful operators can greatly simplify the programming effort for data transformations and improve performance. Some current research efforts on data cleaning are investigating the usefulness and implementation of such query language extensions.

Conflict Resolution

A set of transformation steps has to be specified and executed to resolve the various schema- and instance level data quality problems that are reflected in the data sources at hand. Several types of transformations are to be performed on the individual data sources in order to deal with single-source problems and to prepare for integration with other sources. In addition to a possible schema translation, these preparatory steps typically include:

- Extracting values from free-form attributes (attribute split): Free-form attributes often capture multiple individual values that should be extracted to achieve a more precise representation and support further cleaning steps such as instance matching and duplicate elimination. Typical examples are name and address fields. Required transformations in this step are reordering of values within a field to deal with word transpositions, and value extraction for attribute splitting.

- Validation and correction: This step examines each source instance for data entry errors and tries to correct them automatically as far as possible. Spell checking based on dictionary lookup is useful for identifying and correcting misspellings. Furthermore, dictionaries on geographic names and zip codes help to correct address data. Attribute dependencies (birthdate – age, total price – unit price/quantity, city – phone area code, etc.) can be utilized to detect problems and substitute missing values or correct wrong values.

- Standardization: To facilitate instance matching and integration, attribute values should be converted to a consistent and uniform format. For example, date and time entries should be brought into a specific format; names and other string data should be converted to upper or lower case, etc. Text data may be condensed and unified by performing stemming, removing prefixes, suffixes, and stop words. Furthermore, abbreviations and encoding schemes should consistently be resolved by consulting special synonym dictionaries or applying predefined conversion rules.

Dealing with multi-source problems requires restructuring of schemas to achieve a schema integration, including steps such as splitting, merging, folding and unfolding of attributes and tables. At the instance level, conflicting representations need to be resolved and overlapping data must to be dealt with. The duplicate elimination task is typically performed after most other transformation and cleaning steps, especially after having cleaned single-source errors and conflicting representations. It is performed either on two cleaned sources at a time or on a single already integrated data set. Duplicate elimination requires to first identify (i.e. match) similar records concerning the same real world entity. In a second step, similar records are merged into one record containing all relevant attributes without redundancy. Furthermore, redundant records are purged. In the following we discuss the key problem of instance matching. More details on the subject are provided elsewhere in this issue.

In the simplest case, there is an identifying attribute or attribute combination per record that can be used for matching records, e.g., if different sources share the same primary key or if there are other common unique attributes. Instance matching between different sources is then achieved by a standard equi-join on the identifying attributes. In the case of a single data set, matches can be determined by sorting on the identifying attribute and checking if neighboring records match. In both cases, efficient implementations can be achieved even for large data sets. Unfortunately, without common key attributes or in the presence of dirty data such straightforward approaches are often too restrictive. To determine most or all matches a "fuzzy matching" (approximate join) becomes necessary that finds similar records based on a matching rule, e.g., specified declaratively or implemented by a user-defined function. For example, such a rule could state that person records are likely to correspond if name and portions of the address match. The degree of similarity between two records, often measured by a numerical value between 0 and 1, usually depends on application characteristics. For instance, different attributes in a matching rule may contribute different weight to the overall degree of similarity. For string components (e.g., customer name, company name, etc.) exact matching and fuzzy approaches based on wildcards, character frequency, edit distance, keyboard distance and phonetic similarity (soundex) are useful. More complex string matching approaches also considering abbreviations. A general approach for matching both string and text data is the use of common information retrieval metrics. WHIRL represents a promising representative of this category using the cosine distance in the vector-space model for determining the degree of similarity between text elements.

Determining matching instances with such an approach is typically a very expensive operation for large data sets. Calculating the similarity value for any two records implies evaluation of the matching rule on the cartesian product of the inputs. Furthermore sorting on the similarity value is needed to determine matching records covering duplicate information. All records for which the similarity value exceeds a threshold can be considered as matches, or as match candidates to be confirmed or rejected by the user. In a multi-pass approach is proposed for instance matching to reduce the overhead. It is based on matching records independently on different attributes and combining the different match results. Assuming a single input file, each match pass sorts the records on a specific attribute and only tests nearby records within a certain window on whether they satisfy a predetermined matching rule. This reduces significantly the number of match rule evaluations compared to the cartesian product approach. The total set of matches is obtained by the union of the matching pairs of each pass and their transitive closure.

Tool Support

A large variety of tools is available on the market to support data transformation and data cleaning tasks, in particular for data warehousing. Some tools concentrate on a specific domain, such as cleaning name and address data, or a specific cleaning phase, such as data analysis or duplicate elimination. Due to their restricted domain, specialized tools typically perform very well but must be complemented by other tools to address the broad spectrum of transformation and cleaning problems. Other tools, e.g., ETL tools, provide comprehensive transformation and workflow capabilities to cover a large part of the data transformation and cleaning process. A general problem of ETL tools is their limited interoperability due to proprietary application programming interfaces (API) and proprietary metadata formats making it difficult to combine the functionality of several tools.

Data Analysis and Reengineering Tools

Data analysis tools can be divided into data profiling and data mining tools. MIGRATIONAR-CHITECT (Evoke Software) is one of the few commercial data profiling tools. For each attribute, it determines the following real metadata: data type, length, cardinality, discrete values and their percentage, minimum and maximum values, missing values, and uniqueness. MI-GRATIONARCHITECT also assists in developing the target schema for data migration. Data mining tools, such as WIZRULE (WizSoft) and DATAMININGSUITE (InformationDiscovery), infer relationships among attributes and their values and compute a confidence rate indicating the number of qualifying rows. In particular, WIZRULE can reveal three kinds of rules: mathematical formula, if-then rules, and spelling-based rules indicating misspelled names, e.g., "value Edinburgh appears 52 times in field Customer; 2 cases contain similar values". WIZRULE also automatically points to the deviations from the set of the discovered rules as suspected errors.

Data reengineering tools, e.g., INTEGRITY (Vality), utilize discovered patterns and rules to specify and perform cleaning transformations, i.e., they reengineer legacy data. In INTEGRI-TY, data instances undergo several analysis steps, such as parsing, data typing, pattern and frequency analysis. The result of these steps is a tabular representation of field contents, their patterns and frequencies, based on which the pattern for standardizing data can be selected. For specifying cleaning transformations, INTEGRITY provides a language including a set of operators for column transformations (e.g., move, split, delete) and row transformation (e.g., merge, split). INTEGRITY identifies and consolidates records using a statistical matching technique.

Automated weighting factors are used to compute scores for ranking matches based on which the user can select the real duplicates.

Specialized Cleaning Tools

Specialized cleaning tools typically deal with a particular domain, mostly name and address data, or concentrate on duplicate elimination. The transformations are to be provided either in advance in the form of a rule library or interactively by the user. Alternatively, data transformations can automatically be derived from schema matching tools.

- Special domain cleaning: Names and addresses are recorded in many sources and typically have high cardinality. For example, finding customer matches is very important for customer relationship management. A number of commercial tools, e.g., IDCENTRIC (FirstLogic), PUREINTEGRATE (Oracle), QUICKADDRESS (QASSystems), REUNION (PitneyBowes), and TRILLIUM (TrilliumSoftware), focus on cleaning this kind of data. They provide techniques such as extracting and transforming name and address information into individual standard elements, validating street names, cities, and zip codes, in combination with a matching facility based on the cleaned data. They incorporate a huge library of prespecified rules dealing with the problems commonly found in processing this data. For example, TRILLIUM's extraction (parser) and matcher module contains over 200,000 business rules. The tools also provide facilities to customize or extend the rule library with user-defined rules for specific needs.

- Duplicate elimination: Sample tools for duplicate identification and elimination include DATACLEANSER (EDD), MERGE/PURGELIBRARY (Sagent/QMSoftware), MATCHIT (HelpITSystems), and MASTERMERGE (PitneyBowes). Usually, they require the data sources already be cleaned for matching. Several approaches for matching attribute values are supported; tools such as DATACLEANSER and MERGE/PURGE LIBRARY also allow user-specified matching rules to be integrated.

ETL Tools

A large number of commercial tools support the ETL process for data warehouses in a comprehensive way, e.g., COPYMANAGER (InformationBuilders), DATASTAGE (Informix/Ardent), EXTRACT (ETI), POWERMART (Informatica), DECISIONBASE (CA/Platinum), DATATRANSFORMATIONSERVICE (Microsoft), METASUITE (Minerva/Carleton), SAGENTSOLUTIONPLATFORM (Sagent), and WAREHOUSEADMINISTRATOR (SAS). They use a repository built on a DBMS to manage all metadata about the data sources, target schemas, mappings, script programs, etc., in a uniform way. Schemas and data are extracted from operational data sources via both native file and DBMS gateways as well as standard interfaces such as ODBC and EDA. Data transformations are defined with an easy-to-use graphical interface. To specify individual mapping steps, a proprietary rule language and a comprehensive library of predefined conversion functions are typically provided. The tools also support reusing existing transformation solutions, such as external C/C++ routines, by providing an interface to integrate them into the internal transformation library. Transformation processing is carried out either by an engine that interprets the specified transformations at runtime, or by compiled code. All engine-based tools (e.g., COPYMANAGER, DECISIONBASE, POWERMART, DATASTAGE, WAREHOUSEADMINISTRATOR), possess a scheduler and support workflows with complex execution dependencies among mapping jobs. A workflow may also invoke external tools, e.g., for specialized cleaning tasks such as name/ address cleaning or duplicate elimination.

ETL tools typically have little built-in data cleaning capabilities but allow the user to specify cleaning functionality via a proprietary API. There is usually no data analysis support to automatically detect data errors and inconsistencies. However, users can implement such logic with the metadata maintained and by determining content characteristics with the help of aggregation functions (sum, count, min, max, median, variance, deviation, etc.). The provided transformation library covers many data transformation and cleaning needs, such as data type conversions (e.g., date reformatting), string functions (e.g., split, merge, replace, sub-string search), arithmetic, scientific and statistical functions, etc. Extraction of values from free-form attributes is not completely automatic but the user has to specify the delimiters separating sub-values.

The rule languages typically cover if-then and case constructs that help handling exceptions in data values, such as misspellings, abbreviations, missing or cryptic values, and values outside of range. These problems can also be addressed by using a table lookup construct and join functionality. Support for instance matching is typically restricted to the use of the join construct and some simple string matching functions, e.g., exact or wildcard matching and sounder. However, user-defined field matching functions as well as functions for correlating field similarities can be programmed and added to the internal transformation library.

Data Loading

Data loading refers to the "load" component of ETL. After data is retrieved and combined from multiple sources (extracted), cleaned and formatted (transformed), it is then loaded into a storage system, such as a cloud data warehouse.

ETL aids in the data integration process that standardizes diverse and disparate data types to make it available for querying, manipulation, or reporting for many different individuals and teams. Because today's organizations are increasingly reliant upon their own data to make smarter, faster business decisions, ETL needs to be scalable and streamlined to provide the most benefit.

Benefits of Data Loading

Before ETL evolved into its current state, organizations had to load data manually or else use several different ETL vendors for each different database or source. Understandably, this made the process slower and more complicated than it needed to be — reinforcing data silos rather than breaking them down.

Today, the ETL process — including data loading — is designed for speed, efficiency, and flexibility. But more importantly, it can scale to meet the growing data demands of most enterprises. ETL easily accommodates proliferation of data sources as technologies like IoT and connected devices continue to gain popularity. And it can handle any number of data types and formats, whether structured, semi-structured, or unstructured.

Challenges with Data Loading

Many ETL solutions are cloud-based, which accounts for their speed and scalability. But large enterprises with traditional, on-premise infrastructure and data management processes often use custom built scripts to collect and load their own data into storage systems through customized configurations. This can:

- Slow down analysis: Each time a data source is added or changed, the system has to be re-configured, which takes time and hampers the ability to make quick decisions.

- Increase the likelihood of errors. Changes and reconfigurations open up the door for human error, duplicate or missing data, and other problems.

- Require specialized knowledge: In-house IT teams often lack the skill (and bandwidth) needed to code and monitor ETL functions themselves.

- Require costly equipment: In addition to investment in the right human resources, organizations have to purchase, house, and maintain hardware and other equipment to run the process on site.

Methods for Data Loading

Since data loading is part of the larger ETL process, organizations need a proper understanding of the types of ETL tools and methods available, and which one(s) work best for their needs, budget, and structure.

- Cloud-based: ETL tools in the cloud are built for speed and scalability, and often enable real-time data processing. They also include the ready-made infrastructure and expertise of the vendor, who can advise on best practices for each organization's unique setup and needs.

- Batch processing: ETL tools that work off batch processing move data at the same scheduled time every day or week. It works best for large volumes of data and for organizations that don't necessarily need real-time access to their data.

- Open source: Many open-source ETL tools are quite cost-effective as their code base is publicly accessible, modifiable, and shareable. While a good alternative to commercial solutions, these tools can still require some customization or hand-coding.

Data Transformation Services

Data Transformation Services (DTS) is a group of utilities and objects used to automatically perform extract, transform and load operations to or from databases. DTS is widely used with Microsoft SQL Server databases.

DTS was a feature of Microsoft SQL Server from version 7.0 through SQL Server 2000. It was replaced by SQL Server Integration Services (SSIS) in SQL Server 2005.

DTS consists of a set of utilities called DTS tools and objects called DTS packages, which automate extract, transform and load operations to or from databases.

DTS packages are the logical components within DTS, where every DTS object is a child component of packages. They are used when a user alters data using DTS. Packages also hold connection objects, allowing packages to read data from object linking and embedding database (OLE-DB) compliant data sources. Package functionalities are organized as steps and tasks.

DTS tools within SQL Server include:

- DTS wizards,
- DTS designer,
- DTS programming interface.

DTS transforms and loads data from heterogeneous sources like open database connectivity or text-only files into supported databases. It also automates data import or transformation on a scheduled basis, in addition to performing other functions such as executing external programs.

DTS provides version control and backups for packages when used along with version control systems.

Online Analytical Processing

OLAP is a category of software that allows users to analyze information from multiple database systems at the same time. It is a technology that enables analysts to extract and view business data from different points of view. OLAP stands for Online Analytical Processing.

Analysts frequently need to group, aggregate and join data. These operations in relational databases are resource intensive. With OLAP data can be pre-calculated and pre-aggregated, making analysis faster.

OLAP databases are divided into one or more cubes. The cubes are designed in such a way that creating and viewing reports become easy.

OLAP Cube

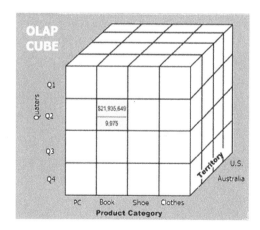

At the core of the OLAP, concept is an OLAP Cube. The OLAP cube is a data structure optimized for very quick data analysis.

The OLAP Cube consists of numeric facts called measures which are categorized by dimensions. OLAP Cube is also called the hypercube.

Usually, data operations and analysis are performed using the simple spreadsheet, where data values are arranged in row and column format. This is ideal for two-dimensional data. However, OLAP contains multidimensional data, with data usually obtained from a different and unrelated source. Using a spreadsheet is not an optimal option. The cube can store and analyze multidimensional data in a logical and orderly manner.

A Data warehouse would extract information from multiple data sources and formats like text files, excel sheet, multimedia files, etc.

The extracted data is cleaned and transformed. Data is loaded into an OLAP server (or OLAP cube) where information is pre-calculated in advance for further analysis.

Basic Analytical Operations of OLAP

Four types of analytical operations in OLAP are:

- Roll-up: Roll-up is also known as "consolidation" or "aggregation." The Roll-up operation can be performed in 2 ways:

    ○ Reducing dimensions.

    ○ Climbing up concept hierarchy. Concept hierarchy is a system of grouping things based on their order or level.

Consider the following diagram:

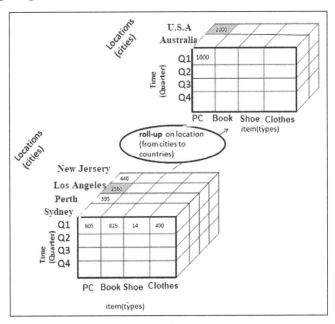

- In this example, cities New jersey and Lost Angles and rolled up into country USA.

- The sales figure of New Jersey and Los Angeles are 440 and 1560 respectively. They become 2000 after roll-up.

- In this aggregation process, data is location hierarchy moves up from city to the country.

- In the roll-up process at least one or more dimensions need to be removed. In this example, Quater dimension is removed.

- Drill-down: In drill-down data is fragmented into smaller parts. It is the opposite of the rollup process. It can be done via:

  ○ Moving down the concept hierarchy.

  ○ Increasing a dimension.

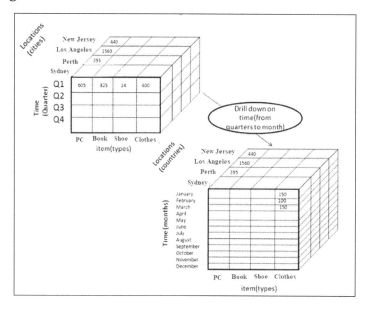

Consider the diagram above:

- Quater Q1 is drilled down to months January, February, and March. Corresponding sales are also registers.

- In this example, dimension months are added.

  ○ Slice: Here, one dimension is selected, and a new sub-cube is created.

Following diagram explain how slice operation performed:

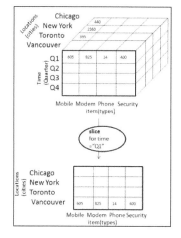

- In this aggregatiDimension Time is Sliced with Q1 as the filter.

- In this aggregatiA new cube is created altogether.

  ○ Dice: This operation is similar to a slice. The difference in dice is you select 2 or more dimensions that result in the creation of a sub-cube.

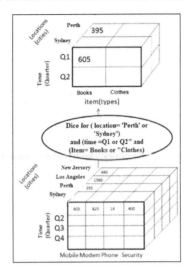

  ○ Pivot: In Pivot, you rotate the data axes to provide a substitute presentation of data.

In the following example, the pivot is based on item types.

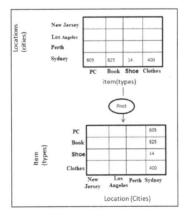

Types of OLAP systems

OLAP Hierarchical Structure:

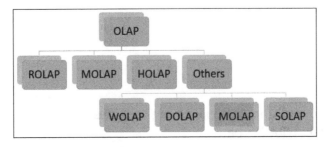

Type of OLAP	Explanation
Relational OLAP(ROLAP)	ROLAP is an extended RDBMS along with multidimensional data mapping to perform the standard relational operation.
Multidimensional OLAP (MOLAP)	MOLAP Implements operation in multidimensional data.
Hybrid OnlineAnalytical Processing (HOLAP)	In HOLAP approach the aggregated totals are stored in a multidimensional database while the detailed data is stored in the relational database. This offers both data efficiency of the ROLAP model and the performance of the MOLAP model.
Desktop OLAP (DOLAP)	In Desktop OLAP, a user downloads a part of the data from the database locally, or on their desktop and analyze it. DOLAP is relatively cheaper to deploy as it offers very few functionalities compares to other OLAP systems.
Web OLAP (WOLAP)	Web OLAP which is OLAP system accessible via the web browser. WOLAP is a three-tiered architecture. It consists of three components: client, middleware, and a database server.
Mobile OLAP	Mobile OLAP helps users to access and analyze OLAP data using their mobile devices
Spatial OLAP	SOLAP is created to facilitate management of both spatial and non-spatial data in a Geographic Information system (GIS)

ROLAP

ROLAP works with data that exist in a relational database. Facts and dimension tables are stored as relational tables. It also allows multidimensional analysis of data and is the fastest growing OLAP.

Advantages of ROLAP Model

- High data efficiency: It offers high data efficiency because query performance and access language are optimized particularly for the multidimensional data analysis.

- Scalability: This type of OLAP system offers scalability for managing large volumes of data, and even when the data is steadily increasing.

Drawbacks of ROLAP Model

- Demand for higher resources: ROLAP needs high utilization of manpower, software, and hardware resources.

- Aggregately data limitations: ROLAP tools use SQL for all calculation of aggregate data. However, there are no set limits to handling computations.

- Slow query performance: Query performance in this model is slow when compared with MOLAP

MOLAP

MOLAP uses array-based multidimensional storage engines to display multidimensional views of data. Basically, they use an OLAP cube.

Hybrid OLAP

Hybrid OLAP is a mixture of both ROLAP and MOLAP. It offers fast computation of MOLAP and higher scalability of ROLAP. HOLAP uses two databases:

- Aggregated or computed data is stored in a multidimensional OLAP cube.

- Detailed information is stored in a relational database.

Benefits of Hybrid OLAP

- This kind of OLAP helps to economize the disk space, and it also remains compact which helps to avoid issues related to access speed and convenience.

- Hybrid HOLAP's uses cube technology which allows faster performance for all types of data.

- ROLAP are instantly updated and HOLAP users have access to this real-time instantly updated data. MOLAP brings cleaning and conversion of data thereby improving data relevance. This brings best of both worlds.

Drawbacks of Hybrid OLAP

- Greater complexity level: The major drawback in HOLAP systems is that it supports both ROLAP and MOLAP tools and applications. Thus, it is very complicated.

- Potential overlaps: There are higher chances of overlapping especially into their functionalities.

Advantages of OLAP

- OLAP is a platform for all type of business includes planning, budgeting, reporting, and analysis.

- Information and calculations are consistent in an OLAP cube. This is a crucial benefit.

- Quickly create and analyze "What if" scenarios.

- Easily search OLAP database for broad or specific terms.

- OLAP provides the building blocks for business modeling tools, Data mining tools, performance reporting tools.

- Allows users to do slice and dice cube data all by various dimensions, measures, and filters.

- It is good for analyzing time series.

- Finding some clusters and outliers is easy with OLAP.

- It is a powerful visualization online analytical process system which provides faster response times.

Disadvantages of OLAP

- OLAP requires organizing data into a star or snowflake schema. These schemas are complicated to implement and administer.

- You cannot have large number of dimensions in a single OLAP cube.

- Transactional data cannot be accessed with OLAP system.

- Any modification in an OLAP cube needs a full update of the cube. This is a time-consuming process.

OLAP Architecture

Regardless of the different types, all OLAP architectures involve building a multidimensional data structure, where dimensions represent business entities such as sales regions and products or natural entities such as time and geography. It is this data structure, called a cube, that users analyze via an OLAP technology. Two issues regarding the multidimensional data structure distinguish OLAP architectures:

- When and how is the multidimensional data structure constructed?

  ○ Some OLAP technologies require an ETL (extract, transform, and load) process, which typically runs at off-peak usage times to build and update a persistent multidimensional data structure. On the other hand, other OLAP technologies access source data directly to build and present multidimensional data on the fly as the user performs analysis.

- Where does the multidimensional data structure live and how persistent is it?

  ○ The multidimensional data structure may reside in a persistent, dedicated multidimensional database, a hypercube temporarily cached in memory, or a star schema/snowflake schema stored in a relational database.

Data Staging

Data in OLAP systems mostly originate from other systems. It is necessary for the active data to be stored in a separate form, data warehouse or data mart, for the OLAP system. Below are the main reasons for implementing a separate data warehouse instead of using the existing operational databases.

Performance

Performance can suffer when executing complex OLAP queries against the operational databases such as OLTPs. Data should be kept in a separate, optimized structure where users can rapidly access, without damaging the response from the operational systems.

Multiple Data Sources

Most OLAP systems require data sourced from various operational systems, possibly including external sources or desktop applications. Since the base systems may use different coding systems or have different periodicity, the process of merging these heterogeneous sources can be very complex.

Cleansing/Adjusting Data

OLTP systems may contain erroneous data which needs to be cleansed before it is in the stage for analysis. Also the different sources may contain data of varying quality or inconsistent representations or formats. In order to adjust data without affecting the OLTP systems, data should be kept separate.

Timing

Since most OLAP systems require data sourced from various operational systems, it is most likely that they are updated on different cycles. Therefore, they may be at different stages of update at a time. In order for the analysis to be based on consistent data, the data needs to be staged.

Operational databases may be missing some data that are required for decision support. They store current data only, but historical data may be critical for some decision making.

Operational data is very detailed, but decision makers need to see it at a much higher level. For efficiency, it's usually necessary to store merged, adjusted information at summary level, which cannot be feasible in OLTP systems.

Data Updating

When the system allows users to modify the existing data, it is important to have a separate database which will not overwrite the original operational data.

References

- Data-warehousing: guru99.com, Retrieved 29 August, 2019

- Components-of-a-data-warehouse- 4213: tdan.com, Retrieved 15 June, 2019

- Data-warehousing-tools: alooma.com, Retrieved 19 May, 2019

- Data-warehouse-design-the-good-the-bad-the-ugly: blog.panoply.io, Retrieved 18 August, 2019

- What-is-data-transformation: alooma.com, Retrieved 16 March, 2019

- Data-extraction-techniques, data-mining-and-warehousing: vskills.in, Retrieved 26 August, 2019

- Data-transformation-services-dts- 1183: techopedia.com, Retrieved 22 April, 2019

- Online-analytical-processing: guru99.com, Retrieved 05 January, 2019

Permissions

All chapters in this book are published with permission under the Creative Commons Attribution Share Alike License or equivalent. Every chapter published in this book has been scrutinized by our experts. Their significance has been extensively debated. The topics covered herein carry significant information for a comprehensive understanding. They may even be implemented as practical applications or may be referred to as a beginning point for further studies.

We would like to thank the editorial team for lending their expertise to make the book truly unique. They have played a crucial role in the development of this book. Without their invaluable contributions this book wouldn't have been possible. They have made vital efforts to compile up to date information on the varied aspects of this subject to make this book a valuable addition to the collection of many professionals and students.

This book was conceptualized with the vision of imparting up-to-date and integrated information in this field. To ensure the same, a matchless editorial board was set up. Every individual on the board went through rigorous rounds of assessment to prove their worth. After which they invested a large part of their time researching and compiling the most relevant data for our readers.

The editorial board has been involved in producing this book since its inception. They have spent rigorous hours researching and exploring the diverse topics which have resulted in the successful publishing of this book. They have passed on their knowledge of decades through this book. To expedite this challenging task, the publisher supported the team at every step. A small team of assistant editors was also appointed to further simplify the editing procedure and attain best results for the readers.

Apart from the editorial board, the designing team has also invested a significant amount of their time in understanding the subject and creating the most relevant covers. They scrutinized every image to scout for the most suitable representation of the subject and create an appropriate cover for the book.

The publishing team has been an ardent support to the editorial, designing and production team. Their endless efforts to recruit the best for this project, has resulted in the accomplishment of this book. They are a veteran in the field of academics and their pool of knowledge is as vast as their experience in printing. Their expertise and guidance has proved useful at every step. Their uncompromising quality standards have made this book an exceptional effort. Their encouragement from time to time has been an inspiration for everyone.

The publisher and the editorial board hope that this book will prove to be a valuable piece of knowledge for students, practitioners and scholars across the globe.

Index

CPSIA information can be obtained
at www.ICGtesting.com
Printed in the USA
LVHW061449270323
742703LV00003B/486